SEEING AMERICA FIRST

Taking That Dream Driving Vacation
To Visit Our National Treasures

By Tony Petracca

Copyright © 2016 by Tony Petracca

Seeing America First
Taking That Dream Driving Vacation To Visit Our National Treasures
by Tony Petracca

Printed in the United States of America.

ISBN 9781498482646

All rights reserved solely by the author. The author guarantees all contents are original and do not infringe upon the legal rights of any other person or work. No part of this book may be reproduced in any form without the permission of the author. The views expressed in this book are not necessarily those of the publisher.

www.xulonpress.com

To Theodore Roosevelt

TABLE OF CONTENTS

Introduction: "See America First" ix
1. Revving Up The Engine: The Countdown Begins 19
2. It's A Beautiful Day In The Neighborhood: Pennsylvania
   And Its Contiguous States. 31
3. There And Back Again: The First Cross-Country Drive. 37
4. The Inaugural Trip: Setting The Template 47
5. Not All Those Who Wander Are Lost: Expecting The
   Unexpected 67
6. Top City #5 – Memphis: I Hear America Singing 78
7. Good Buddies: The Long-Distance Fraternity 86
8. Top City #4 – Chicago: Fire, Wind And Water. 96
9. What's The Frequency, Kenneth? Tuning In When You're
   Out And About 108
10. Top City #3 – Philadelphia: The Cradle Of Liberty
    (And Of An Author Or Two). 119
11. A Lane Change: Or, Deliverance From Banjoes. 133
12. Top City #2 – Seattle: The Town On The Sound 137
13. TR NP: Badlands And Bison 145
14. Top City #1 – Washington, DC: A Capital City 151
15. The Cross-Country Drive From Heck: Snow,
    Tornadoes And Icy Hot. 171
16. The Best Idea America Ever Had: Our National
    Park System 180
17. 50x5: Five Recommended Sights In Each State. 217
Conclusion: A Continent Awaits 285
Epilogue: Theodore Roosevelt 289

vii

INTRODUCTION

"SEE AMERICA FIRST"

If you won a free trip to anywhere in the country, where would you go? LA? Walt Disney World? The Florida Keys in the winter? New England in the fall? Yellowstone in the summer? The Rockies in the spring? I could go on, as I'm sure you could, too. Many places in our great land call to us invitingly: Waikiki, New York City, the Grand Canyon, Chicago, the Outer Banks. Wouldn't you love to see all these places? Wouldn't that be the dream vacation for you?

So my next question to you is, What's holding you back? OK, I'll admit that you need two things for any vacation to work: the time, and the money. But let's assume that you have at least two weeks you can take as a block in a given year. Let's also assume that you could salt away enough cash for that time period. So, what would you do with it? Go down the shore again? Maybe up the mountains? Now I'm sure that, when you're, say, caught in gridlock in Chicagoland, the thought of the Wisconsin Dells sounds great. Still, when you're at home relaxing, perhaps in front of a fireplace, or sitting on your front porch, or taking a pleasant drive to see friends, where do you dream of going? The Dells once again? That lakeside rental north of town? Touring the Loop, one more time?

Don't you ever just want to get away from everything familiar? Don't you wonder what's beyond the horizon? Wouldn't you really like to go to locations you've only wondered about, the places where other people have been? So, I ask again, what's stopping you? If you get onto I-80 in Chicago, it will take you all the way to NYC in the East, and all the way to San Fran in the West. You don't need a passport or a visa to cross into Iowa, or Indiana, or any other state along that route. So, instead of those two weeks in one familiar place, why not spend them in some *un*familiar place? Or several unfamiliar places? It's not necessarily a choice between New York and New England: if you plan your time right, you can see both. Yellowstone, the Grand Canyon, Glacier: they can be done in one two-week loop. Oh, not everything in them, or in-between them, but certainly the sights you want to see the most.

But won't that involve added expense? you ask. Well, on the one hand, gas isn't cheap most years. However, on the other hand, jet fuel isn't cheap, either. So how much would a family of four cost to fly to Walt Disney World, and then rent a car for the two weeks, as opposed to driving your own car to the Sunshine State? Wouldn't the total price tag for gas be less than the cost of the four airfares and a rental? And, as a bonus, you can stop to see the Gateway Arch in Saint Louis, and Graceland in Memphis, and tour the *USS Alabama* in Mobile, then see Orlando, and hit Cape Kennedy on the way back, and Coke World in Atlanta, and Great Smokey Mountain National Park, and Opryland in Nashville, and Churchill Downs in Louisville, and the Indianapolis Motor Speedway. If your vacation is basically 16 days, Friday to Sunday, couldn't what I just outlined represent a workable holiday?

So what have I added to your money and your time to transform two weeks in Orlando into two weeks driving from Chicago to Orlando and back? Just one little thing: imagination. And that's exactly what I want to do in this book: fire your imagination, so that you not only *want* to see such places as these (which I suspect you do already), but that you realize that such a trip is possible, and even within your personal vacation parameters. And really, how many times can you ride Space Mountain, or tour It's a Small World, or see Fantasmic, anyway? When I did WDW, it took me four days. If you have 16 days to travel, that leaves you 12 days remaining for collateral touring: the Tampa Bay Area, New Orleans, Mammoth Cave National Park, Cincinnati. The specific stops you opt for going and coming are your choices: just look at the map, and let your imagination run free, considering all those intervening states, and eventually deciding on the cities, and parks, and sights, you really want to visit. These loci are just waiting for you to drop by.

I'll admit, you're going to be busier on this vacation than you would for two weeks at a cabin in Wisconsin; or even, perhaps, *perhaps*, for two weeks at Orlando. However, do you really think your kids are going to let you relax in Central Florida, once you get there? So if WDW is your destination, you're going to be on your feet, one way or the other. However, instead of buying a two-week Park Hopper pass this year, what not buy that National Parks pass, or one of those combo tickets for a given city, or use those AAA discounts indicated in their tour books?

Just so you don't get the wrong idea: I love Chicago, and the area around it. As you'll see, it made my list of top five cities. In fact, it works both ways: the family living in Orlando could just as readily imagine a vacation heading from there to the Windy City. So for them, part of the fun would be touring the Loop, and the Brookfield Zoo, and the Wisconsin Dells, all for the first time, instead of yet another year at Seaworld and Universal Studios. You see, every state, and every city, is worth visiting. What I would like to see is people, whether groups, or families, or even that strange bird, the solitary traveler (like myself), not go automatically to their own vacation default setting: the Los Angeles amusement parks one more year, or two weeks camping at the local state park. I know you want to see more than that. And if, after reading this book, you don't plan a vacation like the one I'm suggesting within five years of said reading, for from two weeks to a month touring the USA, I will consider the book as having failed, no matter how much you may have otherwise enjoyed it.

That's why I'm writing this tome: to get you on the road. I don't work for a travel agency, or AAA, or the petroleum industry. I'm just a guy who has done a great deal of peregrinating in the USA, and I yearn to share some of these adventures with you. However, I don't simply want you to appreciate the places I have been, and then go back to (Cliché Warning) business as usual every year. Rather, I want you to be so motivated by what I have done that you say to yourself, If Tony could do it, I can do it too. Maybe not every year. Still, the first thing I would like you to do is take that dream vacation, that month on the road, seeing all those wonderful sights, from the Liberty Bell to Mount Rushmore, from the Alamo to Mount Rainier. You may not be able to pull it off in a year, or even two years, given that you may need to save up time, or money, or both, and maybe wait until the kids are at least out of diapers. But you can start planning now.

Then, once you have taken the dream vacation, and are back home, with all the pictures, and the t-shirts, and the souvenirs, I want you to ask yourself, What is keeping me from doing this sort of thing again, in two years, or five years, or even next year? Believe me, you will not exhaust the sights in America in one trip, or two, or five: I have done it over 40 times, and there are still places I have not gotten to visit yet that I'd like to see, so you're not going to run out of dreams, as long as you're still willing to let your mind wander free.

Now, you might say, I could never travel that much, so what's the point of starting? I'll never drive cross-country 40 times, so I guess I'll be going to the Dells one more year. Heck, long-distance truckers drive cross-country as many times as I have in *one year*: should that make *me* stop wanting to see new things? And on that first trip (which I relate in a subsequent chapter), in the winter of 1984-85: I had no idea the domino effect it would initiate in my personal vacation history. I have always just taken one year at a time, one trip at a time, and enjoyed it as much as I could; and I hope to continue doing so as long as the good Lord gives me the health for it.

Some of you may be old enough to remember the sixties ad campaign by the US government, entitled, See America First. It actually had its roots in the early 20th century, with the railroads and the newly-formed National Park Service (NPS) trying to convince wealthy Americans to abandon travel in Europe, a favorite destination, for the western half of their own country, especially to the new National Parks that were being formed to add to the older ones. With the advent of cheaper jet travel in the sixties, more and more *middle*-class Americans were taking vacations to Europe, and even more exotic places. In the midst of all of that international travel, that old See America First campaign resurfaced. Uncle Sam was telling us that there was still plenty to see right here, and for a lot less money. That latter point may resonate with people in these economically troubled

"See America First"

times, so that folks who used to summer abroad may need, for financial reasons, (*Cliché Warning [or, henceforth, *CW]) to cast their eyes domestically for now. What I, and Uncle Sam, are saying, is that, if you do so, you will not be disappointed.

I remember a TV ad, back when this campaign was rolling (I'm not sure now if it was directly connected with it or not, although its point is similar). It involved a gray-haired man, a little portly, talking to the camera, explaining that he always wanted to travel around the country, but never took the trouble to do so. Eventually, he told himself that he would accomplish this dream after he retired; but now that he was finished working, he lacked both the money and the health for activities of that sort. The camera then pulled away, and you saw him, looking through one of those pay binocular devices on the shore, glancing across the harbor to the Statue of Liberty. The point was not that there's anything wrong with the Statue of Liberty. The point was that, he had always wanted to travel outside the five boroughs of New York City; and now that he had the time, it was too late. It brings a metaphorical tear to my eye just thinking about that ad.

That's not the way I want you to think. No, I want you to be another Ignatius of Loyola. Who was he? A Spanish nobleman born in 1491, who had dreams of winning glory for his country on the battlefield, until a cannonball ended his military career. He needed to spend a good deal of time convalescing, and at that point began reading the lives of the saints. What that book did was fire *his* imagination, so that he eventually told himself that he could still win glory, not on an earthly battlefield, but in the service of the Great King. Indeed, he summed up his resolve by insisting, "If Francis of Assisi could do it, and Dominic could do it, I can do it, too." He was willing to dream, but he did not stop with the daydream. No, he put his dream, his vision, into action, founding the Jesuit order, and is now counted among the greatest saints in the Catholic Church's history.

To repeat: that is precisely what I want you to say: If Tony could do it, if some friend or family member could do it, I can do it too. And you can: perhaps not this year, perhaps not next year. But if you want to turn your travel dreams into reality, you need to stash some money away, and save up some vacation time, and procure the travel books, and the maps, and start turning desire into achievement. And if you don't have any travel dreams yet, read on. I plan to fire your imagination.

How? By sharing some of my own travel stories. I have a two-fold purpose in doing so: to allow my own time on the road to bear positive fruit for others by enlivening their desire to join me on the road; and to suggest some specific places to start, to present particular locations like cities and states, National Parks and museums, so that, if you don't have any travel dreams yet (which I sincerely doubt), I will help you get the process started; and if you already have travel dreams, I will make you decide that the time has come to turn the possible into the real.

I recall a National Geographic TV piece when I was a boy, about a certain Pacific tribe that practiced a very distinctive rite through which a boy needed to pass before he could be considered a man: to jump off a tower, head-first, with nothing but a couple of vines tied around his ankles to stop him from smashing headfirst into the ground. Now he could see others accomplishing this feat over the years, and knew that they survived when they did it. However, it was easier said than done. I can feel for those young men, since I remember my first attempt to do a flip off the high dive at our swimming club. I kept walking back and forth along the top, until the yelling of the other kids, who wanted to use the board too, got me to jump off. I managed to do something resembling a flip, but was mainly happy that it was over. Well, this boy's family would follow him up the ladder; and if he hesitated at the edge, they would poke him with a certain type of leaf that made him itch, so that, even if he was afraid of the fall, he would jump, if only to get away from his family.

You can see me as one of those leaves. My stated intention is to make you itch so badly to take at least one cross-country drive, ocean to ocean, in your lifetime, that you will do it, if for no other reason than to shut up my voice inside your head. You don't have to do it every year, or even every five years: just once. I am convinced that if you take that step, the country will snag you, so that you will probably want to do it again some day. However, you may be like my one frat brother, who ran his first marathon race, and that was it for the rest of his life. I've never run a marathon, and probably never will now, since I imagine it's too late for me (he did it when he was in the Marine Corps), like that retired New Yorker. However, on the Internet the other day, there was a bit about a man from India, who took up marathoning in his *eighties*, to deal with his wife's death, and just completed one at the age of 100. Sure, it took him over eight hours, but he did it. And you can do it too.

You see, after reading this book, every time you notice the side of a U-Haul truck, with some US city or state or National Park highlighted, my voice is going to be itching on the inside of your brain. Every time you watch a movie or TV show that takes place in LA, my voice is going to be itching on the inside of your brain. Every time you see a vacation ad in a magazine, or pass by a travel agency, my voice it going to be itching on the inside of your brain. Every time a friend shares with you about his or her travel experiences, or shows you photos of them, or sends you a postcard from elsewhere, my voice is going to be itching on the inside of your brain. Every autumn, when your kids come home from school with stories of where their classmates went on vacation that past summer, my voice is going to be itching on the inside of your brain. Indeed, ever time your GPS tells you how to get somewhere local, my voice is going to be itching on the inside of your brain, telling you that that GPS system that is taking you to Michigan Avenue in downtown Chicago could just as easily be taking you to Michigan's Upper Peninsula, or Florida's peninsula, or the Olympic Peninsula across Puget Sound from Seattle.

If you don't want that annoyance to commence, close this book now and never open it again. Oops: it's too late! You've already dipped your foot into the pool, and the monster in the middle of the lake has been alerted, as in *The Lord of the Rings*, and it's coming to get you. I've already planted the seed, and every time anything reminds you of travel, that seed will be watered. You can fight it – using an increasing amount of energy to remain in denial – that you really don't want to see bison in Yellowstone, or see Old Faithful spurting, or catch a big-mouth bass there; or that, if you watch TV, you really don't need to see the actual Hollywood sign, or go to the original Disneyland, or take the Walk of Fame, since LA comes into your home every evening; or you don't need to go to New York City, since you need to be crazy to want to drive there, and anyway, there are skyscrapers in Chicago, and museums, and municipal parks, and (*CW) if you've seen one, you've seen them all. You can keep resisting; but think of all the energy such resistance involves.

Then imagine yourself using that same energy to plan a cross-country drive. Imagine writing postcards *to* your friends from the Grand Canyon, telling them that you took the mule ride all the way down to the bottom to the Colorado River, and saw the IMAX film of it, and even enjoyed the walk along the edge in the light of the full moon. It's still energy, but it's being used differently. I mean, you could wrap your limbs around a tree and squeeze for half an hour, or you could go for a three-mile run. They both use energy, but which one is more enjoyable and productive? (OK, I admit to having sported a Treehugger bumper sticker on a car I used to own, but never did so for thirty minutes.) So if you want to wait until retirement, only to realize that you only have enough money and health to take the elevator to the top of the Willis Tower (the old Sears Tower) each month to see the panorama, the moment may pass you by. Don't let this happen to you! (*CW) Take the bull by the horns, and start preparing today. How? By reading the rest of this book. It is not a tour book strictly speaking, but AAA provides them free to members. No, this is your motivational spiel, your half-time pep talk.

There was an ad up recently on a billboard near where I live, with the pictures of several individuals other people would consider winners: General and Secretary of State Colin Powell; Notre Dame football coach Lou Holtz; Notre Dame and Forty-Niner quarterback Joe Montana; New York mayor Rudy Giuliani; and first Lady Laura Bush. I didn't actually attend this motivational gathering, but I imagine it was very well done, because I know everyone represented on that ad, and each one has something to say. Well, that's what I want you to become: travel motivators. I want you to become so geared toward touring, even if only once every five years, that you are able to pass the flame on to your relatives, friends and co-workers. Indeed, I want you to fall in love with travel so deeply – not simply the idea of travel, but with real, live, actual travel – that eventually *you* become that itchy voice inside the brains of others, getting them to take the jump into cross-country vacationing, until they do what you have done. Why? Because you want them to enjoy it as much as you did.

And then too, you'll need people with whom to swap travel stories, at least until you write your own book.

Just kidding about the book: the only thing you need to write is a postcard or two, letting others in on the secret you've lately discovered. And that secret? That America is a (*CW) treasure trove of magic, of sights to see, be they National Parks, art museums, magnificent buildings, historical sites, zoos, arboreta, air and space museums ... the list could go on and on. In college I always wanted to see the world, but circumstances conspired to make me travel in the USA, as I shall relate in due time. So what happened? It's not that I lost all interest in the other five habitable continents. It's just that I fell in love with travel in America, and now see it as my own default setting. Perhaps after 40 cross-country excursions, it's time for me to allow myself to be challenged internationally. Maybe so. But as for you, my advice is what that sixties ad tried to drive home, no pun intended: See America First.

Just a note on how to read the book: most of these chapters, once you get past the introductory ones, are generally free-standing, meaning that they need not be read in order. After all, there's no reason you need to digest the one about my third favorite city before you peruse the one about my second favorite city, since the focus within those chapters is simply on the individual towns being discussed. For that reason, you may run into occasional duplication in different chapters. For example, there are several sections dealing with my home state, Pennsylvania (lucky you), and you may pick and choose rather than read them in order. How considerate of me not to edit out such overlapping info (although if you prefer the word lazy to considerate, I won't argue with you). The perfectionist Dr Sheldon Cooper in me wants to have every datum represented only once, but my practical Penny side wants to make the book as easy to read as possible, which at times means repetition, since most of us don't have photographic memories, and so will not necessarily remember, by the time we get to page 251, what we read on page 29. (By my current age of 60, I'd be happy to remember on page 251 what I wrote on page 250.)

Bon voyage!

CHAPTER 1

REVVING UP THE ENGINE: THE COUNTDOWN BEGINS

I was born in the Philadelphia area, and for the first 22 years of my life never traveled farther than a contiguous state away.

Actually, that's not true; and stooping to outright lies in the first sentence of the first chapter of a book is hardly the way to engender a feeling of confidence in anything that will subsequently be written and (hopefully) read. You see, I spent a week in Washington, D.C. during my senior year in high school for what was called the Close-Up program, which gave interested students a broad introduction to various facets of national government. Now I know that the District of Columbia is not a state. However, one day we were driven to Arlington National Cemetery and the Pentagon, which meant that we entered Virginia, albeit barely. A quick glance at the map reveals that, while Virginia *almost* touches Pennsylvania, the thin arm of Maryland prevents their direct contact. However, there is an old Latin saying that goes, "*Parum pro nihilo reputatur*," which means that a little basically counts as nothing (nothing personal, Maryland), a truism that is not universally applicable, as evidenced by such things as diamonds, uranium, black holes, gametes and love.

I'm a Catholic priest, by the way, which is why I guess I just used a Latin proverb. I'll try not to do it too often. That's something I suppose you ought to know, since even though it has not generally been the focus of my travels, it has been one context for them. You see, as it happens, the start of my serious traveling basically coincides with my ordination, although that's not the main reason for them.

So why didn't I travel much before then? Well, until I was 18 I did not have a driver's license, and so I couldn't drive myself (legally, anyway). Pennsylvania allows you to start driving at 16, but since there wasn't a family car to be put at my disposal, it was decided by my parental units to postpone my procuring a license until I was closer to college, so that I earned it in May of my senior year in high school. Thus, my friends got a jump on me for 27 months, although, as you will agree, with over 40 cross-continental drives, I have made up for lost time. (I hope that that hyphenated word did not come across as too pretentious. It's just that I want to show that I have seen almost as much of Canada [in terms of area] as I have of the USA. I'd like to see Mexico, too, but, except for one quick incursion across the border from Arizona, and a cruise to the Mexican Riviera, I have not done it yet. Given the state of my Spanish, I have too little confidence in doing it alone.) And then I got a 10-year-old car for college, which was fine for the 12-mile round trip each day, but which I would have felt uncomfortable trying to drive any significant distance. (That is, assuming I had the money to do so, which I did not, since the money that I did make on summer jobs basically went toward college expenses. Break out the violin, right?)

Thus, my touring depended on others, specifically, my parents. With five children, travel for us essentially meant an annual vacation at the South Jersey shore. The two-hour drive to Wildwood, and in later years the 90-minute trek to Brigantine, seemed long enough with seven people and their luggage in the car (with children of crying age, and bladders that craved attention); so I guess the thought of going anywhere farther, and packing and unpacking the car with regularity during that time, never seriously occurred to my folks. True, my father did some business-related travel; and his talking about his annual Data Processing Management Association out-of-state conventions whetted my appetite to see places like New Orleans, and Montreal (he was there for the World's Fair, Expo '67), and San Francisco (which, once he got there for the first time, supplanted even Montreal as his favorite city). Indeed, I recall one year, when the convention was as close as Chicago, they considered taking all of us by car, and even mapped it out with our home atlas. However, they just couldn't swing it, then or any other year.

Thus, we kids would ambush him on his return each year with the usual greetings, immediately followed by the usual rummaging through his luggage to see what souvenirs he bought us. (My all-time favorite was a wind-up plastic alligator from the Big Easy that scrambled quickly across the floor.) But long after these keepsakes had gone the way of all toys, the pull that his speaking of those cities engendered in me remained, and I knew I wanted to see a lot more of the world than Southeastern Pennsylvania and South Jersey.

Now I just mentioned the world, and you might think that a priest who has been ordained for over 30 years would have been to all the usual international Catholic stops, such as Rome, the Holy Land, Fatima, Guadalupe, Paris, Ireland, Bavaria, Spain. However, in spite of my strong desire to go to all of those places and many more (you could hardly name a place that I would not like some day to visit), my travel off the continent has thus far been limited to Italy, twice, and that rather late in the game. One reason is that I love driving, just love it. The more, the better. Long, boring mile after long, boring mile. And I cannot drive to Europe or Asia or Africa or Australia.

Another reason is that I am cheap, and, when traveling, tend to eat food I carry with me rather than dining in restaurants (although in these later years I at times stoop to the use of the drive-throughs and dollar menus of fast food places). Further, I eschew motels (and *a fortiori* [there's that Latin again] hotels) in favor of other accommodations. Sometimes I camp, and so actually eat hot food (if I'm not too tired to cook it after driving 16 hours and then setting up the tent). Sometimes I stay with priests I know along the way (my second seminary accepted men from all over the country), and so actually eat food that someone else has prepared, which occasionally means going to restaurants. And sometimes I simply pull into a rest stop and sleep in the back seat of my car. To be fair to myself, it's not only my stinginess with money that is involved here. I am also stingy with time, and consider it a waste of *my* time to spend half a day or more (say, if I check in at 6:00 p.m., and check out at 8:00 a.m.) in a place where I know no one, and where all the spots of interest are closed for the day. Then there's the hassle of hoping there's a room during the tourist season (I generally have no idea where I'm going to be tomorrow night, and so do not make reservations), and of actually procuring it (which involves dealing with people I don't know), and checking out the next day. How much easier to pull into a rest stop, climb into the back seat, sleep, get up, and drive away. (If I want a cheap breakfast, there are always the rest stop vending machines.)

Now, the precipitating reason for my taking these cross-country trips is that, during my seminary years, my parents moved from Pennsylvania to California, where they became ensconced strongly and soon. Thus, if I was ever going to see them again, it looked like it was going to involve travel on *my* part. Given how I had for years wanted to do just that, nobody needed to twist my arm.

However, I would not say that even that factor was the ultimate reason for my driving across so many times. After all, there is plane service between Philadelphia and Los Angeles, and I could have flown out each year to see them and saved myself quite a bit of trouble (as I have done on occasion when circumstances required it, such as for baptisms), as well as some of my valuable time. I dislike flying, but I tolerate it. It's not a fear of flying in the usual sense. Indeed, my favorite aspects of the flight are the two most dangerous times – take-off and landing – adding excitement to an otherwise boring several hours. No, what I fear is getting stuck in front of kids who like to kick the back of the seat, or near screaming infants, or next to a bore. (To get a concrete picture of this flyer, rent a copy of *The Accidental Tourist*, and observe the William Hurt character. When my father asked a friend and fellow worker why he drove an hour into work every day in rush hour traffic instead of taking public transit, he received the reply that he was particular about whom he let sit next to him.) And then the air pressure in the cabin tends to make me dehydrated and sick (i.e., queasy stomach, headache). I have generally preferred a window seat, both to enjoy a semblance of privacy, and to be able to gaze at the ground or the clouds the whole time I'm awake but too tired to read. Of course, as I and my bladder age, the aisle seat looks better and better. (I used to be able to avoid pit stops on the road between fuel fill-ups, but, short of using a catheter, which I have at times considered [the less-invasive kind], those days are gone.)

This disinclination to be around people I don't know deserves mention, I suppose, both because it might seem unusual for a priest, who works with people all the time, and because it is yet another factor that impels me onto these long, eremetical drives. It might help you to know that I am a strong introvert, and actually once entered a monastery of hermits for a brief time, and left (so I tell people at least, tongue-in-cheek) because even *they* spent too much time together (twice a week) for my taste. (Allow me to add, with a deadpan face, that the real reason was that I simply wanted to spend a fall in Vermont, where the leaves are dramatically beautiful. The reds and yellows were so bright – even the ones on the ground – that they hurt my eyes. As Pennsylvania proud as I am, I have to give the autumnal edge to the Green Mountain State.) It's not that I dislike strangers so much as find their small talk, well, soporific. I'm not saying that I don't have the same effect on others (ask anyone who's tried to stay awake during my homilies). After all, we all have different things that interest us. However, as I've gotten older, I've discovered that the things that tend to interest me tend to interest hardly anyone else. (Now I know I shouldn't be telling you this, in case you haven't bought the book yet but are only browsing through it in the bookstore. I do that a lot, too, and get books out of libraries, to avoid paying for them.) If you don't believe me, count yourself fortunate that I excised the chapters on the designs of license plates and the shapes of state route signs. Experience teaches well, but not always kindly.

However, perhaps you will see the reflections contained herein as a sociological curiosity: to read about people who, for instance, really sleep in their cars (I don't do this in mid-town Manhattan, you understand, on those rare occasions when my travels take me through densely-populated areas). Because, you see, while I realize that each of us has his or her own tastes, I have (finally) noticed over time that there are what you might call Most People's Tastes, and there are My Tastes. (I've stopped discussing license plates with others for that reason, unless asked to do so, which I never have been. In my younger days I really thought others were as interested in them as I was.) However, rather than believe that the twain shall never meet, I like to think (although I may still be in denial here) that the things that interest me simply have not begun to interest you *yet*, but that reading about them might spark an interest in something you have always wanted to do but could never convince yourself to do: to take at least one cross-country drive during your lifetime.

After all, I have taken more conventional vacations, and they have not killed *me*. In fact, they tend to be relaxing. So if *you* are used to those R&R sorts of holidays, why not try *my* type? You don't have to do it every year. You don't need to do the stripped-down version that I do. But the Grand Canyon looks a lot different from the ground than from the air (as impressive as it appears from above, admittedly, a bonus for traveling from LA to Philly through Chicago rather than Dallas/Fort Worth). And then there's Old Faithful, and Independence Hall, and caribou, and Mission Control, and so many other things between one coast and the other, generally not visible from 30,000 feet (unless you're doing military surveillance). If you've ever wanted to see, not in a book, not on TV, not even in an IMAX theater, but really see, the Grand Tetons; or a buffalo in the wild (a word I still prefer to bison, in spite of a decision that somebody made in recent years for some reason, given the city, and the nickel, and Bill, and the wings, and the chips); or a grizzly bear (at a safe distance, or in a car: not that I've always followed that commendable advice myself with other large wild animals); or the Florida Keys surrounded as they are on a sunny day by *green* water; or Fisherman's Wharf (with the taste of local Ghirardelli chocolate or Boudin sour dough bread in your mouth); or a field of sunflowers; or one of tall hay or wheat glowing in the sunlight; or the almost phosphorescent reds of autumn in Vermont, why not? If you can't see it all, why not at least see something? I still haven't seen it all yet, and hope that I have not taken my last such trip. The other five continents continue to beckon, and maybe I unconsciously think that I'll live for 200 years, and enjoy perfect health the whole time, to be able to do them in the same integral way. Do you really want suddenly to discover that you're too old to travel by car, and that you've missed all the cool stuff? Don't let this happen to you! *Carpe diem* (a Latin phrase I learned, by the way, not in the seminary, but from the film, *The Dead Poets Society*, thanks to Robin Williams, God rest him): Seize the day!

Still, I have found travel in the USA infectious. Indeed, back in 1992, when I was flying (yes, flying) back from California to the East after baptizing my first nephew, gazing down at the vast empty spaces below, misty-eyed that I was passing over the continent so fast, it took a mere sentence two months later from another priest at some diocesan gathering to get me back on the road. What was that sentence? He related that he was leaving early that evening to be able to finish his packing for his flight the next day to Yellowstone for his annual fishing trip. Those words, and the personal memories they evoked, decided me that I had to get out again on what could have been my last such trip before entering the afore-mentioned monastery. It wasn't (I had two more trips after that before entering the next year, believe it or not; and I did not remain there, although I don't *think* primarily because of their vow of stability, which basically means staying put the rest of your life), but it was something I felt I just had to do.

But we have now arrived at the ultimate reason why I keep doing this traveling: the compelling, magnetic, unremitting beauty of this continent. It was on that same above-mentioned impromptu trip in 1992 that I ran into a man from Italy. It was in Zion National Park in southwestern Utah, a ruggedly gorgeous state. I had driven through that Park on the highway once before with a seminary classmate back in 1986, a year after our ordination, without realizing that we would be doing so (we were on UT-9, on the way from the Grand Canyon to Yellowstone), and I was really taken with the place, promising myself that I would return one day, God willing, to do some non-technical rock climbing on all that granite. That promise was fulfilled in 1992, along with one to return to Theodore Roosevelt National Park, in western North Dakota.

In Zion there was one particular hiking option named Hidden Canyon, which was rather rigorous physically. I assumed that the warning about this trail was over-reactionary. Boy, was I wrong. There were lots of people on it early-on; however, the farther up I went, the fewer people, and their footprints in the sandy surface, were present. Eventually there was only one set of feet going up past where I was walking, and I soon met their owner coming down.

This Italian *que uomo* was in excellent physical shape. He had an ebullient personality, or else was in an effervescent mood as a result of the climb. The effort by then, however, was having a different effect on me, since it was becoming not only strenuous but dangerous, given that you were more and more required to scoot up logs propped against the narrowing canyon walls, which led up to precariously thin sedimentary ledges, which sloped downward and which, yes, had sand on them. When I got to the point where I was not sure I could make a particular jump, and then noticed several more such hurdles between myself and the top, I did something I rarely do: made a prudent choice, aborting the mission rather than fall 20 feet onto granite, break something, and languish there above the level anyone else that day would visit (except for a veteran mountain climber from the Italian Alps, and he was already heading down).

Now this individual (in his thirties or early forties) spoke very little English; and the only Italian words *I* knew were the wrong ones to use with physically-impressive strangers out in the middle of nowhere. However, my limited knowledge of Spanish and Latin (see, it does have everyday uses) enabled us to communicate after a fashion, and I soon realized how taken he was with America. He was on a trip across the country to see as much of the outdoors as possible, and he kept repeating the words, "*Que bella!*", "How beautiful!" He commented, however, that there is much beauty in Europe, too, but that the added dimension in America was *size*, as with, for example, the Grand Canyon. And yes, the Alps are tall, too, like the Rockies, but they don't run from Mexico to Alaska. We continued on our respective ways (I hadn't bailed out from the hike just yet), although at the time I did not realize that my first overseas trip, five years later, would be to his country. And while some people might prefer that foreign visitors learn English before coming here, I say, Nonsense. Come on over! After all, that's the way I have seen Italy twice, and I managed to survive. Call me naïve, but I imagine that most people are happy to help a foreigner who has thought enough to visit the United States or some other country in the first place (France being the obvious exception); and I was thrilled to see how happy

Revving Up The Engine: The Countdown Begins

this man was with what he had seen here. In the end, while we did not have a common verbal language, there was another language at work, an aesthetic one resulting from a mutual appreciation of beauty.

Even if you don't consider yourself an aesthete, I would be very surprised if you could visit the Grand Canyon, or the Grand Tetons, or the Grand Banks, or Grand Central Station (well, maybe not) and not feel a sense of awe. We all, I believe, have an openness to true beauty, and simply need to place ourselves into its proximity to appreciate it. I think that innate trait (sorry) is what compels travelers to compare stories: not so much a one-upmanship of places visited (although I enjoy geographic name-dropping as much as anyone, as this book will prove), but a wanting to speak that aesthetic language with someone else who understands. What I am hoping, is that this language not remain the arcane enclave of a few, but that everyone from this country (and from other countries) will become fluent enough to enter this conversation. And becoming at least conversant does not require a hundred thousand miles of travel, but seeing what you can with an openness to the beauty that lies therein. Then you can listen to the stories of others as if you have been there with them, because while there are different particular manifestations of beauty, the same Beauty lies behind them all.

And don't think I am referring exclusively to the (*CW) great outdoors. There is plenty of human-made beauty in art museums; and the inspired aspects of our human history as in the documents of our creation as a nation (again, sorry) show a rational beauty in the human mind and heart: the vision of a Benjamin Franklin, or the bravery of a Francis Marion, or the patriotism of an Abigail Adams. And what of the beauty of creation collected for us in natural history museums? It all represents different aspects of Beauty, and is all worth experiencing.

Now, what I've just said might seem a tad inconsistent with what I've said earlier about my tendency toward solitude. However, one reason for that tendency is that as a boy I was often picked-on by other kids, given that what *they* liked and what *I* liked tended to be different (e.g., basketball vs. license plates). However, when I find people of similar interests, I can become quite the chatterbox (at least until they run from the room screaming). One reason for penning this volume is to try to bridge that gap: to be able to communicate a sense of our country's beauty to people who have so far seen little of it. After all, if you're anything like me, even if you've never traveled much, you would *like* to see all these places if the details could ever be arranged. At the risk of redundancy, I am hoping that after finishing this volume you decide that arranging the details is not only possible but worthwhile.

Perhaps you were like me even in grade school. Each September I would be subjected to the vacation stories of other kids in the class, who had gone to Disneyland or Cape Kennedy or Yellowstone or other places I only dreamed of going, while I had to repeat once again that I had only gotten as far as the Jersey shore. (Lest anyone get the wrong impression, South Jersey has some of the best beaches and the whitest, finest sand in the world; and a hundred years ago Cape May, a wonderfully-preserved Victorian town, rivaled Newport, Rhode Island as *the* summer, east-coast resort for the rich. It may not be far from true that whole neighborhoods from Philadelphia transplant to the same sections of the Wildwoods each summer. Still, there are quieter places, as we learned when we began renting a house in the largely year-round residential community of Brigantine, just north of Atlantic City but a world away. AC has gone through a sort of reviviscence since those days with the arrival of casinos, so that the vacationer has all manner of options between Brigantine and Cape May, including legendary boardwalks [some much more impressive than the fabled Santa Monica pier near LA] and excellent waves for body-surfing. It's just that I longed to see greener pastures, as many as possible. But for most people in the USA, south Jersey [including the Pine Barrens, or, as it is called now, the less-colorful Pinelands National Reserve, an entity encompassing almost the whole southern half of the state] can be one of those greener pastures.)

But back to grade school. I generally teach in the school of whatever parish I am assigned to as a priest, and find myself asking that same vacation question of the class at the start of each year. One reason, of course, is to give me an excuse to talk about *my* latest trip. I do feel a bit bad when some kids talk about spending three months in Orlando, while others mention a day at the Kennywood amusement park in Pittsburgh. Still, I'm not trying to make those latter kids feel bad, because I really enjoy hearing where they all went. And I also want to infect them with my same love for travel, so that, just as I saw very little until I was almost 30, so too they can hope one day to see much more than that which is circumscribed within a 200-mile radius.

Now, allow me to confess that for years I never kept a detailed log of any of my trips (except the ones to Rome, which you will not be reading about here), and generally no log at all (later, this sin of omission was to change). When on my first trip, a short excursion through New England and a couple of the Maritime Provinces in Canada with a frat brother, I noticed that he kept a daily journal. I thought it was a good idea, but for a long time never followed his example. Thus, it was not until about the 11th trip, when they had begun blending together in my mind, that I sat down with my Rand-McNally Road Atlas and tried my best to reconstruct at least the places I had been and the routes I had taken. However, I think now, in light of this current endeavor, that that omission will work as a blessing for you, for you will not be subjected to a mile-by-mile account of an accumulation of drives long enough to circumnavigate the globe several times over. Rather, I will present my travel-related thoughts to you more thematically than chronologically (generally: there will be exceptions). While it might seem at times (not without reason) that I am simply falling into the trap of seasoned travelers – to show off through name-dropping – I hope that this presentation of reflections and recollections will encourage You the Reader to become You the Traveler. Then, if we ever meet, we can do one of the things I enjoy almost as much as touring: comparing travel stories.

One final introductory remark: you may not find the name of your town, or your favorite vacation spot, or historical location, listed here. That fact does not mean that such places are not worth visiting. It simply means that I am simply not aware of them, have not visited them (yet), or simply didn't have room to include them all in a book of this size. What I have seen so far corresponds to some extent to travel circumstances; and what I chose from among them corresponds in no small part to my own personal tastes (although I try to discuss sights that would appeal to a variety of interests). This book is not meant to be the whole meal, or even the main course, but an appetizer and an aperitif, to whet your own appetite not simply to visit the places named herein, but to be able to impress me, when we meet some day, with the places you've found that I so far have not, and so get *me* back on the road.

CHAPTER 2

IT'S A BEAUTIFUL DAY IN THE NEIGHBORHOOD: PENNSYLVANIA AND ITS CONTIGUOUS STATES

We all need to start from somewhere, and I, like Fred Rogers, started in Pennsylvania. Actually, that's not exactly true; and so here I am, starting this *second* chapter with another falsehood. Not very appropriate priestly example. Still, in one sense, my life began in Pennsylvania, since I was born there. However, if you go by Chinese rather than Western reckoning for when to start counting the beginning of your birthdays, then my first state was actually Florida, which is not only not Pennsylvania, but is not even a contiguous state to Pennsylvania. OK, so how?

My parents were married on April 30, 1955, and I was born on February 2, 1956, nine months and two days later. They obviously didn't waste any time in the children department (you know those Catholics). Now, since they honeymooned in Miami Beach, Florida, and drove down from Pennsylvania, then that meant that, assuming a nine-month gestation, I was conceived two days after their wedding. The first night they spent in Philadelphia, the second night at the well-known South of the Border motel complex in South Carolina, on the state line with North Carolina (just getting its start at the time), and the third night, May 2, in Miami Beach (which, as any Jackie Gleason fan knows, has the greatest audience in the world, and is, apparently, the best place to conceive a child as well).

Now I suspect that *these* Honeymooners had something other than The Great One on their minds that week, and so that is where I enter the picture, albeit *in utero*. Still, since my conception in the Sunshine State meant that I was technically in Florida and all the intervening east coast sovereign jurisdictions before getting to the Keystone State, then Pennsylvania was in that sense my *eighth* state to occupy physically. However, as much as I admire the Chinese culture, and hope to visit China some day, I will for the rest of this book take the more customary occidental course and begin my official state count when I actually exited the womb on Groundhog Day of 1956. (Of course, having covered a thousand miles in the first several days of my embryonic existence on the ride back perhaps explains more than anything my long-standing love of driving.)

And here, allow me to make a point. (I hope you'll forgive any mini-homilies to which I may subject you: it's an occupational hazard.) My father worked for one of the big Philadelphia banks for 28 years before he and my mom grew tired of the cold and moved to warmer climes. His office was downtown, and after taking the el (for you people from the Heartland, that is the elevated train) from suburbia each day, he'd walk past Independence Hall, the single most important historical building in the country (you'll allow me a bit of civic pride). However, in all those 28 years, he never once actually went-in to see the Liberty Bell (which at the time was housed there). My mother, a native of the city, finally went to see it, in her forties, during the Bicentennial year, and recalls how the people next to her were from South Carolina; and when they asked her where *she* was from, and she said, "Drexel Hill, about half an hour away," they looked at her oddly. Still, better late than never. My point? It is so easy sometimes, in imagining that the grass is greener somewhere else, to miss so much of the turf your own area has to offer. Thus, while I strongly encourage every American to travel cross-country at least once (but you knew that), I also encourage all of us to know what is within a hundred-mile drive of our home, and visit it.

Now while Philadelphia has a rather high concentration of things to see and do per square mile (museums, music, sports, history, colleges), still, wherever I travel, there always seems to be *something* to discover. In fact, since I have been ordained for the Catholic Diocese of Altoona-Johnstown in 1985, in central Pennsylvania, I have always found something to see and do here. As it happens, my mother fell in love with diminutive Johnstown when she came to visit me. When we were taking the downtown walking tour, we ran into the then-mayor, Herb Pfuhl, who asked us to stop by his office the next day, at which time he gave her a certificate naming her an honorary citizen of that municipality. So if 99% of the country feels that the grass is greener in *your* greater neighborhood than in theirs, then check out why, and see it.

I admit it: it was culture shock moving from Philadelphia to State College. To correct another lie, or at least a possible inaccurate impression: my parents did not move to California from Philadelphia, but from State College, right next to Penn State (yes, that is the name of the town), an intervening stop having to do with work. They arrived in central P-A in 1979, the year I entered the seminary in Philadelphia. (When I began at a second seminary in 1983, reflective of the fact that I changed dioceses to Altoona-Johnstown, they moved to the West Coast, occasioning the usual remarks from classmates that if I found them again, they'd probably move a third time.) Now I never lived in Philly proper, but in the western suburbs, but which were still part of the same urban sprawl. Moving to Pine Grove Mills, a little village outside the small university town of State College, which didn't even have home mail delivery, occasioning a daily jaunt down the street to visit George the postmaster, we entered another world. The old post office, now replaced, could practically fit into the trunk of my car, quite a contrast with the main postal center in Philadelphia, a square block in size. (That one and the same frat brother with whom I toured in 1978, visiting subsequently from the City of Brotherly Love, got a kick out of this little building, to which George replied that he wondered how anything at all ever got delivered correctly in the big city.) At first it was great, since that was around the time I entered the sem, and so only came home for breaks, enjoying life in the country for a couple of weeks at a time. It was after I started my first assignment, in Altoona, a blue-collar town of 50,000, that it began to feel like exile. However, the longer I lived there, the easier it was to get used to things like quiet, and a slower pace, and friendliness, and natural beauty, and safety, and traffic that moved well at all times of the day.

This is not meant to be a slap at Philadelphia, or at big cities in general. It's just that every place has its strengths and weaknesses, and I believe it is best to focus on the strengths and put up with the limitations wherever you happen to be (end of ferverino). So, once the shock of full-time residence in Central Pennsylvania was over, life there proved to be pretty appealing, and has now become my home. I recall vacations in Pine Grove Mills from the sem: walking out the back door of the house, up to the mountain ridge, and onto a hiking trail with no one else on it (recall my hesychastic leanings). At the time this chapter was first written, I lived in the rectory, or priest's residence, in State College proper, from which I could walk in half an hour to Penn State's campus, which is not only beautiful but has lots of things going on most of the time, and is quite relaxing and peaceful the rest of the time (especially when the undergrads are gone). And, during the academic year, after regularly viewing their graduate student weekend foreign film series, I'd walk home after midnight without the slightest concern for my safety (except perhaps running into my pastor at the front door).

Thus, in Pennsylvania, you have everything, from a metropolitan city like Philadelphia to a small town like Pine Grove Mills. There are the Pocono Mountains if you like skiing. Lake Erie, if you like boating. Fallingwater, if you like architecture. Gettysburg, if you like historical re-enactments. The Amish, if you like simplicity of life. Philadelphia, if you like higher education (and a little history). Pittsburgh, if you like sports champions. Elk County, if you like hunting (mainly white-tails and gobblers, although there is now a limited elk lottery each year in the Commonwealth). Saint Vincent Archabbey in Latrobe, if you like monasteries (not far from where Arnold Palmer used to drive his old tractor around, and where Mister Rodgers lived). State College, if you like arts festivals (it has one of the 10 highest-ranked nationally each year, in July). Altoona, if you like engineering wonders (the Horseshoe Curve). And lots else. I'll talk more about Philadelphia in a subsequent chapter (lucky you).

So where else had I been before ordination as a deacon, at age 28, in 1984? There's New Jersey to the east, my boyhood summer home-away-from-home, which I've already touched upon. I have also taken the train through it to New York City, each time seeing the sign when it crosses the Delaware River from Pennsylvania, "Trenton makes; the world takes." And one night I accompanied my aunt to the Walt Whitman International Poetry Center in Camden to hear her at a reading. Yes, there is definitely lyricism in the Garden State.

New York is another contiguous state, the one to the north, although I had only been touring in New York City once. It was my first year in the seminary, in 1980, and the school was sponsoring a day trip, to end with a Broadway play. We also went to the top of the Empire State Building (I regret now that I never entered the World Trade Center towers). Before I arrived at the sem the preceding year I had considered monastic life, and visited a priory outside Elmyra, NY (due south of the Finger Lakes, and not far from the Pennsylvania state line). Talk about a contrast to NYC! This monastery was in the middle of nowhere, on purpose, so that the monks could lead a quiet agricultural life. The atmosphere was very appealing, and there has always been a part of me that has tended toward solitude (but you knew that too). So just like Pennsylvania, you can see big and small and everything in-between in the Empire State.

To the west we have Ohio. I spent my last two years there before ordination, at my second seminary, in Columbus: the Pontifical College Josephinum. I regret that, because I did not own a car then, I did not get out and see much of anything, including the state capitol (I was to see it many years later, and then only after dark). I knew that on the drive out from Pennsylvania the place to look for police catching speeders was Zanesville, but I never stopped even there, either, to view any of the sights I would later travel to tour in the Buckeye State.

To the southwest is West Virginia, but all I saw of the Mountain State in those years was the tunnel on I-70 that runs under Wheeling before they built the I-470 bypass.

To the south is Maryland, across the Mason-Dixon Line (it is marked on I-70). I went on Boy Scout camping trips several times, twice down on the Chesapeake Bay. On one such adventure in March I ended-up in a mud bog up to my waist. On another trip, in January, there were flat-topped pieces of ice floating in the water. Several of us got onto one of these impromptu boats, and soon it began sinking. I panicked, and thought that it would be preferable to jump off and into the water. It was so cold, even though the water was only up to my waist, that I immediately doubled-over, so that now I was wet and freezing up to my neck. Somehow, in spite of myself, I managed to survive those trips (I'm sure my mother's prayers played a big role). Also one summer my family went to visit a retirement home for the religious order to which two of my nun aunts belonged, and it was on that trip that I had a strong sense of being in the genteel South in the Old Line State. That impression was reinforced by the nicest rest stop on an interstate that I have ever seen, on I-95 on the way down, with a restaurant called the Maryland House, where my grandmother walked into the rest room, and soon emerged talking to three friends from years before. You just never know whom you're going to meet on the road.

Finally, Delaware is to the southeast. Nearby Wilmington was always popular with Philadelphia shoppers because there is no state sales tax. There is also no liquor tax in the Diamond State, although it is illegal to buy booze there and bring it into P-A. There was also a great hoagie shop, just across the state line, which actually made and sold these sandwiches with prosciutto (always pronounced *brozutte* by my Italian family), the expensive, delicious (albeit salty) Italian lunch meat, at a reasonable price.

Thus, except for my week in Washington, D.C. in high school (which is cut out of Maryland anyway), and the incursion across the Potomac to Arlington, these contiguous states circumscribed my peregrinations until I graduated college. Indeed, except for one trip that graduation summer, which shall be related two chapters hence, they proved to delimit my world until close to priestly ordination in 1985. Thus, if you are in grade school, or even college, or married with a couple of kids, and figure it's too late to start any serious travel, just look at my life and take heart, since things were about to change dramatically. At age 28 I was in my last year in the sem, and took the first of many cross-country drives. But that excursion moves us to the next chapter.

CHAPTER 3

There And Back Again: The First Cross-Country Drive

My first cross-country drive was not about touring, but about getting home for Christmas (I can hear Bing Crosby singing in the background). It was December of 1984, during my final year in the seminary (recall, in Columbus, Ohio). Three of us wanted to visit family for the holidays, but didn't have a lot of extra cash for plane tickets. One of my classmates (we were all deacons) was planning on driving out to Tucson, Arizona, for which diocese he was studying. Another classmate was going to hitch a ride as far as Gallup, New Mexico, *his* diocese. I was told there was room for me if I wanted it, in a car that would get me as close as Phoenix, where I could hop a cheaper flight the rest of the way to Los Angeles, where my family by then lived.

I need to mention that we took a Dodge Colt, and that we were driving a couple of thousand miles one-way. (Someone might argue that Columbus is not on the East Coast, so that it is not really a cross-country drive, but it was close enough for my book [literally and figuratively]. After all, we did cross the [*CW] Mighty Mississippi.) That was quite a few miles in a rather small auto. Oh, it was great for gas; but with three guys, and baggage, it was close to its upper limit. (There was a fourth friend who almost took the drive, heading into Colorado, but that potential passenger, fortunately, never materialized, nice guy though he was.)

We left Columbus at 2:30 in the afternoon. The car owner was driving, and we went for three hours before stopping on that side of Indianapolis at a McDonald's for dinner, and to wait-out rush hour traffic for the city. (I was to experience in later years, when the I-465 beltway seemed perpetually to be under construction, how wise it was to avoid Indy at that time of day.)

I took over the operation at that point. This was a no-frills ride – no sightseeing stops, but just around-the-clock driving – so that I stayed at the wheel until 3:30 the next morning Central Time, almost 11 hours later. This stretch was no doubt the longest I had ever driven at one time. As subsequent trips were to prove, circumstances were creating a monster.

We were not taking any purposely scenic drive, but rather the most direct route (Colorado would have been somewhat out of our way, not to mention problematic in December, but the compassionate auto-owner found it hard to say No to anyone, and would not have considered snow a big problem anyway, what with his front-wheel drive and stick shift). That intention meant that we took I-70 from Columbus across Ohio into Indiana and then past Indianapolis. We shot across Illinois, and finally picked-up I-44 in Saint Louis, Missouri. The trek up to that point was unremittingly boring, since those states are nice and flat, it was early winter, and it was dark most of that time anyway. To this day I find them boring (sorry), except when fields are newly ploughed, and are dark and shining brown with loam, or ripe with crops. Too bad you generally can't see farmland from the interstates in the east, lined as they are with shrubs and trees (which flora admittedly becomes colorful in the fall).

We stopped somewhere for gas, at which point I announced that I had done enough driving for now (what a lightweight), and was heading into the back. The rear seat was mostly filled with luggage, but there was a space behind the front passenger seat where you could lie at a slant and hope to get some shut-eye. The third passenger had been there for some time; and since he was the only one of us who had not driven yet, it was assumed that he would now take the wheel.

The problem was that at this point he declared that he was unable to drive at night. Hmm. Well, I was too tired to go on, and was ensconced in the back seat by now anyway. So the owner, who had been mostly awake keeping me company while I drove, was stuck with driving again. The last words I heard before falling into a fast sleep were from him: "OK, guys, I just hope my snoring doesn't keep you awake." Cute.

He, a seasoned traveler already, knew from experience that, when there was more than one driver, the non-driver needed to be getting sleep, so that when the driver got tired, he would be fresh to take-over the wheel. He assumed that we had that fresh driver in the guy sleeping in the back, and so decided to stay awake while I drove. Well, in three hours I awoke, and we were not only all still alive, but moving. Barely. It was 6:30, and we had hit Oklahoma City in the rain, at the beginning of rush hour, and with construction going on to boot. It was barely daylight, and everything seemed gray, my first unfortunate experience of the Sooner State. (That was to remain my general impression of that locality for years. After all, it was the quickest route from P-A to LA, and I took it whenever [*CW] time was of the essence. It wasn't until much later, when I drove through it in the spring and all the bushes along the road were blooming, that I learned that there was another side to Oklahoma topography.)

I could see my friend's face from the side, and he looked like he had been up for days. What I also noticed, however, was that my short but deep sleep had refreshed me, so that I announced to that grateful classmate that I was able to take over the driving again. Thus, I returned to the captain's seat until that afternoon. By then we were in New Mexico, and the scenery had gone from gray Oklahoma and northern Texas panhandle winter, to the delightful Land of Enchantment. That's what it says on New Mexico's license plates, and since my first time there I have believed them. In fact, it is within less than five miles of the Texas state line that the change in scenery occurs. (I personally do not consider Texas part of the southwest, which I believe begins in New Mexico, although you could probably argue that west Texas belongs there too. I do like west Texas and its sheer distances, and the way the highway cuts through the hills, revealing layers of rock; and I do believe that El Paso is

SW, but, after all, that part of the Lone Star State runs beneath New Mexico [not that you asked].)

Anyway, I'm now ready to turn the wheel over to someone else, having driven for seven or eight more hours (we stopped for lunch at another Micky D's, and gained an hour crossing into New Mexico and-so into the Mountain Time Zone). The obvious choice is the one who has not driven yet, right? But now he informs us that he doesn't know how to drive a stick.

Well, I had driven a stick once before in my life, when I was thinking of buying a VW off a work-mate of my father's, who taught me how to operate it in about 30 seconds. After all, on an interstate you simply need to be able to get from first to fifth and then glide for hours. That was the owner's opinion as well, who gave our sleepy-head companion a quick lesson on the spot, so that he was able to begin operating the vehicle.

Not that there was much time left for him, since he was, as I said above, to be dropped off in Gallup, New Mexico. But even that projected driving shift was cut short, since the rain that we experienced in Oklahoma City earlier that day was by now turning to snow, and the owner judged that he had better take over the wheel again since it was his car. I for my part, callow traveler that I then was, couldn't believe that it was snowing this far south.

We had picked up I-40 back in O-K City, and were now pulling fairly close to Gallup. A look at the map reveals that the Continental Divide crosses I-40 at mile marker 47, while Gallup is situated around mile marker 20, which spells mountains. So *that* was why it was snowing this far south, I thought to my inexperienced self. Further, at some times conditions approached white-out. Not only that: we seemed to be surrounded by truckers, who were all by now practically crawling. The owner had his trendy CB radio on, of course, and we could hear the way the truckers were skittish about the road surface. But we heard something else as well: that there was an access road just to the north of the interstate. The man at the helm decided to get off at the next exit, and we found this street to be much better for making time, since there was hardly any traffic on it. He just shifted into a lower gear and moved steadily forward.

Yes, we were moving steadily forward, but we were moving slowly nonetheless. The owner was a seasoned snow driver, hailing originally from Massachusetts, but even he knew not to push himself, especially with passengers in the car. I felt tense the whole time, not because of his driving, which was fine, but simply because of conditions. We were expecting to get into Gallup for dinner, and we finally pulled in somewhat after 9:00 p.m., cold, tired and, especially, hungry. Where were we staying? At the residence of the Catholic leader of Gallup at that time, Bishop Jerome Hastrich. Our new stick-shift driver was reporting to him for Christmas break, and the other two of us were to spend the night there as well. He had plenty of room, since he had sold the former prelate's house and moved to the poor side of the tracks, to be closer to the folks, where he built a residence for seminarians that was also his own episcopal home. He was a kindly man, who proved his worth to us immediately by heating up tasty, filling leftovers for us upon our arrival. Thus we were able to sit and chat with him while we ate.

The next morning we attended his mass. He rang the church bell in his black cassock trimmed in red to call the faithful to lauds, or morning prayer, which preceded mass. Afterward we all had a bite of breakfast. Coming as I did from Philadelphia, where the cardinal lived in a mansion and had a large, plain-clothes man from the police department as his personal bodyguard (at least in those days), I was not used to a bishop waiting on table. One thing both men had in common, however, was that they retained a small community of nuns to take care of the cooking and cleaning. The particular sisters here were all German, since he himself was from Wisconsin, and so the car owner was able to practice some of his German out on the good *Schwesteren*. (I was then taking Theological German, but he was far ahead of me conversationally.) It was a most edifying experience.

Then the two of us hit the road. The snow had now stopped, and the roads were clear (it had not been a significant overall accumulation), so once again we were moving close to the speed limit. We could have taken I-40 to Flagstaff, in Arizona, and then followed I-17 south to Phoenix. (I'm not sure why I flew out of Phoenix rather than Tucson, since my friend was heading to the latter, although Phoenix is on the way. Perhaps it was his thinking that the city was bigger and may have had more flights.) However, my kind host had a better idea: to take the scenic route, or at least an even more scenic route. (I have learned since that I-17 is scenic, too, starting with Flagstaff, at 6910 feet of elevation and surrounded by mountains [including Humphrey's Peak, the highest point in the state, over 12,000 feet above sea level {the tallest point in Pennsylvania is Mount Davis, weighing in at a slim 3213}]).

Now I'm not sure what route that was, but I do recall that at one point it involved winding down one side of a large canyon and winding back up the other side. It was harder driving for him, but he wanted me to see some of the beauty of his adopted home state (although it tends to be ubiquitous there, as I would learn over the years). My guess from a semi-confident memory and a glance at the map is that we took US-191 south from I-40, although in the end that would have been no shorter than going via Flagstaff (so time, again, must not have been the reason). The other candidate is the shortest route: following US-191 until hitting AZ-61 as the connector to US-60, which road goes right into Apache Junction, the town where we were staying that night. Either way, I know that it was gorgeous traveling, part of the general experience of this trip that allowed me to fall in love with the beauty of the American Southwest. (I have traversed US-191 recently and was reminded how scenic, and icy, it can be.)

He had arranged our stay in the Phoenix area to be in Saint George Church at Apache Junction, where a mutual friend of ours was stationed as a deacon. I had studied with this man for a year in Philadelphia, and it was good to see him again. We caught up that evening, but it had been after another long day of travel (in time more than miles). (I recall that the owner did most, if not all, of the driving, no doubt to allow me to enjoy the view better, since he had seen it several times before.) These were not easy interstate miles, but challenging scenery miles, with the road snaking up this hill, and down that mountain. Simply beautiful, but taxing. Thus, we hit the sack early.

The next morning I was chauffeured to the airport, where I caught my flight for Los Angeles and my family. We had made it from Columbus to Phoenix in little more than two days, and now on the

There And Back Again: The First Cross-Country Drive

third day I was on the West Coast. That week represented a pleasant stay, during which period I was joined by my friend and his Pinto for a day or two before heading back to school. This way, we were able to go one day to see the magnificent floats as they were being finalized for the upcoming Tournament of Roses parade in Pasadena on the first of the new year.

I do have one detail from that trip that I would have approached differently, if possible. My Dad had somehow gotten hold of a couple of tickets to the Rose Bowl that year, and they were ours for the asking. However, we were on a trimester system at our school, which meant that classes resumed two days after New Year's, the day (back then) of the Rose Bowl game. While my friend may have been open to seeing the game and missing the first day of classes back in Ohio, we'd still have needed to clear the delay with our New Mexican buddy as well. My regret is that I never even considered staying for the game, since classes were always important to me. I was to see the Rose Bowl several years later with my brother, again with tickets from our Dad, but how cool would it have been to return from vacation and telling our testosterone-laden fellow seminarians that we had just been to the Rose Bowl? (To try to see that glass as half full, we were at least able to make it back to school in time for the national championship game, the Orange Bowl, which pitted Nebraska against Miami, which [*CW] went down to the wire.)

We left LA (meaning, of course, the Los Angeles *area*, since my parents always lived in Orange County, in the 'burbs) the evening of the 30th of December. We were to reconnect with the third member of our traveling party, not in Gallup, but at the parish of a priest who had been ordained a couple of years before from our seminary. He was stationed in the town of Roy, in northeast New Mexico, which meant that we had quite a drive ahead of us for one day.

I recall that at some point during the night I was driving and the owner was asleep. In those days, and for quite some time since then, there was a sign on I-40 (we had taken I-15 to I-40) that warned drivers that it was 100 miles to the next gas station (between Ludlow and Needles, although a no-name gas vendor has since established itself [*CW] betwixt and between the two towns). I woke him at that point and asked him how we were doing for gas, back in the days when I tried to push the tank as far as it would go. He glanced at the gauge, declared that we were fine, and went back to his snooze.

Well, halfway or so into the hundred miles, I was not so sure. Then, when a sign announced that there was, unexpectedly, gas at a particular exit, I took it. Now it was the middle of the night, and there was no sign of anything in the dark but the desert. I imagined that I saw a light in the distance, but as far as I drove down the two-lane road, this beacon of hope never seemed to get any closer. Eventually I had to admit that I was chasing a will-o-the-wisp, and made an about-face to return to the highway. My passenger had awakened about this time, probably with the change of speed and direction, and I informed him of how I had added 30 or 40 miles to the odometer while following a mirage. He wasn't even phased, but rather still thought we could make it, although he did gently advise me that he never got off the interstate for fuel unless he could see the actual gas station from the road, a lesson that I took to heart for ever after. (Nowadays there are small indicator signs on interstates to avert a similar scenario, which in my experience work most of the time.) I tried to feed off his confidence as I kept driving. Well, the gas light on the dashboard went on with 15 or 20 miles to go, which indicated that there was a gallon of fuel left, which meant that we would probably be OK, given that he was getting over 30 miles per. Soon we were at the very welcome service station.

The next day, New Year's Eve, was beautiful, since we got to see both Arizona (the best part of it on I-40, the central stretch near all those mountains, and the elk warning signs, although I have never seen an elk in Arizona) and New Mexico, in daylight. A highlight, which I've always looked forward to since then, is the view coming into Albuquerque from the west on I-40. You're driving along, when suddenly, way down below (since the highway suddenly falls away in a seven-mile declivity), the city appears, with the mountains to the east acting as a dramatic backdrop; and that is how that scene has forever etched itself onto my mind. It is probably, day or night, the most breathtaking approach to a city that I have ever experienced (although Tucson is no slouch either in that department as you approach it from the southeast on I-10).

At Albuquerque we probably got onto I-25 north, taking it through Santa Fe on our way to Roy. (The 2010 Rand-McNally gazetteer lists the population in Roy at 234, down from 362 a decade before.) That option would have meant more beautiful driving, at least until sunset, which would have come very early at that time of year. We were to be this other priest's guests for New Year's Eve, and we arrived in good time for 1985 to make its appearance. We all had a sip of something or other at midnight, and I seem to recall some fireworks that our host supplied. He actually had five congregations to take care of, and we arrived early enough to attend evening mass at one of his parishes. He had a large, snow-worthy vehicle, in which he drove us to a very small church at some distance. (For Catholics, January 1 is the feast of Mary, the Mother of God, and is what we call a holyday of obligation, requiring attendance at mass, either that day or the evening before, even if it does not fall on a Sunday. Our own plans were to utilize the evening option, to be able to hit the road once the sun was up.)

Such is what we did, hoping to get back to Columbus, with 'round-the-clock driving, by the evening of January 2, 1985. However, Mother Nature was having her say again. This time it was a major ice storm in Texas and Oklahoma. In fact, there was a section of I-40 that the state police had closed west of Oklahoma City, which of course was the route that we were planning on taking. However, we checked the map (the owner taught me to carry a good road atlas, which I have since always done, my favorite being the Rand-McNally brand, which I prefer to others, since I like the way it colors the different types of highway routes better [picky picky]), and noticed that OK-152 ran parallel to the interstate about 15 miles to the south. We headed that way now, and turned east when we hit it. I was driving at that time, and was surprised how confident I felt, navigating in fourth gear with this new-fangled front-wheel drive. The road was covered with ice, but it was cold, which meant the ice was less slippery (it is the water sitting atop the ice, I would learn, that tends to make it problematic). It was well after dark, and the road for obvious reasons was deserted. Thus, we traveled without incident until heading north to Oklahoma City, where we picked up

I-44. The rest of the drive was smooth, and we pulled-in to school around dinner time on the 2nd.

The Nebraska game (the Orange Bowl) came down to a try for a two-point conversion on Nebraska's part. The Huskers had maintained the #1 ranking the entire season, and only on this night ran into a tough opponent, Miami. The extra point would have tied, but they decided to go for the win via a two-point conversion, and missed it. Another friend and fellow sem, an outstanding overall athlete from Ohio, said what I was thinking afterward: that if they went for the win rather than a mere safe tie, the #1 ranking should have remained theirs, no matter who won the game, since they had dominated all season and may just have had an off night. Illogical it might seem now, but that is what over 2000 miles of driving in three days will do to you (so what was my friend's excuse?).

So that was my first cross-country experience. It was a lot of fun, especially since we had a small window for getting to the West Coast and back, which meant that we needed to do some serious hustling. The touring was minimal in one sense (the Rose Parade floats); but in another sense it was not, for it was on this excursion that I began to realize just how visually spectacular a country we have. Further, this was the trip that hooked me on long-distance travel, and I would spend many years of vacation, in driving between PA and LA to see family every year, trying to view as much of our national splendor as possible in as short a time as possible, with distance being no object.

In fact, I can probably say that I owe this book to that trip, so I will leave it to you to thank the trip or blame the trip, according to your preferences. But I think that everyone should, at least once in his or her life, be able to drive on I-40 in Arizona and New Mexico and realize that I am not making all this stuff up.

CHAPTER 4

THE INAUGURAL TRIP: SETTING THE TEMPLATE

[Even thought this excursion occurred before the one described in the preceding chapter, I mention it here, since it was the first vacation taken for the purpose of touring, as opposed to just going down the shore, or simply getting to LA and back for Christmas. Thus, it helped set the template for my tendency to want to see as much as possible in the time allotted for a trip, while the cross-country drive mentioned earlier expanded my travel horizons to include the entire continent. It may seem like putting the proverbial cart before the horse, but this chapter is the more interesting of the two, and so is a development in subject, even if it occurred earlier in time. Confused? Just read on.]

By this chapter heading, I mean my first trip outside the states contiguous to Pennsylvania (not counting crossing into Virginia during that Close-Up week in DC my senior year in high school, 1974). It occurred back in August of 1978, the summer after I graduated from Saint Joseph's College (now University) in Philadelphia. I was currently unemployed, but for some time had been thinking about entering the priesthood, and-so was hanging in limbo as I discerned the long-term direction of my life.

More specifically, I was thinking about entering a monastery, and there were several addresses that my spiritual director had unearthed for me to contact. I initially visited two of these places, but I was still searching.

Another monastery on that short list was all the way up in Massachusetts: a large place leading a quiet life and supporting itself, among other ways, by producing those Trappist Preserves you may have seen over the holidays. This house was not in a contiguous state, but was a good deal farther away. I had rented a car (a Mazda) to get to the house in New Jersey, and had taken the Greyhound coach to the place in New York. How would I get to Massachusetts?

Around this same time, my fraternity brother and good friend (Bro) told me that he was thinking of taking a trip through New England and maritime Canada. Would I be interested? Is the pope Catholic? But how would still-unemployed I pay for this holiday? It was here that my parents came through, giving me some money for the excursion, since they believed I would be visiting more monasteries. That may be how I pitched the trip to them, or it may have been a miscommunication, and by now I conveniently don't remember which. All I know is that I planned to see only that one monastery in Massachusetts, and even then very briefly for this initial visit (there would be a couple of subsequent stays there of greater length, thanks again to the bus company); and that after I got home and related the details of the vacation to Mom and Dad, they were surprised and disappointed that I had not been doing more monastery-shopping. (I would make up for lost time in the fall/winter of 2001-2002, when I visited 18 monasteries in less than three months ["We – Are – Driven!"].)

It was exciting preparing for the trip. Bro was the one who rented the car, so all I needed was clothing. After all, we would not be doing any camping, and would carry minimal food with us. (One exception was peanut butter, honey and Saltines, a good snack while driving (protein, carbs and sugar), except for the stickiness of the honey, even though we carried one of those plastic bears with a convenient dispenser. I think there was still bee goo on the steering wheel when Bro returned the car to the rental company.) We agreed to split the expenses, naturally, and so would rotate gas fill-ups and motel rooms while each paying for his own food, and then splitting the rental

The Inaugural Trip: Setting The Template

(*CW) down the middle. Bro added that all traffic tickets would be our own responsibility (happily, there were none).

We possessed a general idea of where we were heading, but did not have a lock-step itinerary. In other words, with the exception of the ferry to Canada and a couple of frat houses, we did not have reservations for each night set-up beforehand. We anticipated that we would drive through Massachusetts to the coast of Maine, where we would take the boat to Nova Scotia, and then drive back around the Bay of Fundy (all this within 10 days). It was no drive across country, but it was not a bad chunk of travel for a first trip. (This lack of making arrangements ahead of time may have been formational in my own later practice of [*CW] traveling by the seat of my pants.)

We left on a **Sunday**. In fact, it was August 6, 1978, a date I am sure of, even without notes, as I shall shortly relate. We left Philadelphia early in the morning (I had stayed Saturday night at Bro's house, since he lived closer to New England than I did), and drove straight to New York City. We knew nothing of the Big Apple, but on a Sunday morning we could get away with such geographic cluelessness. It was still early, so traffic was light. We had no idea how to navigate east through to the other side, but we just kept passing major north-south arteries until we saw a "Welcome to Connecticut" sign, announcing that our driving woes were over. (As a piece of local color: there was one car with its two left wheels over one of those tapered concrete barriers in the middle of the highway, evidence that someone had done a little too much partying the preceding Saturday night.)

Well, that was my first new state: Connecticut, the land of nutmeg and constitutions. And therein would be our first sight: Yale University. We had no destination on campus, such as a museum. We were simply driving through the city, so we just parked and walked around for a while. I wanted to be able to say that I saw at least one Eli smoking a pipe (remember, this is back in 1978), and when I spied one perambulating by, I was satisfied.

A more substantial tourist stop was Mystic Seaport. Bro was big on wanting to visit there, and it turned out to be an excellent choice. It was to some extent a floating display, in that there were three old ships in dock that you could board. There was also a conventional museum on land, with a number of maritime buildings. (I do not know if the currently-adjacent Mystic Aquarium and Institute for Exploration, which I have since enjoyed, was up and running then.)

We were spending the night at a frat house. Our fraternity is Phi Sigma Kappa, and we were heading on a sort of pilgrimage to Alpha, the founding chapter (1878). As pledges, we had read the history in our thin, red, hard-covered frat books, but we were the first two brothers from the Lambda Hexaton chapter (well over a hundred foundations later) to visit it.

It was at the University of Massachusetts, Amherst campus, and so, on the way from Mystic to there, we needed to backtrack through Hartford. It was there that I managed to navigate us past the state capitol. Now the first state house I had ever seen was the one in Pennsylvania, in Harrisburg, on a class trip in grade school; but this was the first one I had seen as an adult tourist. We had no thought of stopping in (not that it would have been open on a Sunday anyway), but that drive-by planted a seed that would come to full bloom in 2010, when I would visit my 50th state capitol, in Juneau, Alaska.

We arrived at the chapter house on campus, and were welcomed warmly by the brothers. One older (to us) man, an alum, was in charge, and he showed us where we'd be sleeping that night. Then, after that somewhat circuitous drive from Philly to there, we got back into the car and drove an additional 38 miles to the east to Spencer, to that monastery, where I decided to drop in on the monk to whom I had already written about a possible vocational visit.

It was one of those Eastern summer days of crippling humidity. We found the monastery entrance off the highway (MA-9), and started ascending a road until we arrived at the first building. That edifice turned out to contain an outstanding Catholic bookstore (I would learn about the quality of their selection on a subsequent visit), but one that at that hour was closed. It was constructed of gray New England mountain stone, set in a particular pattern that would characterize all the structures we saw. (I was told later that one monk worked year-round on the plant simply as a pointer.) We figured that the rest of the structures couldn't be that far away, so we parked there are started walking.

The Inaugural Trip: Setting The Template

The road, of which we could not see much at any one time, wound steadily uphill. The sweat began to form on, and then pour out from, our skin. We would turn another corner, and still discover nothing but trees. I did not realize yet that the monks wanted to insulate themselves from noises below, and so were perched at least half a mile up from the bookstore. Well, the main buildings finally came into view, and into the guest house we dragged ourselves. At this point, Bro was not a (*CW) happy camper.

I asked for the vocation director by name, and soon (*CW) a mountain of a man entered, with a patriarchal beard and a big smile, in their signature black-and-white habit, as pictured on the Trappist Preserve jars (I suppose that such a monastery could be called a Trappist preserve). He actually remembered, not only that I had written to him, but that I was from Drexel Hill, Pennsylvania (he must have just consulted a file or something, although he was bright enough to have earned a doctorate in canon law). This was simply a get-acquainted session, but the result was that I told him I'd write back to him to return for a week in the not-too-distant future. I don't believe we saw anything else of the place that evening. (I did not realize at the time how early the monks retired for the night, so that he may have been getting ready for his 8:00 bed-time when we arrived.)

On the drive back (the walk downhill was considerably easier), Bro said that I had looked starry-eyed, but that he had been able to be more objective, noticing, for instance, yellow nicotine stains on Father's fingers. In any case, our minds soon turned to more practical matters: beer. We didn't want to return to the frat house empty-handed, so we stopped at a convenience store that advertised brew on its sign. Imagine our chagrin when we walked in and found that the refrigerators that held the desired bottles and cans had large wooden sticks across them barring access, indicating that, since it was a Sunday, there was no alcohol for sale anywhere in the Commonwealth of Massachusetts. We from the Commonwealth of Pennsylvania were well-acquainted with Blue Laws, but we weren't expecting this routine outside the Quaker State. Well, the brothers had plenty of suds without our proposed contribution, and we quaffed a few with them as they (*CW) regaled us with stories of some people we had heard of back in Philadelphia, and some of whom we had not.

It was a most pleasant end to a long but enjoyable day, even with its several hundred miles of driving; and we limited ourselves on our consumption (to an extent), knowing that we had another long day planned for the morrow.

Oh, about the date. When Bro and I finally emerged at the top of the monastery's property, we were not too tired to notice that the yellow-and-white Vatican flag they flew was at half-mast. We inquired of Father the reason, and he informed us that Pope Paul VI had died that day. Son of a gun! We must not have been listening to the radio, or we certainly would have heard that bit of news (well, maybe not on rock stations). So when I asked earlier, Is the pope Catholic? I guess it was a trick question.

By the way, the reason I started writing this chapter now (i.e., in 2007) is that I was just visiting my parents, and saw that they had some photographs and postcards out, including the ones that I had mailed home from this trip. That occurrence not only gave me the idea for the chapter, but helped jog my memory about it, such as weather details and the like. The first one appears now:

The front says **Mystic Seaport Waterfront**, and the back reads, **Hi, I'm in Amherst, Mass, at the frat house. We've visited Mystic Seaport and Spencer. Today we drove 400 miles so we'll be in bed early. The weather is still rainy but the car runs fine. Love**. These words tell me that we must have left Philly in the rain, and that the humidity at the monastery was the sort that settles into a green area after a summer shower, since the weather front had not blown through yet (although it was not raining when we walked up and down the hill, thankfully).

A final note on the day: we had rented a Dodge Diplomat. I recall praising the car so much after we returned home that within the year my Dad procured one for his business, which served him for many years.

Well, by **Monday**, that (*CW) cut-it-with-a-knife humidity had turned back, not only into rain, but into a steady downpour. It was in that deluge that we arrived in Worcester, MASS (pronounced WUS-ter by the locals), where there was a rare book shoppe (Isaiah Thomas) that Bro wanted to see. Too bad the guy was closed on Mondays. (English-major Bro did manage to find another used bookstore on our travels, in Maine, and wrote in his journal one night about how he had rediscovered Jack London through one of his lesser-known works.)

Our next destination was as uneventful: Martha's Vineyard. The passenger ferry to the island left from Wood's Hole, not far from the town of Falmouth. (We agreed that there should be a sign on the way into that municipality that read something like, "Welcome to %#@*ing Falmouth.") We parked the car and hopped onto the ferry; but once we made the crossing we discovered that there was nothing to do there without a car, or at least a bike, and we weren't in a peddling mood, so we hurried back and caught the same ferry as it made its way to the mainland. Bro had imagined that we could find all sorts of whaling stuff (like scrimshaw) on nearby Nantucket Island, but Martha's Vineyard was little more than a name to us. This experience may have been formative of my tendency to visit places just to say that I saw them and then quickly move on to the next such sight.

We did move on, passing through the much larger East Falmouth on our way to Cape Cod. (We had already passed through both North Falmouth and West Falmouth before Wood's Hole. Too bad there's no South Falmouth of which I'm aware. [I am not making this up. Check the map if you don't believe me.]) It was here that the norths, souths, easts and wests of places multiplied, as a glance at the Rand-McNally will reveal. It was here also that we stayed hunkered down in a motel for the night, indicating to me that we must have left Amherst later than I realized, since it was dark by the time we arrived for the evening (not that the weather helped brighten things much), and the elbow of the Cape is not all that far from Amherst.

We had decided ahead of time that we would splurge and have two nice meals while we were away, and this dinner was to be the first. I recall that when they brought my lobster to the table, they had the head removed and sitting on a raised circle of metal, so that the decapitated crustacean was gazing up at me dolefully. It was a cute presentation, but it did not prevent me from eating it, my first ever. Bro commented on how I went for every last milligram of it, even cracking open the legs to extract whatever lay therein.

My postcard for this day reads as follows: the front says **Martha's Vineyard**, and the back continues, **It's still raining, but I had my**

first boiled lobster (on Cape Cod, no less). I also got onto Martha's Vineyard. I'll have to find a monastery with fresh shellfish. Love.

The next day, **Tuesday**, was somewhat trying. The weather had not markedly improved, so there was either rain or high humidity. We decided to head up Cape Cod the rest of the way. Of course, I needed to go to the very end of the Cape, past the artsy Provincetown and any roads, along the beach, to the lighthouse. I told Bro when I left him for this solitary trek that it wouldn't take long, but what did I know? It took a while; and even though I felt good doing it, as if I had accomplished something akin to an explorer cresting a mountain, there was a gnawing doubt (*CW) in the back of my mind about whether it was a good idea in the first place. Of course, when I could look back from the end at Long Point and see land across the way, I felt that I had succeeded in my quest.

That doubt became full-blown, however, when I returned, and found Bro as steamed as the preceding night's lobster. We drove back around the Cape with (*CW) nary a word spoken between us. Bro was driving, and there was as little discussion as possible, even when we stopped to see Plymouth Rock, which proved at the time to be something of a disappointment. There was this rock down in a sort of shelter, with the year "1620" engraved upon it. Wow. (Of course, my feelings at the time could have been the result of the tension in the car. I stopped there many years later and had a more positive experience of Plymouth, both the boulder and the town.)

Well, now it was time to head up to Boston. I was driving, and it was later than we wanted to be hitting the city on a weekday (I wonder why), which didn't help the overall mood. We were heading to another frat house, on a campus that will remain nameless in this account. We finally found it, but received a tepid welcome when we arrived, with all but one brother continuing to sit and watch afternoon TV. Then we were escorted by that brother to a top floor attic, where there were no screens on the windows (resulting in flies in the room, and probably mosquitoes at night), and no bedclothes on the stained mattresses.

What a contrast to Amherst! The good news was that this common plight broke the tension between us. We quickly agreed that we were not going to stay in that flophouse, and so Bro gave them some story when we returned downstairs, and off we went. None of them seemed sad that we were not staying. (When we later related this incident to the Amherst bros on the way home, unfortunately, they were not surprised.)

So now we needed to find some place to stay. Remember, this is Boston in the summertime. We checked the AAA book, decided on a hotel, and sped off as fast as we could during rush hour. After creeping along Commonwealth Avenue (or Comm Ave, as the locals say), a street which stops being called that, and then starts again somewhere else (you just need to know that geographic curiosity), we finally found the hostelry. It looked quite nice, and we smiled as we emerged from the car hot and tired. We made it!

Not so fast, part two. We approached the desk and inquired about a room. A man inquired in a Caribbean accent if we had reservations, and then seemed to stifle a laugh when we replied that we did not. He then turned to another man and asked, "Where are we sending them now?" This latter individual provided the name of a competing establishment, and we were soon out the door, armed with directions.

By some miracle, we found the motel with relatively little trouble, but realized right away that we were going to be spending the night in a fleabag. (OK, so it wasn't so bad as all that, but it was definitely low-rent.) We had no choice but to stay. Still, we were planning on enjoying *two* nights in Boston (meaning that we had at least some idea of an itinerary), so, once we were ensconced in our room, we got right onto the phone to one of the places recommended by AAA in the area and made reservations for the following night.

We cleaned ourselves up and then headed out, going to Cambridge, to the Harvard area, just to bop around. We found a great restaurant called the Wursthaus (I am told that the landmark has tragically since been leveled because of some urban renewal project). Of great interest to us frat types was the beer menu, of several pages, organized by country. I had heard of this legendary brew from the then-Czechoslovakia called Pilsner Urquell. I ordered a bottle, and soon it became my favorite non-dark beer. In fact, the place impressed me so much that I bought a mug with the name of the eatery/drinkery on it, which I kept for years. Following the enjoyable meal we walked around the area to work off our wursts, and then headed back to the motel.

The next day, **Wednesday**, a full day with no traveling, was dedicated to Boston. We first tried to get to the sight of the Boston Massacre, but unyielding one-way streets would not allow us to find it, so we finally gave up (to this day I have never seen it, even with several more such trips under my belt). You see, Boston driving was in a class by itself, even given that we were from Philadelphia. Beantown is within a couple of decades of being 400 years old, and the main streets there now, had started as Indian trails and cattle paths and such. It was called the Hub of the New World, and rightly so, since the towns around it seemed to radiate from a center, meaning that there was definitely not a grid pattern to the streets. Then add the Boston drivers, who seemed to lean on their horns a millisecond after the light turned green if we were not moving, even though we had foreign plates on the back of the car, and that completes the picture. Thus went the Boston Massacre sight.

We somehow knew that Bunker Hill was represented by an obelisk, which we were able to identify from where we were, so we just made for that point, crossing the Charles River in the process. We congratulated ourselves on getting there, but then realized that we had no idea where we now were, since Old North Church, our next stop, while having a bell tower, was not perched on a hill, and so, practically speaking, did not have its own conveniently tall location indicator.

Eventually we were parked up a side street, completely flummoxed, with the map out, when a man stopped by the driver's side of the car and asked, in a thick Boston accent, "Are you lost?" We both thought for a second of answering sarcastically, given that we had a P-A license plate and the afore-mentioned cartographical product completely unfolded inside, but decided instead that this must be the one nice driver in town, and so replied along the lines of, "As a matter of fact, sir, we are." He asked us where we were heading, and we told him. He then inquired if we had seen Old Ironsides yet, the historic nickname of the *USS Constitution*, and we said No, but that we didn't have time. He put in a plug for the Revolutionary War-era ship, and then added that he would *lead* us back across the river and put us onto Hanover Street (he placed the accent clearly on the second syllable), from which we could find Old North Church. We

The Inaugural Trip: Setting The Template

thanked him profusely. He still gestured at one point down to where Old Ironsides was waiting for us (can you believe it? I've still never more than seen it from that distance), but we kept driving, a decision I regret now. Still, you can't see everything in one day. (I need to add that on subsequent trips to Boston, two in 2004, another one in 2010, and yet a fourth in 2013, I found the drivers much more pleasant. It must have been the weather, and the lack of a GPS.)

Well, his directions were right, but they did not seem so at the time. You see, when we arrived at where the Old North Church should have been, we found a firehouse next to a little park of trees. So we circled the block, then circled it again, but found nothing different (as if the terrain changed every few minutes). Thus, we decided to ask someone. There was a very dark, Italian-looking young woman walking by, so we called over to her. We expected her to talk like Rocky's girlfriend Adrienne, a fellow denizen of Italian South Philly; so when she said, "Pah-don?" we were taken aback. Of course she would sound like Boston, we realized, and then asked her where the church was. It was her turn to be taken aback, and, looking confused, she directed us to the men sitting in front of the firehouse. We asked them, and they shouted back, "It's right *here!*" Then we looked *up*, above the trees in that little park, and saw the steeple. Bright.

We parked and walked through the verdure, passing old Italian men seated playing checkers. We arrived at the church, and saw what Bro was most interested in: their Vinegar Bible. So what's a Vinegar Bible? you ask. A large, old, hardcover book of scripture with a typo, replacing "The Parable of the Vineyard" with "The Parable of the Vinegar," the most famous printing mistake ever, apparently. The book, of course, was opened to that very page behind the glass. After checking out the rest of the place, we moved on.

We also hit the Boston Commons that day. We saw the boats shaped like swans, as well as the swans (not shaped like boats). One stop around that downtown neighborhood was to yet another rare book dealer, where I saw a framed signature of Nathaniel Hawthorne, along with a very nice woodprint of the author, for a mere $625 (in 1978 dollars), a tad (*CW) rich for my blood.

It was that evening in the motel room, after we had taken a dip in the indoor pool in the nicer motel, as we were watching the local news, that we saw the weatherman, who announced that the bad weather that we'd been having would be leaving, moving to the northeast. That, of course, was the very direction that we were heading the next day. Oh well. At least it wasn't a nor'easter.

Thursday was to be our last day in the Boston area. We moved out from the center of town now, hitting the city of Salem for lunch. We were interested also in seeing the House of the Seven Gables, of Nathaniel Hawthorne fame, which we did by walking across town (why we didn't drive I'm not sure). There was plenty of witch-related tourist stuff, but we seasoned travelers eschewed all of that (which means I'll need to go back someday to see it). We had found an excellent place to eat: a fish market that had a restaurant around back. I recall ordering steamed clams, and getting 32 of them, which was plenty of local magic for me.

We then drove out to Walden Pond, of Henry David Thoreau fame, and were very disappointed with what they had there: little more than poster boards reminding people that that author had lived there once. (I understand they've improved the place since, although I've never been back.) We also headed out to Concord town, of Paul Revere fame, where we drove around. There was simply no time for Paul Revere's other (*CW) claim to fame, Lexington.

This was, even after local touring, a big travel day for us; and at this juncture we pointed ourselves through northeast Massachusetts and headed toward that small stretch of New Hampshire and so into Maine (two new states in less than half an hour). Our goal was Portland, some 40 miles into Vacationland, where we planned to catch the auto ferry to Yarmouth, Nova Scotia, saving quite a bit of driving. I remember at one point rumbling down a road near or in Portland, where there was a German shepherd lurking by the right side of the road, ready to pounce. The dog actually went for the car, causing me to swerve wide to the left to miss it (and I thought Boston residents were inhospitable). Thankfully there was nobody coming the other way. There was another time when I needed to stop fast, and all our luggage in the back seat (we each had two pieces) hit the floor (one of several such happenings during the trip), since we were both consulting the map while moving and didn't see the stopped car in front of us (no comment needed).

The Inaugural Trip: Setting The Template

We arrived at the ferry in good time for its 9:00 p.m. departure. Now Bro had previously suggested procuring a cabin to sleep in, but I had balked at the extra expense, so we had a reservation for the car but not for a stateroom. However, once we got onto the ship, I relented, especially given the current outside temperature. You see, we had planned to sleep on the deck, on beach chairs, and now that brainstorm looked pretty lame. We got onto a waiting list, and, well, waited, as a loudspeaker called out names in light of cancellations. Finally we were summoned, which was something of a Godsend, since when we went outside that evening to check on things, the wind was whipping across the deck from the sea that now surrounded us (Redundancy Warning) on all sides, and across the handful of people who were trying to get to sleep among the elements. (Not Honda Elements, which had not been marketed yet: I had thought of sleeping in the car, but there was no access permitted to your vehicle during the voyage.)

That was the first time I ever saw the Milky Way. I thought that what was up in the sky was a cloud at first, but then I realized that it was stars, so dense that they looked like a haze. Remarkable. Still, the wind was cold, so back in we went, where Bro (*CW) tried his luck at the casino, since we were now in international waters. He also was able to buy a couple of Cuban cigars for his enjoyment while in Canada. The cabin was tiny, but it was better than nothing, and after a long day of touring and driving it did not take me long to fall asleep.

That day's postcard read, on the front, **Plymouth Rock**, and then, **#2. The weather has changed for the better. We saw the top of the Cape and Plymouth Rock. Today we leave Salem, then head to Maine to take the ferry to Nova Scotia**. Unfortunately, I can't find #1. The front of the card pictures Plymouth Rock inside iron bars with "1620" incised into it, which occasioned my mother to say when I got home, "The rock is in jail!" When I visited it again years later, I made a call home, leaving a voicemail with the cryptic saying, "The rock is still in jail." (Needless to say, Mom had no idea what I was talking about.) (Those paying close attention will note that the weather seems to have gotten better on the Cape before getting worse again in Boston.)

I awoke **Friday** morning in daylight, within easy view of the shore. We were heading along the coast of Nova Scotia to Yarmouth. Our landing would be my first step into another country. I have since been to every province in Canada, but that day was the start of it all. The sky was blue, meaning that we had managed to leave the bad weather behind after all, which was fine with us. We were soon in the car, and then driving off the ferry onto Canadian soil. It was also the first time I had ever been in a different time zone, so we made sure our watches were set for Atlantic Time.

There were several marked touring routes in Nova Scotia, and we took the Lighthouse Trail, since it moved us to where we were heading that day, the capital, Halifax. (I can't recall if we started making reservations ahead of time for rooms after our Boston fiasco or not. I do know that we didn't run into any more problems with finding rooms. Either we got smart, or simply got lucky.) It was 186 miles directly up the coast along NS-103, but the Lighthouse Route took us closer to the water, where the lighthouses are (duh). The postcards I sent that day were from Peggy's Cove, which is close to Halifax. I don't recall now if we actually saw the lighthouse there, but I would have wanted to for my mother's sake, who not only liked lighthouses, but whose name was Peggy. The entire time the water, both fresh and sea, was a deep blue.

What a contrast between Halifax and Boston! It was so easy driving here, and there were patches of green even at the center of town (by then we must have forgotten about the Boston Commons). We had already fallen in love with the province, and now we became infatuated with the capital. It was later in the afternoon, and we soon found ourselves at the Citadel Hotel (with or without reservations). This place was palatial compared to the spots where we had stayed in Beantown, and was not all that expensive either. We dropped the luggage in our room, and then went to the hotel restaurant for dinner, a most pleasant room with plenty of natural light and indoor greenery.

The only blotch on our time there was the man who resembled a bodybuilder, with an accent from the Islands, who came by our table to ask us if we wanted to buy some acid. We assured him we did not, and turned back to our Molsons. Indeed, I discovered on this trip that the USA allows beers only to a certain maximum percentage

The Inaugural Trip: Setting The Template

of alcohol to be imported, so that often the foreign brew needs to be watered down. But nothing was watered down in Canada, and I discovered that a couple of bottles of suds were usually plenty for me. That was good for Bro, since he insisted on paying for my drinks both evenings we were in Canada, so excited was he to be back in the country. (Who knows to what extent his travel fervor influenced me in later places such as Seattle, as related below.)

(I recall a time when Bro and I were patronizing one of our favorite watering holes in Philly, the Khyber Pass. They had live jazz on the weekend for a dollar cover, and stocked Guinness on tap [need I say more?]. On this particular occasion we found ourselves sitting with another couple of people, since there were not private booths but simply long tables for everyone. This one gent asked if he could take a taste of one of our Guinnesses, and as he pulled a sip, his face puckered into a grimace. We explained that that strong of a beer was an acquired taste (strong meaning bitter), adding that that was one taste well worth acquiring. Well, when the jazz band took a break, this bloke, and a couple of his friends, produced instruments from somewhere, like Tolkien's Dwarves near the beginning of *The Hobbit*, and began playing what sounded like authentic Irish music. After they finished, we asked him if he was from the Emerald Isle, and he replied, "Aye." We then asked how it could be that he had never tasted Guinness before, and he explained that he was quite familiar with Guinness, but that this water-down %&@* was not quite the same thing.)

That day also I sent two postcards, both, as mentioned above, of Peggy's Cove, one taken at sunrise and one at full light. The first read, **Lighthouse at Sunrise, Peggy's Cove, Nova Scotia**, and then, on the back, **Hi. How is everyone doing? I have crossed over on the ferry and am now in Halifax, Nova Scotia, Canada. The weather has lately been very nice. The scenery along the southern coast is breathtaking, and the water is actually blue. We also visited Oak Island ...** Then, the second: **Lighthouse at Peggy's Cove, Nova Scotia**, at what looks like sunset (OK, make up your mind), then ... **where there is supposed to be buried some pirate's treasure. They are sure that it is there but they can't dig down to it because of flooding, collapse, and so on. Today we're off to St. John, and**

the next day we'll be back in the states (Maine). Love. I do not remember visiting Oak Island, although I had heard of it from back in high school; but apparently, unless the Molson was a lot stronger that I realized, we visited it that day. It clearly made quite an impression on me. (Oh, and neither one of us had figured out yet that water is blue when the sky is blue. And we both graduated with honors.)

On **Saturday** our main occupation was to drive from Halifax, Nova Scotia to Saint John, New Brunswick, a distance of 265 miles along the highways (as opposed to the ferry, and not including side trips). However, we wanted to see the Bay of Fundy, which we did at one point, since it has the highest tides in the world. When we viewed it the tide seems to have been out, which is when you can really appreciate how far it goes. Indeed, there was quite a length of shoreline that looked wet, as if it had recently been underwater, so the boast it made seemed credible to us (I'm sure the people of Canada slept better than night as a result of our unofficial acquiescence to their documented claim).

Saint John impressed us as a blue-collar town without a great deal to do after dark. Thus, even on a Saturday night we found it hard to find any place open where we could get a Molson's. As a result, we were forced to return to the hotel. There was a club there, but it would not allow Bro to enter as long as he was wearing jeans, albeit designer jeans (I mean, he hadn't been digging ditches all day in them). He was not happy, since it *was* possible to enter wearing polyester, but we went back to our room for Bro to change. We returned, to discover that it was little more than an empty discotheque, so we returned to the hotel proper and went into their lounge. There, like Dorothy Gale, we discovered that there is no place like home, since it was just what we were looking for: a quiet place to chat and have a couple of beers.

Bro was soon back in his typical Canadian good mood, and once again announced that he wanted to pay for the brewskies, to which largess I offered no objection. We each had three over two or three hours, which back home would have counted as abstinence; but here I recall, to the extent that I recall anything, almost stumbling as we made our way up to the room. Gotta love that genuine Molson's. (I can only imagine what the people around us were saying about typical Americans who can't hold their alcohol. I mean, we could really go the distance at frat parties, until the keg was kicked. Well, it wasn't the keg that got kicked that night, that's for sure. [My drinking days have long since ceased, by the way.])

I'm not sure if we attended Mass or not for **Sunday** (heathen that I apparently was then). My notes do remind me, however, that we ran into a couple of nuns *somewhere* that morning, from of all places Villanova University, outside Philadelphia, the arch-rival school of our alma mater, Saint Joe's (*CW: small world), offering us a little reminder of home.

The day's postcard: **Head Harbor Light ... along the New Brunswick Shoreline**, then, on the back, **Hi! We left Saint John and are about to cross the border from New Brunswick to Maine. Today we hope to see Acadia National Park. Love.**

The business of the day was to get back to the States (had we been away that long, that I'm using British terminology?) and to tour the above-mentioned Acadia National Park. There was one stretch where we needed to stop and ask for directions while still in NB. A highway worker (on a Sunday? perhaps it was in fact on Saturday, in NS) told us that the freeway that we wanted was six or seven miles down the road. Well, in 6.5 miles, according to the car's odometer, we hit that road. I wish all the directions I have ever received (or given) were that accurate.

I recall being in Acadia, but do not necessarily connect it with this trip. However, it's mentioned on the postcard, and logistically it is between Saint John and Bangor, where we stayed that night, so I think that this is the day I visited my first full National Park. There was one closer to Philly – Shenandoah National Park in Virginia – but I would not see that one for several more years. (Nowadays there is another relatively close one, Cuyahoga Valley National Park in Ohio, but it would be even longer before that one was promoted from a National Recreational Area.) I'm surprised that I did not send a postcard from Acadia (then again, maybe I did, and it got misplaced). I only have one memory of Acadia that trip: looking down from a height and seeing mist of cloud *below* us as I viewed the water. Perhaps we were on Cadillac Mountain. You would think that the first National Park would have made a greater impression on me, but there it is. (Actually, to think that would be anachronistic, since I had not been bitten by the National Park bug yet.)

I remember the restaurant that evening in a little more detail (obviously indicating where my true priorities lay). We arrived in Bangor, settled into a motel, and then went to an eatery to dine. This was to be our second of two really nice feeds, and the one thing on my mind was Maine lobster. We sat at the bar as we waited for a table, and there we met someone *else* from Philadelphia, a guy who had been working up there outdoors for some time, in lumber or something. Small world *déjà vu*. I had a (*CW) fond hope that once during the trip I would be filled with lobster, and this turned out to be the day. I had ordered a large stuffed lobster, brimming with crabmeat, which I polished off after a generous appetizer of steamed clams. By the end of the meal I could eat no more.

Monday was to be a day of driving. We planned to spend our last night on the road at the Amherst frat house again. I don't remember whether we had set this up beforehand when we were there or not, but Bro tended to handle those sorts of details, so he probably did. This time beer was for sale in Massachusetts, so we did not show up *sans* ales. Still, we were given more than we brought, in good brotherly fashion, and passed an enjoyable evening.

On **Tuesday** Bro made the mistake of saying, in the car, "Four states and two provinces: all right!" and slapping my upraised hand. The problem was that I had somehow assumed that we would end up seeing all six New England states. I thought about it, and he was right about his calculations; so I asked if we could go north on I-91 until we hit Vermont, then turn around and drive home. He wasn't happy with the idea but he suffered it, after I agreed to pay for the extra gas that it would take (as if any place in New England is far from any other place in New England).

For those of you following along with your maps, you know that that leaves Rhode Island. My subsequent notes for this day say that we cut its corner at some point during the trip. The logical place would have been when we were at Mystic Seaport, in eastern Connecticut, since that's about six miles from the state line, but I'm not sure I was conscious of wanting to experience all the states that

The Inaugural Trip: Setting The Template

early in the trip. I have no clear recollection at this point about the Ocean State one way or the other (sorry, dudes).

However, it does occur to me now that I was early on (*CW) showing my true colors, in good Cindy Lauper fashion. In a conversation years later after a cross-country trek with my sister, we agreed that when she travels she is focused on people, while when I travel I am focused on places. Bro was so happy when he shook my hand in triumph; and if I had any sense I would have left it at that, savoring the moment of friendship, and assuming that some day I would return to New England to see what I missed on this trip. But my default setting already was to see the states we had missed, rather than savor a moment of bonding. Oh well. Experience has taught me to alter my earlier perspective.

In any case, by the time we got back to Philadelphia, we were on an amicable footing again. When we were crossing the Delaware River (I was driving), Bro made a point of stretching to see the statue of Billy Penn on City Hall, at the time by law the tallest building in downtown, and-so visible for some distance (see below). He said viewing it made him feel that he was really back home. He later mentioned that when he returned the car, we had almost exactly doubled the mileage on it (roughly 2900 to start, and 5800 to end, a 2900-mile trip), which apparently impressed the guy at the desk.

Apart from those couple of examples of tension, it was a most enjoyable time. On one of the days at Amherst we stopped on campus to see the marker that indicates when our fraternity was founded there, a reflection of the brotherhood that we shared, and which proved stronger than the tension. Driving was a big part of the trip, too, and I realized that I liked to drive as long as the other guy would let me. (I also must admit that I like to sleep in the morning, being a night person in those days, and that it was usually Bro who got us moving each day before they threw us out.) But probably the biggest piece was the very idea of travel, of getting out and seeing new things. We weren't just moving from motel pool to motel pool, but were hoping to see the sights in-between. And a couple hundred thousand miles later, I still get excited at the thought of taking another such journey. The first trip, then, set the template for the rest, even if it was not that intense yet: see as much as you can in the time given you. And I guess that that's a major part of what I'm trying to tell you too: Go for it! Just don't forget about the people traveling with you in your quest to see new things. I have a high tolerance for solitude, recall. However, among my most memorable trips are the ones I took with family and friends. People and sights are not mutually exclusive. When you travel with others you may see less of what you want to experience in terms of the number of attractions visited; but you will have more joy, since you will be experiencing the trip not alone, but through the eyes of your fellow vacationers as well.

CHAPTER 5

NOT ALL THOSE WHO WANDER ARE LOST: EXPECTING THE UNEXPECTED

This saying happens to appear on my favorite bumper sticker, the one I for years had displayed in the rear window of my car, until the sun's rays caused it to disintegrate: "Not All Those Who Wander Are Lost." It was blue with white letters, and was mounted on cardboard, so that it was not actually attached to the inside of the car, but sat against the concave side of the glass. I bought it in Washington, DC, on the National Mall, from the bumper sticker guy. I have spent twenty minutes at a time standing there, reading them all and notating the ones I like, always buying at least one, of course, for rent, as it were, of the space (and so that he's still there the next time I'm in DC).

The saying comes from JRR Tolkien. It is part of a song in *The Lord of the Rings*, and applies to Strider, one of the main characters. This individual is a diamond in the rough, a man of high pedigree who spends much of his time in the wilderness, protecting hobbit enclaves and hunting bad guys. He dresses for the wild, but is highly cultured. He wanders quite a bit through Middle-earth, but always knows where he is going. Hence, "Not all those who wander are lost." (I have since had one custom-made, again in blue and white, perched in the back of my vehicle.)

When I was visiting a monastery in Latrobe, Pennsylvania, one of the monks who knew me walked past me in the parking lot, noticed the bumper sticker, and commented on how appropriate it was for me. He's right. I spent my last 30 years of vacations driving in 50 American states and 10 Canadian provinces, generally knowing where I was going thanks to Rand-McNally (and now Garman GPS) but always going some place unexpected, some locale I had never visited before, thanks to my AAA travel books.

So where do I get this *Wanderlust*? Well, as I have already explained, it started in the womb, since I accompanied my parents back from Florida that way. My folks have each made distinctive contributions as well. My dad was always going to his annual business conventions, to new cities each time. My mom, starting with our national Bicentennial, was always looking for some place she had never been before in Philadelphia, trying to find attractions that may not have been well-known but were definitely worth visiting. In later years she and my dad got together in SoCal (that's Southern California, if you live outside the Golden State) to go visiting new sights on the weekends between San Diego and San Francisco, and saw, among other things, a number of the 21 California missions. (I have never kept a formal running list of my own such visits, but I believe that in 2011 I finally got to my last remaining unvisited missions, ironically the two closest to LA.)

Then there were the other kids in grade school, tykes who used to describe the places they visited over the summer. Our default setting, as I mentioned above, was the South Jersey shore, which provided plenty of (*CW) fun in the sun but was not all that interesting. In contrast, the two kids next door to us went all the way from Philadelphia to Disneyland back before there was a Walt Disney World, which gave them a certain cachet in the neighborhood ever afterward. I was always jealous of classmates who got to travel, hoping that some day I'd be able to join them on the road.

So I started collecting postcards. If I couldn't go to those places yet, at least I could think about them, and experience them vicariously through the travels of others. I also started buying postcards of places that I visited, to act as a sort of photo album of my nascent peregrinations, such as class trips to historic Philadelphia in grade school. Those early colorful pieces of light cardboard are (*CW) long gone, although recently I discovered a collection of later ones that my mother was saving, sent by me from trips that I have more recently taken. I always try to find the right postcard for the person to whom I am sending it, and then enjoy composing the tailored message (it was a small experience of creative writing, my personal inexpensive version of buying them souvenirs, since I was sharing a tiny bit of my person with them in the process).

I never bought travel books while dreaming of going on safaris in Africa or walks along the Great Wall of China. I have always wanted to visit just about every place on the globe, but I knew that wasn't going to happen for a while, and so must have decided not to torture myself in the meantime by musing on these exotic locales. That's just as well, since my travels outside North America, as you recall, have been limited to Italy. There's quite a bit to see in Rome and its environs, but it's just one place.

What do you think-of when you hear the word, "vacation?" For some people, indeed, I'll warrant, most people, it connotes getting time off from work to go some place and relax. Maybe it's down the shore (which is what we in Philadelphia called the beach in South Jersey). Maybe it's up the mountains (for us, the Poconos, summer or winter). Maybe it's at the other end of a car ride or a plane flight. But for many folks, the (*CW) lion's share of the time is taken up at some destination, where said persons can stop traveling and simply enjoy the different environment.

I have family in both Los Angeles and Las Vegas, and so, along with many SoCal denizens, have often made that drive to Sin City. We live in the age of mega-casinos. In that batch of post cards that I found at my parents' place, there was actually one from the 1960s, sent by those same neighbors, from the Stardust Casino. I used to see those billboards on the way to Vegas when I'd go to visit my family from SoCal, advertising Wayne Newton. Well, the historic Stardust has been imploded in the name of progress toward the Bigger and Better. The new side of the strip has these new megaliths: the MGM Grand, the Luxor, Mandalay Bay, New York New York, the Venetian. They tend to be planned and built around a theme. They are self-contained, with lots of rooms, an assortment of restaurants and buffets, specialty shops, shows, plenty of square-footage for gambling, and other amenities such as spa and massage service. You go there, and you don't need to think about your car in the free underground lot, or ever leave the building, until you depart.

Now that's a nice, relaxing idea, and you can do it all over the country: drive to a resort (such as in the Poconos), stay there the whole time, and then drive home. You do a lot of running around between work and home life, so the vacation should not entail all that much more running around, but, rather, plenty of relaxation. As I said, a nice idea.

But if that's such a nice idea, why don't I do it? I think that part of the answer lies in some version of the Protestant Work Ethic that I, a Catholic priest, have inherited as a citizen of the USA. It's hard for me to justify going somewhere and essentially doing nothing for a week or two. It would seem that I need to accomplish something on these trips. (I had a pastor once who used to say, "Father, when I work, I work hard; and when I play, I play hard." You could say then that I got it from him, except that I was that way long before I met the man.)

Another part involves getting away from a daily and weekly routine and simply being my own person for a while, with each day being its own mini-adventure, with my own momentary whims making entries on my daily calendar. I consider where I slept, glance at the map, consult AAA's books, and plan the day from there.

Then there is my cheap side, which balks at how much money I would need to spend to stay at a resort for just one week. With the price of gas always its own unpredictable adventure (except for generally being higher in the summer, of course), driving is less and less cheap, admittedly. Still, gas purchases tend to justify themselves by making it possible to visit a number of places on the trip, instead of simply the one where the plane lands. And in a car, five can travel as cheaply as one, and as comfortably as third class, anyway.

Thus, by seeing many sights on a trek, I can prove to myself and to others that the vacation was not time wasted. After all, I can tell myself, I was in 23 states on my last trip. No laziness there. (The fact that I need a week to recover from the drive back home is beside the point, as is the fact that I have been told that I do not truly know how to relax.) And by eating (mostly) nonperishable food that I carry with me, and sleeping in my car, I can really keep expenses to a minimum.

OK, now wait a minute: did you really just read that? Eating food that I carry with me, and sleeping in my car? Well, that's part of why traveling with me is so distinctive. You can ask my family about my ritual when I leave the West Coast back for Pennsylvania. My typical vacation is three weeks: a week on the road, a week at home out West with them, and a week on the road back. And, true, right there you can see that I do spend some time at one place relaxing, although I still like to see new things in SoCal or LV while I am there. But it was the eye of the driving hurricane, with something between six and ten thousand miles surrounding it. And my parents would not charge me for food, or for sleeping on the sofa, for that week, as I recovered from one drive while preparing for the next.

So, this ritual? On my last full day home I buy the foodstuffs (and my parents would even pay for that, God bless them, when my Mom was alive, and my Dad could still shop with her): a whole package of Orowheat whole wheat bread, to make a loaf's worth of peanut-butter-and-strawberry preserve sandwiches (I have since discovered Nutella), which I would seal in plastic baggies and then place into the original loaf wrapper to keep them doubly fresh. My mother's ritual was baking a double batch of chocolate chip cookies, the Toll House recipe on the back of the Nestles semi-sweet chip pack, which I would divide into baggies and then place into a metal tin for more double freshness. (I might use sugar-free preserves and drink diet soda, but cookies were [*CW] another story.) Mom always put walnuts in them for me, which meant that I would be the one breaking the nut halves into pieces until my sister-in-law showed her that it could be done simply by placing a bunch on the counter and chopping them with a butcher knife: a lot faster and easier. I would ration them at one pack a day. I also carried cans of tuna (packed in the latest thing, extra virgin olive oil flavored with herbs) with an opener (before they became self-opening) and a metal fork, and a couple of cases of diet caffeinated soda (preferably Mountain Dew for the near-double caffeine, or Dr. Pepper for a change-of-pace, until I discovered Diet Sundrop, with more caffeine than even the legendary Dew, and Pepsi Max, with even a tad more than that). (The rest of the ritual concerns packing the car, which I used to do intensely and in silence, to get everything where I wanted it. My long-suffering family knew to give me a wide berth that day back then.)

And that was it. I get protein from the peanut butter and the tuna (which I simply eat out of the can), and quick energy from the soda and the cookies. And while I tend to stop driving while I ingest the fish (occasionally sardines in mustard), the sandwiches and cookies get consumed while I drive, so as not to waste time. I keep them in back of the front seats, so I can simply reach around and grab them when I get hungry. Who needs to stop to eat? Who needs to waste that time and money? It's too much of a luxury to dine at a restaurant, even a fast food place (although I will admit that in 2010, the Year of Fifty States, I was too lazy to make the sandwiches, and my mother had died, so I bought snack cakes and drove through fast-food windows for "nourishment"). True, I was known even before then to pass next to the take-out window of Krispy Kreme to procure a dozen of the white-cream-filled, chocolate covered doughnuts for the road after they opened a shop in central Pennsylvania (which unfortunately folded in the wake of the concerns about high-carb diets). But as everybody knows, when KKs enter the picture, (*CW), all bets are off. Much of my driving represents long interstate miles, and that's perfect for a leisurely meal of PB&J and CCC, with lots of soda sloshing around in me. Just keep driving. I carry several gallons of water, for me and the car, but never drink it. It is primarily for the radiator (which has never needed it, thankfully), or potential emergencies.

Unless it is summer, I carry that entire loaf of peanut butter and jelly (well, strawberry preserves) with me. My mother taught me that if I apply the peanut butter on both slices of bread (well, now PB on one and Nutella on the other), the jelly won't leak through. I usually eat two of these sandwiches per day as I drive. Except in the middle of the calendar year, when they begin to break down chemically in the heat, they stay fresh the whole way back. And I never get tired of them. (In college I took three a day to school with me for four years.)

Over time my preparations for cross-country trips have been refined to a science. I was thinking about everything I needed to have when I left, and then focused on packing the car just right, with the Kenedy [sic] Directory of all parishes in the country under the passenger seat, for instance (no longer needed with a smart phone), and the soda in the space in front of that seat (or later, in back of the driver seat). I'm good at packing, and have never owned large cars, so all the stuff somehow needs to fit, and I can always make it fit. You see, I carry a lot of stuff normally, in case of breakdown (such as antifreeze, windshield washer fluid, jumper cables, food [e.g., cans of tuna] and water), and camping gear (such as a small heating stove for cooking).

In fact, I cart my high-tech Cordura, waterproof, tear-proof East-Pak backpack in my car all the time, especially in case of Central Pennsylvania winters. Soon after another seminary friend and I were ordained in 1985, he convinced me to invest in some equipment for the outdoors, so that we could get together at a state park equidistant between us. At first he said that all I would need was a sleeping bag, which became the running joke when the pack, and what was in it, and the parka, and the tent, and the other items, were all added. This pack contained my mess kit, matches, a deck of survival cards (playing cards with outdoor hints on each one), clothing such as polypropeline long underwear and my LL Bean Mad Bomber hat and leather gloves, and whatever.

I've already mentioned the soda, which I carry solely for caffeine. (While traveling long miles, I make it a practice never to drink anything except soda, for the sake of my bladder, which has grown weaker over time. Liquid needs to earn the right to be consumed by me by having caffeine in it. If I'm thirsty, I'm thirsty. Tough. Thus do I purposely dehydrate myself overnight to be able to hold more liquid the next day outside my bladder.) I eventually came to save the cans as I traveled, dropping them off at the next recycling container I see, often at a rest stop or a National Park.

As I said, in 2010, the Year of Fifty States, this science was perfected. I did stop making the PB&Js for some reason (laziness), and started using the fast-food drive-throughs. I would buy a McDonald's Sausage Egg McMuffin for breakfast, eat a couple of Little Debbie oatmeal pies for lunch, and wolf down a pair of Wendy's double stacks for dinner from their dollar menu, so I was still living relatively frugally, if less healthily. I used a daypack for daily items, and a suitcase for changes of clothing, which fit just right into my trunk, so that it took even less time than before to pack. As a result, I did not become so intense in preparing to go. In fact, during that year, it almost felt like I was on the road more than I was at home, with the prep morphing beyond a science into a lifestyle. Indeed, it got to the point where I did not need to think about it at all. I simply kept my toiletry items during that year in my daypack in my room, so I would not need to repack them in another week. Thus, I could drive three weeks to the opposite ocean and back, and never want for anything. Preparing for your cross-country trip may not be so easy, but for that one time, packing and planning will be part of the excited fun. Remember, you don't need to do it the way I do it to enjoy doing it. Let it be an un-hobbit-like adventure!

Then there is the matter of accommodations. True enough, on certain trips I would bring my tent and sleeping bag and camp some nights. I would carry a greater variety of food (such as oatmeal with olive oil and salt for breakfast, and Ramen noodles for dinner), and actually cook it over that small butane stove with my metal mess kit. Also true enough, sometimes I will stop and see priest friends along the way, and eat and sleep in their rectories (in later years I would often make a donation to the parish for the courtesy). But I rarely plan such stops, since I would generally not know how far I will travel on any given day. It would just be that I find myself in the neighborhood (read: state) of some guy I knew in the seminary, and take a chance and look him up (I carried the handy seminary alumni guide, which was conveniently updated every two years).

However, most of the time I had no plans for sleeping, other than driving far into the night, then pulling into a rest stop along the interstate and diving into the back seat for a few hours of shut-eye. And nothing feels quite so good as stretching out in the back seat after 750 miles of cruising along, or seeing five sights that day. Oh, you can't stretch out all the way, but it has always been good enough for me, leaving me refreshed and eager for more driving the next morning (which as often as not begins before dawn).

And what better place than a rural rest stop? I admit that I'm less-than-sanguine about pulling this stunt too close to a city, given the clientele who would be stopping throughout the night at this particular sort of establishment. But I'm talking about rest stops in the middle of nowhere, where the only things close are the highway and lots of open fields. The place has restroom facilities, which always come in handy. There are usually also vending machines if you want food or cold drink (obviously, I have no problem with swilling down soda at car temperature, fortunately, although I recently bought a small cooler). There's sometimes information about the locality (if there is one), if you want to do some regional sightseeing, although this phenomenon is more common at rest stops that double as welcome centers at the state line. There are picnic tables, and places to walk pets, along with trash cans and the occasional recycling bin.

I've been very blessed in never having run into any trouble at a rest stop. Part of the reason is God's grace for sure, and my mother's prayers; but a contributing factor is that I mind my own business when I'm there. Especially at night, I don't see rest stops as the sorts of places to strike up a conversation. There may be a trucker fraternity, but that's among themselves. (Still, the way I drive, I'm probably a long-distance trucker at heart. And rigs these days have everything in them but showers, and the truck stops have those.)

No, at rest stops I keep to myself. I also have another ritual. Most of the time, once I've finished eating for the day, I'll stop at one rest stop to go inside to brush and floss my teeth. I used to bring a red shoulder Snap On tool pack that my other brother gave me, with any toiletries that I needed (although by 2010 it was worn out from use, believe it or not, so he gave me another such carry-all from a locals casino in LV). I also bring-in a hand towel, so that I can wash my face and neck, and dry myself and my tooth brush when I'm done (most such bathrooms have hot-air blowers [the most effective tends to be the XLerator brand] rather than paper towels these days). I also make it a point to empty my bladder. This done, I get back into the car and move down the road to the next rest stop. The Rand-McNally marks such places on interstate routes in blue, so I have an idea when the next one is coming up (if it is not closed for repairs, or shuttered due to state budgetary considerations). When I pull into this last rest area for the night, I usually park at the end, and then move directly into the back seat without leaving my car, so as to be as little noticed as possible, so that my behavior does not strike people as odd. (Of course, by that time of night, it is only such types as myself who are usually around, anyway, and they instinctively keep to themselves.)

I have mixed feelings about lighting at rest stops. On the one hand, it keeps the places that have it well lit (duh), and so safe. On the other hand, it doesn't help you fall asleep. I may hook a towel at a strategic angle above me so that light is not falling directly onto my face. (I guess I could get an eye mask, like some airplane travelers.) I usually carry a pillow case, in which I keep a large towel in case I need it, and it is on that that I put my head to sleep (although during the Year of Fifty States I started carrying an actual pillow, so often did I need it, which practice I have continued). I sleep under a bed sheet and, if necessary, a woolen blanket. It is rare that I'm traveling at a time of year when that's not warm enough for me, although it can get pretty chilly in the Rockies even in the summer.

I usually wake up while it is still dark, although that practice depends on how much sleep I have been getting the previous couple of nights. I head into the rest area once again to empty my bladder, and to shave. (I used to use an electric shaver, but eventually shifted to closer-cutting blades and so shaved every second day. Before, I would use the electrical outlet, when one existed, to save the battery, although if necessary I could shave while driving. These last few years I have sported a short beard, obviating the need to shave.) I also changed my unmentionables (which I carried in the Snap On pack) in one of the stalls. A gargle with some blue Listerine and I'm (*CW) good to go. "On the road again …"

Now you can't travel this way if you need to shower every day. Daily bathing is very American, of course, but it's not a universal phenomenon (the monks of the monastery I lived-in during part of 1993, mostly non-Americans, only showered twice a week). I seem to be put together differently than most Yanks, not sweating much and, frankly, not stinking much (which even my Mom admitted). I use plenty of deodorant, and run a brush through my short hair to keep my scalp massaged between shampoos. If I stop to see someone on the way, that's where I can grab a shower. Otherwise, I will break down and stay at a motel if necessary.

So much for my rituals. It is helpful that I am a monk at heart, so that I can travel with as little by way of frills as possible. Of course, monks don't vacation; but that may be why I no longer am one.

I seem, if you'll pardon the pun, driven when I travel. I genuinely like visiting new places, and thus far have never gotten tired of doing it. I like seeing old seminary friends in other states. I also like to amass vacation stories, so I can compare notes when I encounter fellow sojourners. I get excited as I'm heading to the next sight as if I've been planning that visit for months, even if I only read about it that morning in my travel book. (I have a general idea where I'm heading on these trips, but sometimes I'll get near a city and then see what the place has to offer.) More to see, more to learn, more to meet, more to experience.

Still, something else helps a lot: loving the act of driving. I thrill about getting behind the wheel and pointing the car toward the opposite coast. I can drive hour after hour on wide open interstates and not get bored with it. Half the fun for me is the people and things I get to visit, but the other half is the act of getting there. Flying happens too quickly, and doesn't make enough stops (indeed, the fewer, the better). I find those long hours of interstate driving relaxing and restful, especially for my soul, as I listen to music, read an audio book, or simply remain quiet with the Lord, meditating or whistling familiar hymns. There are aspects of a mini-retreat and aspects of a whirlwind tour paradoxically wrapped into one.

So, if you make that cross-country drive once in your life, you may do it and enjoy it in spite of all the driving. My sister, after our trip from California to Florida and back in 2004, said that she would never *drive* to Florida again. She loved what we did in the Sunshine State, but not the many miles it took to get there. That's probably normal. I'm the exception, and that's why I've driven cross-country over three dozen times, and still would like to do it again. But as I say elsewhere, don't think you need to travel the way I do to travel cross-country in the first place. Not everybody needs to have a Not-All-Those-Who-Wander-Are-Lost bumper sticker. A lifetime of wandering may not be appealing to you, but I recommend such an experience once to everyone.

(Déjà vu) *Bon voyage!*

CHAPTER 6

TOP CITY #5 – MEMPHIS: I HEAR AMERICA SINGING

❋

[What will begin now is a list of my Five Favorite Cities. However, for a long time such a list was for me unthinkable. You see, I used to avoid urban areas in my travels. My focus was on National Parks, which (except in the case of Hot Springs National Park in Arkansas, and Saguaro National Park, which is bisected by the city of Tucson, Arizona) tend to be refreshingly far from civilization. How did I know where the National Parks were? I was, after all, visiting them before their website was up and running, WWW.NPS.ORG. Further, since I only recently noticed that there is a magazine entitled, *National Parks*, that resource obviously wasn't helping me before, either. Did I just aimlessly drive the interstates and look for those signature brown signs along the way?

[Actually, the way I discovered the National Park System was through the tool I first bought to get me from Pennsylvania, where I was working, to California, where the rest of my family lived: the Rand-McNally Road Atlas. On the map of the USA, before the individual state maps begin, there is a list above the map of just about every full National Park in the system, with said locations indicated in purple on the map below. Such is how I discovered, on my cross-country trip with my priest friend in 1986, where places like Grand Canyon National Park, Zion National Park, Grand Teton National

Top City #5 – Memphis: I Hear America Singing

Park, and Yellowstone National Park were. On subsequent vacations, I began to use that atlas as a way of planning my trips (to the extent that they were planned at all) to see other well-known National Parks, and then less-well-known National Parks, until I decided to visit them systematically. Hence, in those years I stayed as far away from cities as possible.

[Eventually I ran out of National Parks, at least in the contiguous 48 states, so I needed other things to visit on my annual treks cross-continent. I had done the same thing with the map of Canada, at least with the western Parks. I hadn't yet fixed on the idea of seeing the 50 state capitols, which could be done simply with the road atlas as well, so what was I to do? The answer came from the American Automobile Association, commonly known as triple-A, or AAA. It turns out that they offer an excellent set of travel guides, for each state, and that they are free to members, which I first became in 1985, the year I was ordained a priest.

[It was due to these excellent volumes that I was forced to shed a misconception: that there was very little worth seeing east of the Mississippi River. After all, the great majority of National Parks are in the West. Thus, in traveling cross-country, I would make a straight shot toward the sunset (for, say, 24 hours) and then start looking for things to visit once I got there. What an anti-urban snob! I had come to view cities, if not as evil and dangerous, then at least as overcrowded and insipid, so that there was no good reason to go there; and that if I would go there, I was in for major traffic delays, kind of like travel black holes that eat-up all your vacation time. For instance, if I was concentrating on the northern part of the country, I would congratulate myself on how I once again managed to circumvent Chicago and its maze of Mickey Mouse toll roads.

[It turns out, as many of you are undoubtedly already aware, that not only is there a great deal to see east of the Father of Waters; but that some of the most interesting places to experience in the USA, east and west, fall within the municipal boundaries of cities. Better to learn something late in life than not to learn it at all. Thus, it became my plan, indeed, passion (some might say, obsession), to visit every AAA-recommended sight (i.e., GEM, an acronym for Great Experience for Members) in the country, which is how I finally came to acquaint myself with our nation's great cities. (After years of approaching this goal, when I had the travel books marked according to which GEMs I had seen, AAA went and expanded them, so that my overall percentage of GEMs-seen dropped. That's really a blessing, since there's now more recommended stuff to experience; but when you're neurotic it seems like a curse.) It is true that I still plan drives around urban rush hours. But now at least I'm willing (*CW) to bite the bullet and take my chances on, say, the Cross Bronx Expressway, one more time, which I did, not once but twice, in 2010.

[It is not a great stretch to understand how, during these urban visitations, I came to like some cities more than others. Why this city and not that city? It's probably just a matter of personal taste. Note that I am not claiming that the five cities that follow are the best cities in the country, but that they are simply my touring favorites. I encourage you to do some traveling and come up with your own list. Still, you need to start somewhere, and these chapters are as good a place as any so to do, especially if you happen to live in one of the municipalities in question, or the states in which they fall. That statement may seem odd, but my mother, as mentioned above, who was born in Philadelphia in 1931, did not visit Independence Hall until the 1976 Bicentennial celebration. After all, one of the reasons I like certain cities better than others is the tourist sights they contain. There may also be something harder to define in the atmosphere, like Memphis' musical heritage; still, each of my choices has some definite and interesting places to visit. Nonetheless, it's not simply these sights, since few metropolitan areas have more to see than Los Angeles and New York, but neither one of them made the list. So, enough chatter: let's get to the ranking.]

Until recently, my only time in Memphis (the one in Tennessee, not the older one in Egypt) was to see Graceland, a real piece of Americana. (I had driven through the city before on I-40, noticing the Saint Jude Hospital for Children to the north as I crossed the Mississippi, but this was the first time actually I stopped there.) It was, of all things, Paul Simon's song from his Grammy-winning album *Graceland* that (*CW) put the bug in my ear to go there; and now years later I was finally doing it. True, it's a little pricey, but you do get to see the Jungle Room, walk through two jets, and pray at the tomb of the King and his parents. It is southeast of the city proper, in what seems to be a neighborhood past its prime; still, they provide an appropriately-named hostelry, the Heartbreak Hotel, nearby. I was fortunate enough to be there waiting in line with a couple of Elvis impersonators, big sideburns and all, in front of me. It was there that I discovered that Elvis kept up his martial arts discipline his entire life, and that he had earned an eighth-degree black belt in two styles: Tae-Kwando and Kenpo (or Kempo: I've seen it both ways). Pretty impressive for a guy who was fighting weight gain during the latter part of his life. (There's certainly an irony in his death, as I look at my Beatles cap on top of my CD rack. The Fab Four did get to meet the King on one of their US tours, and apparently made a bad impression on him, who afterward informed the FBI that they were too deeply involved in drugs to walk free. That may be true, but it was drugs, prescription and otherwise, that did Elvis in, at the tender age of 42. As Nancy Reagan taught us, Just Say No.)

However, there was one other sight I wanted to see in the city, which attraction would precipitate my return there in 2010: the National Civil Rights Museum. I blocked-out a day, but now realized that I would need to see that museum on a second day. So then: what *did* I see on my first day? There is a huge old house that has been expanded and filled with various interesting items, the Pink Palace Museum, in a well-heeled section of town to the east. I got there with two hours to see everything, and realized too late that I had taken my time with the animal section, with its interesting collection of skeletons, birds, and an ever-popular triceratops, along with colorful minerals, not realizing how much more there was to experience, even apart from their theater. I moved quickly through the history of Memphis (very interesting) before the place closed its doors for the day. To do that museum right requires twice the time I allotted for it.

I also wanted to enjoy the Rock and Soul Museum, given my interest in music, and given the prominence of Memphis as a musical city, especially in the development of the Delta Blues, with a number of musicians coming from Mississippi, including the legendary B.B. King (they featured one of his autographed Lucille guitars inside). The museum moves in chronological order, with a helpful audio device that at times allows you to choose actual songs from the particular era (which is how I discovered that George Thorogood's number about being sent to the doghouse after cheating on his wife was not originally his, but was a blues standard he covered). Before I knew it, another two hours had flown by, and it was time to close. However, the friendly guy behind the counter told me that my ticket would be good tomorrow as well, so I left with the intention of beginning my day there the following morning. Now to find a cheap place out of the city (I was close to the center of town now) to crash for the night.

With this thought in mind, I headed to the garage, connected with the adjacent FedEx Forum sports venue (home of the Memphis Grizzlies basketball team), where I had parked two hours before. It was now 7:05, and the place was gated shut. What the ... ?! Then I took a closer look at the sign I had passed on my way in, which explained that on non-sporting-event nights, the garage closed at 7:00 until the next morning. Great! I went to the nearby security room, but it was empty and dark. What to do? I started walking until I noticed a police car nearby, and made for it. I must admit, I was a little self-conscious, not only because this predicament was going to reveal me as a real traveling lightweight, but because I carried a bag from the Rock and Soul Museum with a white, stuffed wiener dog in it, a gift for a friend who owns a real one. The police were nice enough but not particularly helpful, since all they managed to suggest was to try the security room, and then the venue itself, to look for a night guard. The first I had already done, and the second I now tried, with no more success. I descried a second police cruiser and caught it, resigned to the fact that I was going to have to stay downtown for the night, with nothing but an albino dachshund and the clothes on my back. This time I asked for directions to a cheap place (as opposed to the nearby four-diamond Westin Memphis Beale Street), and they steered me to a much-less-expensive flop house, where I booked a room for the night.

So anyway, I thought, since God, or fate, or karma, or sheer stupidity, had stranded me in downtown Memphis for the duration, I might as well make the most of it. I left my wiener dog in the room and walked back to the infamous Beale Street, only a block north of the Rock and Soul Museum. It reminded me of Bourbon

Street in New Orleans, in that it was quiet and calm during the day, but after dark exploded with music and people coming from everywhere. I passed a small park at one point, where a live band was playing, while many bars and restaurants blasted tunes from inside through open front doors. I found a place that claimed to serve genuine New Orleans food with a Memphis flair, so I entered and ordered a huge combo dinner, which was great except for one anonymous item that was simply too spicy for me to finish. There was a guy at the piano playing and singing jazz, so it proved a most pleasant meal experience, better than the fast food I probably would have scarfed down elsewhere. And I didn't need to worry about parking, ironically, which can be a real nightmare on Beale Street, just as on Bourbon Street (when I was in New Orleans that same year I miraculously found [well, the tourist office did] a facility in the French Quarter, the Place d'Armes Hotel on Saint Anne Street, for about $80 a night [including tax], with free, off-the-street parking, a major bargain). On my way back to my motel (which was right across from another sports venue, where the semi-pro Memphis Royals played, and where I could hear the announcer calling the baseball game), I passed the small W.C. Handy house. I remembered him from a US postage stamp, back when I used to collect them, as the Father of the Blues, and was not now surprised to find him connected with Memphis. The city had some informational plaques in front of other buildings on Beale Street as well, announcing their part in the city's musical heritage.

    The next morning I did as planned, spending an hour to see the rest of the Rock and Soul Museum. Right across the street was the Gibson guitar factory, but the next tour wasn't until noon, and I had a couple of other places I wanted to see, so I satisfied myself with perusing the gift shop. My next stop of the day was another piece of Americana, unique in my experience: a scale model of a river, in this case (*CW) the Mighty Mississippi, right on an island (well, like Coronado "Island" in San Diego, it too is really a peninsula) in the river itself, the Mud Island River Park. I was impressed by how well it was done and at how long it was (a good half-mile), with interesting historical tidbits the entire way until terminating at the fountain that represents the Gulf of Mexico. You take a monorail over to see it, and on my way back I found myself in conversation with a sixty-something English couple, in the USA for their Nth time, very friendly and very happy to talk to me about their home country. (Too bad I was in too much of a hurry to see much of the five-storey Mississippi River Museum, which contained everything, from Native American history, to a full-scale Union gunboat, to a history of local music [*déjà vu*]. I really need to take a few days next time and do this city right.)

Well, the time had finally come (since it didn't close until 6:00) to see the National Civil Rights Museum. Its location was no accident: the old Lorraine Motel, the very place Martin Luther King was staying when he was assassinated back on April 4, 1968, as the song from U-2 reminds us, "Pride (In the Name of Love)." A middle-aged black woman sat nearby at a little booth where apparently she had been protesting for years, insisting that the motel should have been kept open for poor people to stay at, and not turned into a museum. I was glad she was out there, standing for something, but I was still happy that the motel was now a shrine (on the outside, the room that Dr. King was occupying has a wreath of flowers on the corresponding section of railing, up on the second floor). The venue is put together very well, documenting the movement for civil rights chronologically, starting with slavery and ending with the Rev. King's death. It took me the remaining afternoon to go through it with the attention it deserved, beginning with a film in a large theater, the preliminary to the informative displays.

As it happens, I had been to several venues stressing civil rights in 2010, including the Martin Luther King National Historical Site in Atlanta, where he was born; the Henry Ford outside Detroit, which houses the actual bus Rosa Parks refused to yield her seat in, in Montgomery, Alabama, in 1955, leading to her arrest and the bus boycott (she was recently featured on another US postage stamp); and the Lyndon B. Johnson Presidential Library and Museum in Austin, Texas, the man who signed the Civil Rights Act in 1964. But this place had the most information, with some video footage accompanying it. They even featured a small display on Mahatma Gandhi, from whom King borrowed the idea of non-violent resistance. There were several gay activists at the end of the tour (where you could see the actual bedroom Dr. King occupied), talking to a couple of staff members, seemingly trying to convince them that anti-gay sentiment needed to be fought through a civil rights movement of its own. They were still debating when I left. Thus ended two enjoyable and informative days in Memphis.

There were some other places I would have visited if I had time. According to AAA, there is a Danny Thomas/ALSAC Pavilion at the Saint Jude Hospital (he was a devout Maronite [Armenian-rite] Catholic), which, in beautiful surroundings, presents information about his career and the hospital's work, and where he and his wife Rose Marie (I didn't know they were married) are buried (and the institution, like the Shriners' hospitals, never charges anyone for treatment). The Memphis Brooks Museum of Art, the GEM I didn't get to see, would be another stop, with pieces that span the time from Greece and Rome through the Renaissance to the 19th century. The Slave Haven Underground Railroad Museum, which preserves an actual house with a hidden area for runaway slaves heading to Canada, would be a natural for this city as well. There are two record companies with museums also: the Stax Museum of American Soul Music, with background information and artifacts of the stars; and Sun Studio, where different music legends (most notably Elvis) got their starts, and where (as at the Experience Music Project in Seattle, Washington), you can make your own recording (here for an added fee). Last but not least, of course, would be to go back to Beale Street and see the inside of the W.C. Handy House, then walk south and take the Gibson factory tour.

In the end, I budgeted one day, took two, and needed several more to do this city completely (and these are only the highlights). However, after only two days, I was able to imbibe the spirit of the area, and know that, especially with its musical roots and its civil rights heritage, it is definitely some place I want to get to know better. I hope you do too.

CHAPTER 7

GOOD BUDDIES: THE LONG-DISTANCE FRATERNITY

You cannot drive too far on US interstates without encountering trucks, and truckers. They form a subculture all their own, of which Americans in general first became cognizant in 1975 with the song, "Convoy," by C. W. McCall. Yes, we were now aware of citizen's band radios, commonly called CBs, and many of us went out and bought them for ourselves. Articles appeared in newspapers about CBs, listing some of the jargon utilized by truckers and other denizens of the airwaves.

My father even bought a basic one, mainly, I think, in case of accident or breakdown, before the advent of cell phones. It sent and received for quite a distance. One summer we were heading down the South Jersey shore from our Philadelphia suburb. As soon as we drove across the Delaware River via the Walt Whitman Bridge into the Garden State, he got onto the CB and asked if anyone in the Atlantic City area was within earshot. When someone answered, he asked what the weather was like. The voice queried where he was; and when my Dad said outside Philadelphia, the other replied, "It's snowing." Wiseguy. What we didn't realize was that a regular CB only threw for a few miles, not the 60 miles from Philly to the coast. Years later I asked a man in a CB store about it, and he said that what we had, even though it was bought in a regular store, may have been illegal, and that he might need to report the conversation (woah!), although I assured him that it had been discarded years before. So what was it that we owned then? A Get Into Jail Free card, apparently.

My only other personal interaction with a CB was through my priest friend's old Pinto. He was in the practice of driving from the East, where he went to school and where his parents lived, to Arizona, where his diocese was located, and so saw how a CB could come in handy on long, uneventful drives. When I drove cross-country and back with him in December of 1984 and January of 1985, he didn't need the thing for company, but he did show me how it worked. I always thought having one made a great deal of sense (before the advent of cell phones, anyway), especially out in the middle of nowhere in case of a problem, but I never ended-up buying one. I was happier to invest my money in a radar detector, until I finally slowed-down.

Well, it's hard to imagine a trucker without a CB. It's an important aspect of membership in the long-distance club. I've driven cross-country at least three dozen times, and am happy if I can pick up a good radio station. However, high-mileage truckers drive that way all the time, always on interstates, rarely seeing any interesting sights along the way. Because of schedules, they need to drive far and fast, even as federal regulations try to limit how long they can operate without a break. (I've been told that truckers keep track of their own driving and breaks in a log called informally a cheat book, for obvious reasons.) I'm also told that, in addition to caffeine, the occasional trucker uses some other anti-sleep aids to keep going when the body gets tired, hence the reason for the regulations in the first place. After all, no one wants a sleepy auto driver on the road, let alone someone pulling several tons of weight behind him.

One set of clues that there is a trucker subculture, or club, is at truck stops. (Some of the better-known chains include Love's, TA [Travel Centers of America {although some brain cell of mine wants to insist that it used to stand for Truckstops of America}], Pilot, Flying J and Roady's.) Now truck stops allow regular drivers, too (as implied in the more four-wheeler-friendly change of name for TA) to use the bathrooms and shop in the large convenience stores. However, you often find at these places an area called a trucker's lounge, where, to gain access, you are expected to produce driving credentials, which act as an admission ticket. (They usually don't check such things if you look like a trucker, in your jeans and t-shirt and baseball cap with some truck-related product displayed, have a couple of days of beard on your face, and sound like everyone else. Still, they could if they wanted to.) There the trucker can sit and relax with colleagues on these breaks, sharing and exchanging stories that only other truckers would really appreciate from the inside. Other signs of a truck stop include coin-operated showers, traffic ticket negotiators, and dog food for sale. (I remember one truck stop, where there was a special booth for traffic tickets. This poor guy, looking impotent and distraught, was respectfully letting off steam while this woman in uniform listened helpfully. Auto fines are high enough; I can't imagine what a trucker would need to pay for speeding. Plus, if he hauls for a company, that citation could potentially affect his job.)

However, my usual interaction with truckers occurs not at truck stops but on the road. It is true that at truck stops gas is generally cheaper than at most other places (although, with over 250,000 miles on my last car, I became more and more picky about the brand of fuel I injected into my tank). It is also a place, when state rest stops are lacking, where I can pull into a car slot (after all, the workers need to park somewhere), jump into the back seat, and grab some sleep, knowing that no-one is going to bother me, since the place is full of truckers doing the same thing. I just make sure I buy something before I leave, either food or gas, as a sort of rent payment. I feel that I can understand their lives to some extent when my brain is scorched from 18 hours of straight driving; still, I don't do it as my living (although in 2010, when I was filling in all those travel gaps for this book, I came pretty close).

No, for me truckers are the people who drive those big things on the road. And there are lots of them. On an interstate in the evening, the majority of vehicles will be rigs. You can see the small lights that frame their cargo boxes in a line ahead. What is my experience of them? Generally, of other drivers who are just trying to get along while minding their own business. I figure that they're talking to each-other while they're driving and not paying any attention to me. (I wonder if, in light of state legislation about not driving while holding a cell phone, if anyone is going to go after CBs. Do they come in hands-free varieties?) My concern about troublemakers refers to other cars, not trucks (i.e., I never feel that trucks are toying with me, except the one time in Tennessee when the guy kept passing me and the slowing down, even though it was not hilly; even then, I figured that he was just a *strunz*, with nothing against me as a Pennsylvanian).

I remember driving in Arkansas back in January of 2002. I had just left from visiting a monastery in Oklahoma and, in the interest of time, decided to try my luck taking the short cut by going north on AR-7 through 53 rugged miles of the Ozark National Forest, as I headed to another monastery buried away in rural Missouri. I stopped at a surprise rest stop (a rarity off the interstate), after ice had begin to appear on the highway (and this was in a rear-wheel drive car). As it happened, the toilet was locked, so I went in back to knock the dew off the lily, just as I could hear a rig gearing-down (of course). However, when I stepped back out, I found a young guy, friendly, willing to tell me how the road was north from there, since he had just come that way. He replied that there was some ice, but if you took the curves slowly, you would be all right. It was a good encounter, and I made the rest of the drive with no problem. (It was a stretch of road that made the windy Sierra Nevada Mountains highways in California seem like I-80 in Nebraska. Scenery often comes at a price.)

However, at other times I've found truckers to be clannish, and-so not particularly open and friendly to drivers of other types of vehicles. This is not to say that they are *un*friendly. Nor is it to say that they are different from me, since I'm not too friendly to strangers when I'm driving, partly because of my personality, partly for reasons of safety (you never know who this other person may be, especially at a lonely rest stop).

The ultimate example in my experience of a trucker who regards auto drivers with disdain came back on that first cross-country drive, from Columbus, Ohio to Phoenix, Arizona. It occurred, as you may recall, during my deacon Christmas break, with two other then-deacons now-priests. We were heading into Gallup, New Mexico galloping along (sorry) until we ran into a white-out. The Ford had front-wheel-drive and a stick shift; and the owner, being from

Massachusetts, knew how to drive in the snow. This was one place he did get onto his CB, to see what there was to hear (so to speak). At one point we exited onto that parallel side road, less crowded than the interstate, where we could drive faster, because of that listening. In eavesdropping, we overheard a conversation among several truckers. They, of course, weren't happy with the snow, as we could see by how slow they were going around us. But there was this one guy who did nothing but complain about automobile drivers, whom he derisively called four-wheelers, and how they were cluttering up the road for the truckers, even though the semis were clearly more adversely affected by the weather. Eventually one of the other truckers called him on it, asking what he drove around in when he parked his rig between runs. The guy had an answer, replying that when he was home he rode his horse. I guess it takes all kinds. Still, the point isn't that all truckers are like this one guy, but that most of them are not. But there are guys like him out there. It may not be the point of the movie, *Easy Rider*, either, but sometimes you can sense the resentment.

I recall another episode, the only time I found a guy with an 800 number on his truck doing something that I could have reported. (Have you ever noticed that the trucks that drive poorly, or aggressively, never have those "How am I driving?" signs on their backs? With cells phones, they know that you can report an incident the moment it happens.)

Well, this other time, there was heavy traffic in two forward lanes. A car changed lanes in front of a truck, then changed lanes again, trying to move ahead faster (a ploy that seasoned drivers know rarely accomplishes anything). However, the truck was soon able to pull parallel with the car, at which time the driver poked his head out the window of his rig, looked directly at the car *at his side*, and give him the finger with a big "I got you" smile. Now what about the vehicle in front of the truck? He didn't hit it, but I was tempted to call his number and report him. Why didn't I? Perhaps since I wouldn't like someone to report *me*. Do unto others and all that. And he hadn't given *me* the finger. But, yes, those guys are out there, and are certainly not limited to truckers. (I recall one time outside Omaha, Nebraska, on a four-lane highway, where I was changing a CD, and then noticed traffic stopped in front of me. I steered out of the lane to the right, but then needed [*CW] to thread the needle between two highway signs while fishtailing on gravel until I came to a stop, miraculously unscathed. Yes, I admit it: sometimes *I'm* that other driver.)

(By the way, do you remember those commercials some time ago showing, in one case, a woman putting on her make-up in a mirror, and, in another, a guy taking off his sweater? Then the camera pulls back, and you realize that they've been doing those things while operating a car. Then comes the comment, "He's [she's] out there." Well, I've been known to change clothing while driving, eat while driving, and even read while driving, not to mention following the paths of swamp birds with my head in Florida, a practice that drove my sister crazy. I confess it, but don't recommend it. I've simply been lucky, or blessed, in spite of myself. And now I tend to pull over to change clothes (such as from a dress shirt to a t-shirt). And the only thing I read while driving is a map or tour book. Well, it's a start. So you see why I hesitated to rat that other guy out: potential hypocrisy. If I did, it would [*CW] be a case of the pot calling the kettle black.)

We knew a trucker growing up, a father of nine, a really nice guy; he always gave me the impression that truckers drove conservatively, conscious of how much of a load they were carrying around. He complained once that, when he gave the vehicle in front of him enough space as following distance, some car would jump in, forcing him to back off even more. I suspect that there are more truckers like him than like those two clowns I just mentioned.

There is one thing that makes me happy on interstates: the occasional states that post lower speed limits for trucks. Now I know that that statement will not make me popular with long-haulers, but I think that it helps (*CW) level the playing field between cars and trucks. If both are given the same speed limit, such as in my home state, Pennsylvania, trucks will tend to barrel past, making me feel unsafe. In California, where I have family, cars may do 70 while trucks may do only 55. Given how much trucks speed up anyway, and how they tend to avoid the police by their CBs, it means that I generally pass them slowly but steadily if I am doing 75. As I said, I don't like to travel slowly; but I'm not carting ten tons behind me if I do 80 in a 75 zone on a long flat interstate in the Mountain Time Zone.

The very worst experience I've ever had with a trucker, however, came a number of years ago, when I was starting an excursion from Pennsylvania to California. There was highway construction for miles, from P-A into Ohio, on I-70, down to one lane either way, with the speed limit reduced to 55, and after dark. I was doing 60, and this truck was right on my tail the whole time. There was no easy or safe way I could pull over and let him pass, so I just kept driving until the construction ended, staying at 60 to avoid a possible ticket. Well, during that time he must have gone from annoyed to angry to furious to vengeful. So now, with the construction zone behind us, he actually pulls back some distance, and is joined by another trucker, who pulls alongside him. Then (I can see all this in my rear-view mirror) they start racing, (*CW) neck and neck, increasingly picking up speed as they approach me. Then the one on the outside passed me, followed by the one directly behind me, who changed lanes at the last instant. They shook me up and almost caused an accident. (This incident, of course, would occur at the beginning of the drive, and so I wondered about meeting those maniacs again.) What I noticed was that this truck had no emblems of any sort, nothing that could identify him, except for his soiled license plate. I didn't expect an 800 number, but at least I could have gotten a company name. Nothing. That's one phone call I definitely would have made: to the police.

But again, I don't mean to imply that all truckers are like that. No, I'm citing him as the rare exception, like those guys in the pick-up truck from Durango, Colorado [**cf. "A Lane Change" below**]. It's said that America moves by truck, and trucking can be a hard and lonely job.

Sometimes I'm happier with them, as when they flick their high beams after I pass them to let me know I can return to the right lane safely. This practice is something they almost always do for each-other, and occasionally for cars (I have noticed it more up north, on I-90 and I-94, where it can get awfully lonely at 4:00 in the morning). When I drove a U-Haul truck cross-country one year, I was able to understand why they do it for each-other: no center rear-view mirrors. It does help guys (and gals, although I have almost never seen a female trucker in 32 years of long-distance driving) with only side-view mirrors. (I always extend this courtesy to long vehicles that pass me, such as trucks, busses and cars with trailers; and, when they flick their tail lights as the recognized way of saying "Thank You," I give them a blessing. [They always flick back for other truckers, and maybe half the time or less for cars.])

Sometimes I'm less happy with them, as when they pass an even slower truck uphill, and-so slow down traffic in the fast lane. (A mechanic explained to me once how a diesel engine needs to be [*CW, although in this case it is literal, not a metaphor] going full throttle all the time, so that truckers need to pass each-other that way rather than slow down and so be required to downshift.) It still annoys me (especially when they *jump* in front of me to do this, slowing me down for a minute or two as they crawl past another truck), but at least I can understand it better: that they're not doing it just to bother cars. What really annoys me is when, in the passing lane downhill, they tailgate me, and either flick their lights or blow their horn, since they're not at maximum throttle. (Sorry, but I'm not getting a ticket just to make you happy.) Then sometimes they're correct when they flick their lights at me in opposing traffic when I have my high beams on; but sometimes they're wrong when they keep their high beams on until I lower mine (I always lower them if the guy only flicks, but can be slow to do so when he leaves his on, the very things he doesn't want me to continue, as if it's a game of chicken). (Cars are much less sensitive about opposing high beams; and when they do anything to communicate with opposing traffic, they almost universally flick.)

There is one thing I would like to know: why do truckers keep their engines running through the night at rest stops? (Pennsylvania is the first state I've noticed, by the way, that explicitly forbids this practice, with sayings like, "Gentleman, Stop Your Engines" posted inside and outside the buildings.) With a number of trucks parked together, the engines form a symphony, which of course does wonders for the air, although this is usually not a problem at rest stops in the middle of nowhere. (I attended Pope John Paul II's mass at the Los Angeles Memorial Coliseum in 1987, and throughout the whole ceremony, the many busses in the lots kept their engines running. The air was so bad afterward as I walked back to the coach that my eyes were literally tearing, and I was choking.) One reason I have heard is that, if it gets cold enough, a diesel engine won't start (so why do they run them in July in Florida?). Another, less plausible explanation I was given once is that it takes so much fuel to start a diesel engine that running it all night still uses-up less of the tank. I wonder if perhaps they run the engines to keep their batteries charged, to allow all the creature comforts like TV and air conditioning to operate in the cab. (Trucks are a lot more advanced in that regard than years ago. In the National Steinbeck Center in Salinas, California, where novelist John Steinbeck was born [in the town, not the center], there is an agricultural museum, which has a rig that you can actually walk into, to see the sort of living space a present-day trucker has; it may be small compared to a motel room, but it's bigger than the back seat of my car, which is often my bed on the road.)

I can still recall one particular night at a rest stop. I had been to Theodore Roosevelt National Park in North Dakota, and was now heading to Zion National Park in Utah. I headed west on I-94 until it spilled into I-90 in Montana, and continued west toward Butte, where I planned to take I-15 south into the Beehive State. I remember stopping at a rest area in Montana to cook something on my small butane stove, and noticing how chilly and windy it was. (I heard on the radio afterward that that night in Butte they received a foot of snow. It was August.) However, by that night I was ensconced in a rest stop in Idaho. The weather, while not snowy, was still dramatic. As I drove south from Montana, I witnessed even farther to the south the most impressive electrical storm of my life, with lightning striking the ground almost continually as I drove, but safely at a constant distance. I probably would have driven into it, but stopped for the night to sleep. Anyway: at that small rest stop in Idaho, there were no other cars, and only two trucks. One was carting cattle (you can tell on the road, first by the smell, and then by the holes in the trailer); and as I tried to fall asleep with a quart of caffeine still in my veins, the noises I heard were *not* the engine, but the sound of hoofs on metal, and the occasional moo. This was definitely not Midtown Manhattan.

But no matter what, they're on the highways, more often than cars after a certain hour in the evening. They inhabit their own world, and I try not to bother them. But I guess that in general I can thank them for doing their job.

People have asked me why I never thought about being a trucker, and I reply that the easy part is on the interstate, while the hard part is driving on regular roads and making turns at intersections in traffic. That's where they really earn their money, in my opinion, and that's what keeps me from going to trucker school: I think I'm too old to learn to drive the rigs in small places, or even learn how to back-up. (I always had trouble in the monastery reversing the tractor that pulled the grass-mowing blades, and more than once that aforementioned mechanic needed to come out from his work and get me out of a jam when I went to the storage tank to fill up with diesel.) Of course, you never know: some people go to those schools as second careers, in retirement, I'm told. What a job for me: getting paid to drive cross-country. Stranger things have happened.

If I do end-up driving a rig some day, I hope I'm like the folks who drive for people like England, and UPS, and the post office, and Wal-Mart, and FedEx, and Covenant Transport, and Swift (who are not), to mention a few: never above the speed limit, and always non-aggressive. Covenant even sports a bumper sticker declaring, "It is not a choice – it is a child." (They also state, "Award-winning drivers are safe and courteous.") But couldn't I learn even to drive my car better by doing the limit and being non-aggressive? I'm much better than I used to be, but there's probably room for improvement.

Keep on truckin'.

CHAPTER 8

TOP CITY #4 – CHICAGO: FIRE, WIND AND WATER

I had the good fortune to live in the greater Chicago metropolitan area, affectionately known locally as Chicagoland, for almost two years when I inhabited a monastery in the western suburbs. Now, as a monk, and especially as a novice (i.e., a new monk who is on probation), I was not free to come and go as I pleased. Still, I did get to see some of the Second City while there, and have made several stops there (when I did not avoid it while traveling west, but actually headed there on purpose), to take in the sights.

My first trip to Chi-Town was way back in 1982, while a seminarian in Philadelphia. I was thinking once again about the monastic life, and had been very impressed by a Trappist monk from Iowa who addressed our class for a spiritual conference the preceding year. I made arrangements to visit his monastery outside Dubuque, at the beginning of the summer, and so was able to hitch a ride with a friend who was heading home to Arizona (not the guy with the Pinto) and who was kindly willing to go a little out of his way north for my sake. It was a great week with these monks, but I had come to realize at the time that the contemplative life was not for me, so I returned to the seminary that fall.

However, I did not have a free ride *back* to Philadelphia in 1982, where I would be working at the seminary for the summer, so I needed to take public transit, which meant a bus to Chicago and a train from Chicago. The bus depot and the train station were not all that far apart, fortunately, so I decided to walk from the one to the other with my minimal luggage to save cab fare. I did make a point of detouring out to Lake Michigan, the first time that I had ever seen a Great Lake, but for the rest of the layover I contented myself with reading while waiting four hours for the train. It did not occur to me until afterward that I could have done something constructive with that down-time downtown, since, if memory serves me correctly, I walked right past what back then was called the Sears Tower (it is now called the Willis Tower). I could at least have traveled up to the top (to what is now called Skydeck Chicago) to enjoy the magnificent view that it affords of the city and lake. (Curiously, an ad in the 2010 AAA tour book refers to it as the "Sears Tower Skydeck," while another ad in that same volume speaks of the "former Sears Tower"; I guess the Willis name just hasn't caught on. Still, no matter what you call it, it has been until recently the tallest building in North America, a whopping 1451 feet high, almost three times the height of the 555-foot Washington Monument. [Was, that is, until the new World Trade Center tower was completed in NYC in 2013, with its enormous antenna that places it at a patriotic 1776 feet in height.]) It would be years before that visit would transpire; and when it did, I was so impressed, not only with the view, but with the historical timeline inside, that I would now recommend it as the starting point for anyone who wants to tour this great city. (I recall, that day in 1982, walking through the part of downtown called the Loop, and how the local theaters were advertising *Rocky III*, focusing on the fact that Mister T was a Chicago native.)

Allow me to mention as well the John Hancock Observatory, atop a stunted edifice of merely 1127 feet, which also presumably offers great views of that same city and lake (at least when it is not fogged in, as it was the day, years later, that I went up). Indeed, Chicago is known for its architecture, since the city needed to be rebuilt after the Great Chicago Fire of 1871, just when people like Louis Sullivan and, a little later, his protégé Frank Lloyd Wright, were getting started. I finally took the three main Downtown Architectural Tours, which highlight this important aspect of the city's past, in 2013. (The concern involved is the Chicago Architecture Foundation Shop and Tour Center, and offers old and new skyscraper walking tour options, plus one on the water [not walking {unless Jesus shows up}].) So which one should you take? All of them, of course, which I found uniformly interesting, with articulate guides speaking under a rare clear blue Chicago spring sky. (As it happened, in perambulating from the main office to where the boat tour commenced, I passed the new Millennium Park, where a youth orchestra was playing one of my favorite pieces of classical music [I'd tell you what it was if I remembered]. It doesn't get any better than this.)

While visiting yet another monastery in the area years later, I walked to a local sight in the town of Lisle – the Morton Arboretum – where you can hoof it or take a tram tour. They pride themselves on labeling the various flora, to the tune of 4100 different species. It is not simply a bunch of trees; rather, they alternate types of landscape, from wetlands to cultivated gardens. There is even a section for kids to learn while playing. It is a good place to come and just relax for a couple of hours, alternating strolling and resting.

No, I didn't get to see a great deal of Chi-Town my first time through, but I did come back again, armed this time with my AAA travel book. At the top of my things-to-visit list was the Art Institute of Chicago, both because Edward Hopper's best-known painting, *Nighthawks*, which my brother had displayed in his place, was there; and because it had been featured in the film, *Ferris Beuler's Day Off*, where the three high-schoolers are posing next to a sculpture by Rodin, of the French novelist Balzac. Happily, *Nighthawks* was on display that day, along with a lot of other great stuff, including what sticks most in my mind, some excellent stained glass windows by Marc Chagall (I am looking at a poster of one of his paintings, from the Philadelphia Museum of Art, right now). On another visit I went around outside to the back, where I saw an old stock exchange arch. This museum contains one of the premier art collections in the country, perhaps second only to the Met (so that the Second City is once again playing second fiddle to the Big Apple), although Philadelphia might have something to say there. In fact, since I was there they have added a new wing for modern art, designed by Renzo Piano (whose work, not unlike Dale Chihuly's ubiquitous glass pieces, seems to be everywhere these days, such as the building for the Menil Collection in Houston). (Subsequently, it was great to see at least the outside of this museum, with its carved lions [which I am sure are nicer than the ones outside the New York Public Library, so there], appearing in another Chicago movie that I really enjoyed, *The Time-Traveler's Wife*.)

That same film (or at least the book, which I read twice) features another prime sight, which I took-in another year: the Field Museum of Natural History. This is simply an incredible place, the best museum of its kind in the country (although after subsequently touring the American Museum of Natural History in New York City, I might have to amend this judgment), the natural history equivalent to the Metropolitan Museum of Art in NYC (even in general shape). This entity, too, exhibits a pair of lions, real lions, although taxidermied. They were ravaging a village in Africa, according to an audial broadcast I heard years ago, and were thought by the locals to be possessed. A well-known hunter was brought in, who finally killed them both. The radio article ended, saying that they were both now in the Field Museum in Chicago, and that if you went there and looked them in the eye, "You will know fear." Scary stuff! I did it, and lived to tell the tale. I'll leave it to you to make your own decision. In three hours, I only saw about half of what they feature, but needed to move on to see more sights in my one day in town. Among its highlights are exhibits on history in the Western Hemisphere; Africa; DNA; and, of course, dinosaurs. They also have the usual collections of things I enjoy seeing, like minerals and animal bone models (which is why there are no mice there: too scared of the cat skeletons).

So what did I rush off to see that day? Another excellent venue, the John G. Shedd Aquarium, literally next door as you walk north along the lake. Now this is just about the nicest aquarium I have ever seen (I seem to be in a superlative mood, which Chicago will do to you). Here you will find tanks filled with (*CW) denizens of the deep, such as a shark collection, a coral reef, giant octopi and sea turtles. However, what put it over the top for me was the section featuring performing marine mammals: not only otters and sea lions, as cute as they are, but dolphins and Beluga whales as well. You probably don't have them in you tank at home. Thus, if you're not in a hurry there, you'll get a small taste of Seaworld for less than half the price.

What was next on my itinerary? The nearby (another, slightly longer short walk along Lake Michigan) Adler Planetarium and Astronomy Museum. I would not place it in the same class as the other two, even though it ranks as a GEM, but it is still worth seeing if you're in town. As the name implies, there is a planetarium there, indeed, two space theaters. There are also interesting exhibits for those who like space and the space program, as I do. One highlight is an actual space capsule. Of course, there may be more to see and experience here than I remember, or have the space (OK, that's enough!) to relate. Recall that I had been to two significant attractions already that day; and although driving was not an issue, I may have been simply squeezing this particular sight in at the end of a long day, through no fault of its own. My advice, then, is simply to get either a CityPass (you've doubtless seen them in other urban areas), or a Go Chicago Card, and take the time you need to see these sights (it may still help to bring your own brown-bag lunch, to avoid lines and so save precious minutes). If there's some time left over at the end of a day (!), or you want to wait-out the rush hour traffic, you could do what I have yet to do, since it is a new GEM: go north a few blocks to the refurbished Navy Pier and enjoy its carnival atmosphere.

The day I saw those three sights was a beautiful summer day, with a blue sky over blue water, and a gentle breeze (another local meteorological coup). For some reason, there were quite a few dragonflies in the air, more than I have ever seen anywhere else. (My mom used to call them devil's needles, adding that if you didn't cover your mouth when they flew by they would sew your trap shut. You can easily imagine how traumatic this particular day was for me.) It was great to be able to walk from one to the other, and then, in the early summer evening, through nearby Grant Park, just south of Millennium Park, the whole time enjoying the fading sapphire blue above and to the east. There is a statue of a seated Abraham Lincoln in Grant Park by noted artist Auguste Saint-Gaudens. Millennium Park, a recent GEM, has lots more bells and whistles, as my visit in 2013 revealed. (This sort of consideration is important to me in choosing a list of favorite cities, as will be made clear when I discuss the National Mall in Washington, DC.) North of Grant Park is Lincoln Park (this is not a rock group: they are named after a similar entity in LA), the other local park GEM, with another Saint-Gaudens statue of Lincoln, this one standing, along with a monument to my favorite Secretary of the Treasury, Alexander Hamilton (the improbable subject of the recent popular Broadway musical of that name). Near Grant Park but to the west there is a pair of small (when compared to the skyscrapers), curious, Gothic-looking buildings, one standing there with the other edifices, but the other right in the middle of the street, the old Water Authority structures, the more conventionally-located of which contains an historical display of the city.

Philadelphia may have the largest municipal park system in the world, but Chicago obviously has nothing to be ashamed of in this department, quality-wise. No fewer than six parks are noted by AAA, two of them GEMs, which is quite unusual for one city. All this verdure is no coincidence, of course. The long-time mayor when I lived there from 2002-04, Richard M. Daley, son of long-time mayor Richard J. Daley, was known for wanting to beautify the city. I went to pick up one of the monks at Midway Airport once and was pleased to discover a number of flower beds around the area, one typical instance of attractive public space in the Second City. Indeed, in a 2010 visit to Nebraska City, Nebraska, the home of Arbor Day, I discovered that Mayor Daley-*fils* is listed by them as one of the heroes of trees, getting special mention in that part of the arboretum along with the likes of Johnny Appleseed and John Muir.

While I was in the monastery, the Novice Master took us on field trips, as it were, at least three times (although not to the Field Museum). Once was to go to the small lake house in neighboring Wisconsin to relax for the day, at least after cutting the grass, which was filled with that white stuff that falls from aptly-named cottonwood trees. Another time it was to the flagship department store of the Chicago-based Lord & Taylor chain. It was an impressive edifice, which was also where we had lunch. (One of the older monks later said that Father Master should have treated us to a fancier restaurant, but I agreed with the latter's judgment: monks should not be eating [*CW] high on the hog.)

However, it is the third such trip that is cemented into my mind, since it was a real treat for me. Our goal that day lay on the campus of suburban Wheaton College: the Marion E. Wade Center, which focuses on the lives and works of noted British authors C. S. Lewis and J. R. R. Tolkien. There are four colleges of which I am aware of that feature Tolkien study centers: Oxford, in England; Notre Dame, in South Bend, Indiana; Marquette University, in Milwaukee, Wisconsin; and this school. (The two middle schools are both Catholic, not surprising, since Tolkien was a devout papist. Oxford was where both men worked. Wheaton is not Catholic but Evangelical Protestant, which was eventually Lewis's faith. I cannot explain the happy coincidence for denizens of Chi-town that three of these centers are within driving distance of the city. Oxford would require more of a travel commitment.) Father Master had even set-up a meeting with one of the managers, who gave us an overview of the place, and then answered our (well, mainly, my) questions. I have to admit, I was happy that I was able to show-off for this guy how much I knew about Tolkien. The *Lord of the Rings* movies were in the process of coming out, and there was a good bit of literature in print about Tolkien in those days, much of which I had devoured. He then showed us what he called a first edition of *The Two Towers*, the second volume in the *LOTR* trilogy. However, when he handed it to me and I opened it, it indicated that it was in fact a second printing, whereas all book collectors, when they say "first edition," mean the first printing of the first edition. I probably shouldn't have called him on it, since he was doing us a favor, but when I asked him if we could see a first printing, his response was silence.

Then we were turned loose on the place, which is primarily a library of all sorts of books by and about Tolkien and Lewis, and even books that they had read in formulating their imaginary worlds (they were close friends, and influenced each-other to no small extent). All too soon it was time to depart, but we were allowed a swing through the gift shop, where I found a poster of a Tolkien color drawing (he was a competent amateur artist as well) of the land in the west where the Elves lived. I received permission from Father Master to buy it; but then another man, divining that we were monks, insisted on paying for it himself, God bless him (when I think of it I say a Hail

Mary for him, too, as I am doing now). It is now framed and exhibited at the top of my bookcase. The place does not have much in the way of (*CW) bells and whistles, unless they have radically changed it in the past dozen years. However, if you are a Lewis or Tolkien fan, and want to learn more about them while you're in Chicagoland, I strongly recommend this locale.

But back to downtown Chicago. If you read the old AAA guide books, before they started multiplying GEMs, you will still find another museum mentioned (which therefore must be super) in downtown Chicago, just south of the detailed map they provide: the Museum of Science and Industry. I had been meaning to get there for years, ever since I visited the rest of downtown, and finally did so in 2013 as well, spending an entire day inside. AAA's superlative description proved accurate, what with 14 acres worth of displays (around 800 total), including lots of high-tech interaction. The centerpiece of the place, which was certainly high-tech for its day, is the only German U-Boat captured during World War II (for an added fee). Still, if you want to see coal mined, robots man an assembly line, or baby chicks hatch (Department of Redundancy Department), this is the place for you. (Indeed, I now rank it as by far the best venue of its kind in the country, another Chicago gold medal.)

I decided at one point to see it for sure in 2010, the Year of Fifty States; but when I got to Chicagoland, I decided to visit another attraction first that I had wanted to investigate since I lived there, close to the old monastery, in Naperville, called the Naper Settlement (don't ask me why I never saw it while I inhabited the next town over). It is a collection of old structures, gathered from the general area, refurbished, and displayed together. There is quite a lot to see, starting with an informative history of Naperville in the basement of the main building, illustrated with paintings from a revered local artist throughout, which show graphically what the descriptions are discussing. Some of these buildings have costumed interpreters to explain what is found inside. For instance, there is a small brick mansion (is that an oxymoron?) belonging to a Chicago brick magnate (gotta love Chicago common brick), which allows for a half-hour tour. The newspaper building demonstrates how an old printing press was used, and even allows (*CW) children of all ages (*CW) to try their hands at printing a sheet of paper. I was particularly interested in the old chapel. This trip into history, which required three hours, costs only $8.50, so that even the price is antique.

At this point I had a choice to make. I was behind because of trying to find the Naper Settlement, ensconced as it is in a non-grid neighborhood; and then I took longer there than I expected. So, do I drive into Chicago proper, try to park, and then see the Museum of Science and Industry (a laughable plan now, given its scope and breadth), and subsequently get stuck in rush-hour traffic? Or do I head south to Joliet to see a new GEM? I must admit that I chickened-out, not wanting to negotiate Chi-Town traffic, and ended-up in the much smaller city, which has a museum of local history, the imaginatively-named Joliet Area Historical Museum. It's well done, although it helps to have an interest in the past in general to want to go there in the first place. Still, even the general tourist will enjoy seeing rooms taken out of his or her past, with artifacts that would have been in use 25, 50 or 75 years ago. The area was known for the mining of limestone, and there is one large impressive display that seemingly opens up an old canal before the waterway was finished. Another nice feature of the museum is that it is located in an old church, with stained glass windows intact, demonstrating a creative way to maintain historical buildings in a way that pays for themselves. (The fact that a ticket costs $57 is of no consequence – just kidding.) Right at the end of my time there I came upon a temporary display of great interest to me, which documented the contribution the Catholic Church has made to that general locality. I had about five minutes to breeze through what deserved at least a half-hour of my time, but (*CW) all too soon it was closing time. I thought I would wait-out the local rush-hour traffic (yes, even in Joliet, although some was overflow from Chicago, since it went both directions) by having dinner downtown, but I soon discovered that downtown closed at 5:00. I only found one restaurant in several blocks of walking, and it was only open for breakfast and lunch (lots of brown-bagging at work, I guess). Oh well: off to Wendy's; and even that took several stops off the highway to locate.

Of course, we can't overlook the Brookfield Zoo, one of my favorite animal collections in the country, located in a suburb of the Windy City (named that, not because of meteorological conditions there, but because of long-winded politicians when trying to convince others to vote to hold the 1893 Columbian Exposition there, which they succeeded in doing). They charge for parking, but miserly I simply drove to a nearby municipal park (love that park system) where African-American families were picnicking, parked, and walked back to the zoo. Among my memories is a good hoofed mammal collection, one of my favorite groups of animals. It is noted for having cage-less enclosures (I know, that sounds like an oxymoron, too, but they do try to mimic the animals' natural habitats). Among the various exhibits is one that adds some local flavor by reproducing life in and around an Illinois River. I was most interested in the African forest buffalo, a slightly smaller close cousin of my favorite animal, the Cape buffalo, and the only ones I have ever seen. They even provide motorized guided tours.

A couple of non-GEMs of personal interest to me were both in another suburb, Oak Park. One was the Frank Lloyd Wright Home and Studio. I am always happy to see another FLW building, and this one was no exception. Indeed, it was his first independent work. I was particularly struck by the way the ceiling in one open area was designed (I guess you need to see it to appreciate it). My regret is that the day I was there I did not have time to do the whole Architectural Tour in that neighborhood, which is a GEM. (The guide to the house-and-studio tour remarked that Wright lost his job with Louis Sullivan for freelancing, which Sullivan did not allow, even on one's own time. Sullivan drove through this neighborhood one day, and his trained eye could recognize the hand of Wright in a number of houses, which led to his ouster and the beginning of his solo career.) That is one reason to go back to Oak Park. (I have seen other FLW buildings over the years, including the Guggenheim Museum in New York City; the Hollyhock House in Los Angeles [with my mother]; the Dana-Thomas House in Springfield, Illinois; a synagogue in the Philadelphia area (Beth Shalom in suburban Elkins Park) with my seminary art class, where the predominating symbol was the triangle; his two personal homes, Taliesin, in Spring Green, Wisconsin, and Taliesin West, in Scottsdale, Arizona; and of course the celebrated Fallingwater in southwestern Pennsylvania, with my parents. I viewed yet another one in 2010, thanks to a new AAA GEM, in Florence, Alabama, the Rosenbaum House.)

The other sight in Oak Park is actually two: the Ernest Hemingway Museum, and the Hemingway Birthplace Home, separated by a few blocks. Again, because of time constrictions, I walked to the front door of the birth house, but did not have time to wait for the next tour. Rather, I hurried to the museum. In fact, in my experience, while I've visited some authors' houses (Willa Cather in Red Cloud, Nebraska; William Faulkner in Oxford, Mississippi; and Sinclair Lewis in Sauk Center, Minnesota; not to mention John Steinbeck's house in Salinas, California), Hemingway and Steinbeck are the only two authors to whom I've seen actual museums, apart from a residence, dedicated. (It was in the Hemingway Museum gift shop that I bought a khaki cap, which simply says, "Hemingway: Oak Park," obviously for the cognoscenti. I am wearing it as I revise this chapter in the afternoon sun.)

Other sights that I'd like to experience include the National Museum of Mexican Art, with a section helpful to us novices, tracing Mexican culture over the centuries (where there are, of course, works by Diego Rivera). There is also the Smith Museum of Stained Glass Windows, which contains pieces both religious and secular, some designed by the likes of local favorites Frank Lloyd Wright and Louis Comfort Tiffany. For those of the roller coaster persuasion, there is a Six Flags Great America Park in Gurnee, visible from the interstate, which also features its own water park.

My biggest regret about Chicago, besides not seeing everything while I lived there, since I assumed that I'd be in the neighborhood forever, was not visiting the blues clubs in this musical city. It is almost due north of Memphis and the Delta Blues; and I have read, while living in Chicagoland, that even the Rolling Stones, when they are in town for a concert, check out these haunts, as much on the sly as they can manage. My friend and frat brother travel partner from Philadelphia, a blues aficionado, has taken fellow workers to them when in town for conventions, but I never thought to pick his brain about it. I could still do it technically, but it's not so Handy (pardon the pun) as it would have been when I lived there. I guess I'll just have to go back.

Indeed. I'd like to go back, not only to see the new stuff, but to see the old stuff all over again at a more leisurely pace. Then too, it would be nice to stop and see the monks again. I don't know if I could convince any of them to go to the blues clubs with me. If I don't end-up going with Bro, I'll have to wait for the next time the Stones are in town and head on down with Mick and Keith.

CHAPTER 9

WHAT'S THE FREQUENCY, KENNETH? TUNING IN WHEN YOU'RE OUT AND ABOUT

Anyone who drives as much as I do listens to a lot of radio. And anyone who has driven to as many places as I have has heard a number of different radio stations, and musical formats. The fact that there are so many types of radio station selections, such as adult contemporary, alternative, Christian, classical, classic rock, country, jazz, light rock, National Public Radio, oldies, pop, R&B, rap, and talk (these are listed alphabetically, and I'm sure there could be more) indicates just how much humans really love music (and, occasionally, chatter).

Let me say right away that I am one of those many music-loving humans; I enjoy all kinds of tunes, everything from alternative to zydeco. (Yes, I had a zydeco CD once, when my disc collection was at its 600-strong height. It was by C. J. Chenier, the son of the Clifton Chenier whom Paul Simon sings about on his Grammy-winning album, *Graceland*. When my priest friend from Arizona was visiting me in Pennsylvania, and saw my CD collection, which I explained held a great variety of musical genres, he challenged me to produce a zydeco album. The joke was on him, since, to his chagrin, I not only did so, but obliged him by playing it. No wonder he left the next day.) I've effected three great purges of them since, getting the number down to around 50. (It goes without saying that I don't belong to any CD clubs any more.)

Oh, I travel with a few CDs, for use when I'm driving late and need loud, familiar music to keep me going. I don't carry any classical, and certainly not any relaxing Indian flute music, but only rock. I find the more tired I get, the more familiar the music needs to be to keep me awake. During the day I can listen to all sorts of stuff, including songs I have never heard before and will never hear again; but such eclectic experimentation ends after a certain hour. Still, the CDs were only brought for when there was nothing on the radio that was keeping me wide awake. I still prefer local radio, as I explain below; still, when there is nothing familiar on the airwaves at 3:00 in the morning between, say, San Antonio and El Paso, CDs comes in handy. (Recently I have also discovered audio books, and completed four of them on my trip in 2016 for my Dad's 87th birthday.)

Yes, I love listening to the radio. It can be the same old classic rock, or the same new current pop hits, or the same old oldies, or the same old retro, or the same new current rock. It can be the same old composers, with classical music familiar and unfamiliar. Or the country hits for the year that I am just learning.

Being from the 'burbs, country was for me an acquired taste. My sister first got into country, followed by my brother, after we moved from the Philadelphia area to State College in central PA, where you have either Penn State or the surrounding farms, but that location never influenced my listening. I was forced into country when, between cities late at night, or even during the day the farther west I drove, and the farther away cities got from each-other, and I forgot CDs that trip, I was desperate for anything, and found either country or nothing. (Occasionally the only choice was nothing. You haven't lived until you're driving in mountainous West Virginia and hit the Seek button on your radio, and it just keeps going around the dial time after time.)

I used to imagine that country music was for hicks, but eventually discovered how good it is (or else I turned into a hick in the process). There are even different types of country formats ("This is not your father's country station!"), just as there are several types of rock formats, from oldies to dance music. Thus, most years I would come into contact with the country hits, since the different stations across the country tended to play the same songs within the same formats.

As I began to shed my ignorance, I discovered several things about country. One was, as I just said, that there are different sorts of country music, from the old weepy stuff to current rock crossover songs. Another was how much humor there is in country music (such as that one song, "There Ain't Nothin' Wrong with the Radio"), whereas humor is very rare in rock, as if it takes itself too seriously. Finally, a country song has a much better chance of making me cry than a rock song, since it is generally in touch with the heart (no doubt one reason it is so popular). And in the car on a lonely interstate, late at night, fried from the road, with too much caffeine in me, I would let myself cry as I drove. It never lasted long, but what a contrast to the average rock song.

There are a couple of other things about country music. One is that, somehow, the singers can sing with an accent, a Southern drawl. It seems like every English-language singer in the world sings like East Coast Americans, so that individuals with the thickest British accents (from the Beatles, from Liverpool, to Tom Jones from Wales), who can hardly be understood in America when they are being interviewed, all sound the same on records (I know that I'm dating myself by this reference to vinyl). But somehow country singers defy the experience of the English-speaking world by singing Southern.

Another is that the DJs generally sound the same, as if they could all be from the East Coast, in that non-accent (OK, I know, we have an accent, too). I expect country music to sound like the South, but the DJs do not. And that gets me to a more general point: how similar everyone on the radio sounds across the continent. It's like there's a DJ school somewhere in Gary, Indiana that eradicates any tinge of a regional accent, so that rock or country DJs in Pennsylvania sound like rock or country DJs in Texas. How has this happened?

Well, at the same time I began more and more to notice a couple of things in radio-land across the country. The first was that many radio stations name themselves. If there's water flowing through the city, then the station may be called The River. A city in the hills may contain a station known as The Mountain or The Peak. If you're by the seashore, the local station may be The Coast. An alternative station may tout itself as Your Music Alternative, or call itself The Edge (no, not the U-2 guitarist), or The Revolution or The New Rock Alternative, or The Zone, or the Buzz. It's like there are these 25 names, and you must choose one from that list only. I've heard Eagles and Coyotes, Bandits and Stars, Foxes and Points. The lighter stuff presents itself as Sunny or Magic or, simply, Lite. (Indeed, light rock is its own format, and will clue you in by declaring things like they have "The best variety of yesterday and today," or "Today's hits and yesterday's favorites," or songs from "the eighties, nineties and today" or "all of the hits without the metal and rap.") Pop is often something like Kiss (although I've also heard Kiss Country) or Hot or the Mix or, before, Power. (Just today I saw a bumper sticker on a car for a Christian radio station called The Fish, since the fish is an ancient and revived symbol for Jesus Christ.) So it's not enough that the songs are the same: even the DJ non-accents and the station names are the same.

The second is that the conglomerates that own many of the stations began tipping their hand, I don't know why. So you hear now that this station is a Clear Channel station in different cities, or connected with I-Heart, no doubt with identical play lists, developed at some corporate headquarters elsewhere. It's like there are 10 general stations, period, and that every specific station in the country is just an avatar of one of the general stations, simply with different call letters. There is even a Trucker Network, and Racing Country USA (NASCAR info and news), both with country music. However, I think this phenomenon was seen most clearly in the Froggy country stations. They have cute bumper stickers in different cities, always the same, with that smiling frog face that looked like our favorite Muppet. Their DJs were all programmed, too, with names like Polly Wog, Peat Moss, Kelly Green, Cricket, the Frogman, and Captain Kermit the Weather Hermit. And they all regularly announce that they are about to hop over to the radio to play their next song.

Third, what is happening to the DJs? There are stations now that do not use live DJs. My brother, who used to be in radio in State College, PA, is happy with this trend, since he thinks DJs have big egos and all. That may be true. Still, to me, eliminating live DJs is letting some corporate Big Brother be the DJ. One example is the popular Jack FM stations, with the same voice everywhere in the country telling listeners that they do not take requests because they're "Playing what we want." Another is a station in Salt Lake City that tells the listener every song and artist (which I appreciate, a [*CW] pet peeve of mine for many years), but which uses a woman's recorded voice to do so.

I like the thought that there's a (*CW) flesh-and-blood *person* at the other end of the airwaves. And I like the thought that he or she sounds like other people in that given geographic area. (I suspect one reason is the great mobility of DJs, who are rarely from the city where they are currently working.) I mentioned a Southern drawl earlier, but there are a number of Southern accents, and so-on around the country. People may think that all Philadelphians sound like Rocky, but that's just *South* Philly (home of great cheesesteaks). People from my Mom's old neighborhood in *North* Philly sound distinctly different. And neither one was what we spoke in the western suburbs. And so on. (Of course, as a boy, I believed that we had no accent. In seventh grade a religious sister came to our school from the South with a thick drawl; but when someone commented on how funny she sounded ["That Sister Jean is Kentucky fried!" a remark that she overheard], she countered with good humor that many people around the country think that Philadelphia has the most distinctive accent of all. We were dumbfounded and incredulous. Another sister [this one from Chicago] teaching in a high school when I was a seminarian, provided examples of words we pronounced uniquely in Philly, like "Eagles," "fifth," "Schuylkill," and the quintessential "water," which we pronounced WOOD-er.)

This is why I love local radio whenever I happen upon it on the airwaves. (There was a brief time years ago when I wondered about getting satellite service that would pump music into my car continuously, [*CW] 24/7, by genre [for example, Sirius/XM]. The advantages would include being able to get any sort of music, anywhere in the country, even if well between cities. But that's not radio, with the immediacy of someone there to [*CW] put a face [well, a voice] on it.) So when I find some guy who did *not* go to DJ articulation school giving the lunch specials at local restaurants, or taking calls from people with items for sale between songs, or relating the current farm report, I am ecstatic. To get real local people talking reminds me, Toto, that I am not in Pennsylvania any more. And isn't that why I would occasionally *leave* Pennsylvania in the first place?

Of course, there is an exception to the radio accent rule, sort of. I'm talking about Christian stations, which are legion in the South, but which exist other places as well. In the South you expect some version of a Southern accent; but in Montana? No matter where, it seems, there's a Christian preacher speaking, he's doing it with a Southern accent. That must be an elective course in DJ articulation school. There are different takes on the Gospel message, but the voice always sounds the same.

Which brings me to format. Every radio station in existence has a format. They play certain types of music, or present certain kinds of talk. There are many different types of formats, but if two stations have the same format, they're going to sound in many if not in most ways the same. And almost every radio station has a simple format, what you might call a specialty: one thing only.

I have found a refreshing exception to this rule in Canada, in CBC (Canadian Broadcasting Corporation) radio. They have a good bit of talk, like NPR in the USA. But they will play music sometimes just for the heck of it, as a break from all the yakking. What an idea. An NPR piece may have music included in it, but they just don't play music between talk pieces, except for an occasional 30-second Muzak filler at the end of an hour. I guess the radio school is different up there, eh?

There are rare stations and networks that have unconventional formats. I was leaving Reno, Nevada once when I first stumbled upon Alice Cooper, now a syndicated DJ. I have since heard him elsewhere around the country, and it is in fact the former rock star himself. He plays a refreshing mix of rock musical types, and speaks intelligently about them, offering musical factoids for our consumption. (My one-time home station, KROQ in Pasadena/LA [*not* pronounced CROCK, but rather K-ROCK], speaks intelligently about music, too, but it's the same play list of current and nineties alternative hits [to use an oxymoron].) (A couple of other syndicated DJs whom I like are John Tesh ["Intelligence for your life"] and Delilah [with advice for the heart].)

Then there's a station I was able to get on I-40 around Winslow/ Flagstaff in Arizona. It was KLOD, 100.1, The Cat, coming out of Sedona. (By the way, if you're there and can't find this station, or it sounds different, know that radio stations at times change format, although they'll almost always have one clearly-defined one. [For instance, K-Mozart, one of two classical music stations in SoCal years ago, is now country.] In other words, don't blame me.) It seems to be the brainchild of Robert Shields, of mime team Shields and Yarnell fame, and exhibited a format that included, in the hour I was able to tune them in, blues, jazz, world music and more I didn't write down. Now, all of these may sound the same to rock, pop and country people, but they're distinct genres. Was it a special hour show each week? My impression was that that was the way they always played music. (These days, of course, [Altered Cliché Warning] you're only as far as your computer, as this stuff comes [*CW] streaming over the Internet [but not in your car that readily, until they design car radios with cellular modems standard].) It was as cool as cool gets. (Quite recently I heard a similar non-format in western P-A, called Ecclectopia. I was in heaven.)

I read an article once about a radio program director who had all sorts of stuff in his station collection, which at least implied a mixed format as well (or several consecutive ownerships). I wish I remembered where (San Fran?). Then there was the trip through New York City where I found a talk show hosted by the once and future California Governor Jerry Brown, that day interviewing poet Alan Ginsberg, hardly a right-wing talk show. A huge market like New York can support really specialized stations with distinctive formats, but that's a luxury found only in the megalopolis, not in the spaces between cities.

Another phenomenon in radio is the Morning Show (and now, more and more, the Evening Show). Whatever happened to music in the morning? (as one good alternative station in LA, 98.7, laments each day, refusing to kowtow to this trend). If I want music, I don't want to hear talk. If I wanted talk, I'd switch to AM. It is true that, when on the road, I may find talk as more of a stimulant to staying awake at night. Still, I am not usually falling asleep in the morning, unless I am pulling an all-nighter. People must want these cute shows. I guess it's (*CW) whatever floats your boat. Some of these morning shows are even syndicated, so that Kevin and Bean are heard, not only on KROQ in LA/OC (Los Angeles/Orange County), but around the country; another local boy who has made it big is Ryan Seacrest on KISS FM in LA. If I'm tired, I'll take the morning show for the mindless chatter to keep me awake; otherwise, I want to hear music. (There is even at least one syndicated country morning talk show that I've heard around the nation, featuring John Boy and Billy [although I don't believe it originates in Walton County, Virginia].)

When I travel, I like to find things that are distinctive in each area in the local culture; and one of those things is radio. There are times, I admit, when the familiar is attractive, as when I buy my gas at national chain stations, or eat an occasional burger (a sensitive admission for a sometimes-vegetarian) from Carl's Jr. In the same way, if I am tired and some classic rock station is spinning all the usual suspects (which would normally drive me crazy), that helps me to stay awake better. (In this regard, the ultimate driving song is "Radar Love" by the Golden Earrings, and it knows it. That song's like a can of Mountain Dew Code Red at three in the morning.) But I don't learn anything from the experience, and would tend to like to listen to what the people of the area want to be listening to, rather than what some corporation a thousand miles away thinks they *ought* to be listening to.

The car I gave my sister when I was about to enter the 1993 monastery, while she was leaving another monastery, lasted for a number of years, but eventually got tired and worn-out. Specifically, the radio was shot, which meant that she could not listen to music while she navigated SoCal freeways. I could just as easily imagine a car without an engine. If I couldn't afford to buy a new car to replace a broken radio, I would get a small battery-operated tape player and play cassettes, or a small radio to catch local air waves. For me in general, and on long drives in particular, except when I might turn off the radio for 15 minutes to pray a rosary, or enjoy the scenery that the Creator has provided, driving and music have become synonymous. I'm not saying that that needs to be the case with you. Still, I recommend considering making radio, and especially local radio, part of your cross-country experience. (Forgive me, but I just thought of a relevant pun: When I drive cross-country, between cities, I sometimes *cross* format to *country* music. Sorry.)

I think that the Federal Communications Commission should hold a series of hearings, investigating why radio all over the country sounds the same. In 2010, the Year of Fifty States, I logged more highway miles than in any other 12-month period in my life, as I sought to fill-in travel gaps for this book. The whole time, I had the radio on, listening to what each city, and the spaces between cities, offered. I happened at that time, by way of exception, to like the current pop songs, so I gravitated in that direction. It was the same tunes in every town, dictated by the *Billboard* Top 40, or Hot 100 (although the industry actually uses another, lesser-known publication for its musical direction, *Radio and Records*). I think Theodore Roosevelt, the Trust Buster, or his successor in office, would be interested to know that there is practically a monopoly in radio ownership, leading to regularization in the sounds that eventually leave the towers, aimed at your home and car. In this regard, perhaps I am a latter-day Upton Sinclair. Maybe the president will read a review of this chapter, as Teddy Roosevelt did about *The Jungle*, about meat-packing, while he was eating his morning sausage, and get similar results.

Two exceptions to the leveling law in formats are jazz and classical stations, as rare as they are. They have (*CW) flown under the radar so far. One reason: the two jazz stations I am most familiar with, the one in Philadelphia (WRTI, at least during the day now), and the one in Los Angeles, are both situated on college campuses (Philly's is located at Temple), with money coming not from advertising, but from their fans. The same applies to classical stations as well. Now classical music, and jazz, may sound all the same to people who don't listen to it, but there is a great deal of diversity in both genres. In fact, the LA jazz and blues station, KKJZ ("K-Jazz"), from Long Beach State, plays everything from big bands to Sinatra to Miles Davis to fusion to Latin jazz to what was issued just this year. I am in the habit of saying that there is no such thing as bad French food or bad jazz, and the same could be said for classical.

You run into such independence occasionally in the rock world. One alternative station in Oklahoma 20 years ago had a motto for their new tunes: "Because they're still making music in the nineties." (That same station featured two DJs on one afternoon [curious timing in itself], discussing the latest movie from fellow Philadelphian Sylvester

Stallone, predicting that the next Rocky film should be, *Rocky 6: Rocky Meets Rambo*.) Then there was that station in North Carolina in the middle of the night, playing all three live versions of Joe Jackson's, "Is She Really Going out with Him?" which are as different as three songs can be, from his then-recently-released live album. Or how about that advertisement on top of a cab inside the Washington beltway I saw in 2000 for the Hard Rock Café: "Great for the Mommas and the Pappas, and the Offspring too." (It may not have been a radio station, but that ad, besides being clever, captured the spirit of what I am trying to say.) Then there was the station in the Mendicino area of California that played, in succession, Yo Yo Ma and James Taylor, almost as if it was classical *and* classic rock. Or the Portland, Oregon rock station that advertised for a performance of Tchaikovsky's *Nutcracker's Suite*. Or the station further north in California that combined "Amazing Grace" and "The House of the Rising Sun" in a tune by the Blind Boys of Alabama. Or the station from Louisville, Kentucky that bragged, "We don't play the same 200 songs." Or the station that carried Bob and Tom in the morning, and had local Catholic Schools sponsor the weather in the evening. Or the station in Cumberland, Maryland that played a song from *O Brother, Where Art Thou*, by the Soggy Bottom Boys, same voices and everything, but with different words. And for you *Wizard of Oz* fans (this is not code for Black Sabbath), there were country stations as I drove from Virginia into North Carolina who unwittingly (?), within about an hour of each-other, juxtaposed Garth Brooks' "Scarecrow" and Kenny Chestney's "Tin Man."

I'm talking about disc jockeys who refuse to talk through the introduction to "Roundabout," as I actually heard once to my confounded amazement, proving that they deserve the epithet, "AM jocks." I mean, even FM DJs talk over the music now, which only AM jocks did back in the sixties (when AM still played music). Another station that mixes its format somewhat is what calls itself the Highway Stations, 98 and 99, between Los Angeles and Las Vegas, with two different towers and hence frequencies, that broadcast the same show, so you can get it the whole way to Sin City and back. No one lives in that isolated area between Barstow and Baker, so they are geared to drivers. The music is a mix of rock and easy listening, meant to appeal to more than one format expectation, since they want to catch as many of these drivers as possible. They also offer news about Vegas shows and concerts. And for talk, can you beat "Car Talk," on NPR on the weekend, with my *paisanos* Click and Clack (one of whom recently went on to his well-deserved reward), who, while demonstrating their wide knowledge of automobiles, keep me laughing out loud from beginning to end? The antithesis of what I am getting at is summed up conveniently by a Columbus, Ohio station, that reassured its listeners that it played "no unfamiliar nineties music, just classic rock hits." Dudes, the seventies music was once unfamiliar, too. To make it familiar, all you need to do is listen to it. (These days the Pittsburgh classical station [WQED, along with its translator in Johnstown, PA, WQEJ] likes to say, "Remember: all music was once new.") What I'm talking about is exemplified by another Columbus station, the Blitz, claiming that "It's all about new rock."

To experience some real mixing, drive near the Mexican border. I was in Organ Pipe Cactus National Monument one year, which is literally at the southern extreme of Arizona, and got a station where the DJ spoke both in English and Spanish. Commercials for familiar American products were in Spanish, including not only Coke but the Army (!). The format? I called it Mexican Muzak. (I don't listen to Salsa, or any Latino music [although I liked Ricky Martin with his crossover hit, "*La Vita Loca*"], so I can't really comment on it, except to mention that, whenever I am flipping stations near the border and find it, there always seems to be an accordion in the mix.)

And finally, where else are you going to hear about local concerts while you're on the road, which has enabled me to hear a number of diverse acts while traveling, from Eric Clapton to Avril Lavigne, Three Doors Down to Deep Purple, Joe Satriani to Train?

So then: if you drive alone, or even with a carful, you may very well give your radio a consistent workout on a cross-country jag. What you choose to play is up to you: a matter of taste. However, if you travel away from home in order to see the local sights, and taste the local cuisine, and hear the local accents, why not also sample the local air waves, so that, by changing the stations with frequency (sorry), you can discover our diverse land in yet another way.

CHAPTER 10

TOP CITY #3 – PHILADELPHIA: THE CRADLE OF LIBERTY (AND OF AN AUTHOR OR TWO)

OK, I can already hear you yelling "Foul!" since this city is my hometown. But remember, I'm discussing my five faves, not necessarily the objective best (although local publishing sensation Ben Franklin would no doubt have agreed that Philadelphia would be on that list as well, HA!). I was reminded of how much I love the City of Brotherly Love (what the name literally means in Greek, as it appears in the Bible) on the occasion of my uncle's death back in 2010. I drove down for the funeral in October, and re-discovered enjoying simply cruising through the old neighborhoods. Not even the flooding, in the wake of a hurricane, which turned traffic into a nightmare that morning, could dampen my spirits (sorry). For a brief moment I actually felt at home again, a nostalgia supported by tuning-in to WMMR (93.3) on the radio once more (during what they call Rocktober). I love the world-famous K-Rock (KROQ, 106.7) from SoCal, which I listen to at times now on my computer or phone. Still, it was curious timing that one of the long-time disc jockeys, Pierre Robert (row-BEAR) (note the continuity: he was on in the seventies, when I was in college) had just been to a ceremony, during which MMR received a Marconi Award for the best rock station in the country. I'll admit that I prefer the KROQ format, which plays more newer rock, the way WMMR used to. Still, the Philadelphia DJs were giving out a lot of interesting factoids about the music and the artists they were playing. (One example: they had recently imploded the Spectrum venue [former home of the Flyers and 76ers] in South Philly, and Eddie Vedder of Pearl Jam, who loved that place [Philadelphia was, and no doubt still is, a legendary rock concert city], played a set of shows for five nights straight, as his way of paying tribute to it and saying good-bye [indeed, there's a tear in the corner of my eye as I write this; I mean, I saw {Cliché Warning} the one and only Led Zeppelin there back in college].) The other new rock station from my college days, by the way, WYSP ("We're Your Station in Philadelphia"), 94.1, has gone the way of classic rock.

I have already admitted that I love music; still, it's going to take more than one radio station to get me to rank a city in the Top Five. What else does Philadelphia have to recommend itself? The indigenous food, of course. Cheese steaks and hoagies, soft pretzels and scrapple, all get my mouth watering. There is the South Philly of Rocky fame, with its Italian restaurants, and Italian ice (especially with pieces of lemon rind in it). (The funeral luncheon for my uncle was in this area, and included some delicious pasta.) Further, Philadelphia may not be New York City when it comes to delicatessens, but it has plenty of them, places you can buy those Italian lunchmeats: prosciutto, capicola ("gabagool"), salami, pepperoni and provolone (OK, so that's a cheese). In fact, for years, the Number One rated restaurant in the country was Le Bec Fin, a French eatery I could never afford to patronize. If you like ice cream, you can't beat the local brand, Breyers, my mother's favorite. And what tastes better than a Dietz & Watson hot dog at a Phillies game, washed down with a Frank's cream soda? Then, while you're in South Philly, stop at Amoroso's for some still-warm Italian or Kaiser rolls just begging for butter, with an Italian rum cake for dessert.

OK, so what do you do when you're not eating? Boston and Philadelphia tend to vie with each-other over who really deserves the phrase, "The Cradle of Liberty." I'm not going to try to solve that friendly disagreement here, but simply speak for the Philly end. After all, it was in Independence Hall that the Declaration of Independence was signed in 1776, and where the Constitution was later ratified. And if you want a single physical icon to represent the American love of liberty, you can't do better than the Liberty Bell, crack and all (although the Statue of Liberty, a gift a hundred years later from France, would probably come in second). The city fathers and mothers had a brainstorm when they decided to move the Liberty Bell from its old roost in Independence Hall to its own pavilion for the Bicentennial (in 1976, but you knew that). That move not only helped with crowd control, but gave Philadelphia two historical destinations where there had formerly been one (although a Bostonian might with some justification accuse us of using smoke and mirrors to do it).

Now Independence Hall has lent its name to a larger federal entity, Independence National Historical Park (from where I also have a hat), comprised of no fewer than 19 structures, six of them (including Independence Hall) GEMs. The place to start here is the relatively new National Constitution Center, which I visited with an old high school buddy and his wife somewhere in the summer of 2004. Through several media, from bronze statuary to computers to live performance to film, you are introduced to the issues of those days, and how the USA nowadays still deals with constitutional questions. From here I would recommend the Independence Visitor Center, the ultimate tourist orientation stop. It will direct you through this NHP (National Historical Park) and Greater Philadelphia, and will even help you with concerns like room reservations. It is here that you can plan what you want to do for the day (or the week). You can also procure GPS help for navigating the NHP There is even a film by one of my favorite directors, John Huston (son of Walter Huston, father of Angelica Huston), appropriately entitled, *Independence*.

The biggest challenge will be getting into Independence Hall itself, since there are a limited number of timed tickets available (they're free), and since you need to stand in line again at a metal detector. In fact, we three needed to undergo that drill more than once, since seeing the Liberty Bell requires the same screening. You really can't be in a hurry to see these national treasures. (If it's any consolation, it was hot and muggy even for Philadelphia during the meetings to finalize the Declaration of Independence, as related amusingly in the musical, *1776*, which even my old seminary staged one year.) Just pretend you're in the Army ("Hurry up and wait."). At least there are for the most part no out-of-pocket expenses.

Another building we hit that day was the Second Bank of the United States Portrait Gallery. It was Alexander Hamilton (on the sawbuck) who was responsible for starting the First Bank of the US, and Andrew Jackson (on the twenty, at least for now) who was responsible for closing the Second Bank of the US. Someone decided that a collection of pictures of famous Americans might be more interesting to the touring public than an exhibit on banking, so there you are. It is really (Adapted Cliché Warning) a walk down our collective memory lane, with almost 200 of these paintings ready to tell you who the (*CW) movers and shakers have been in our early national history. It too is free. Congress Hall, our final NHP stop of the day, was where the US Congress met (Aha!) until the first US Capitol was built in DC. It witnessed the inaugurations of George Washington and John Adams, and still contains the two chambers of the legislature. The good news: it's free. The bad news: there is another security screening. History is definitely alive in Philadelphia, but it is in no hurry.

The last GEM (although the other sites in the NHP are worthwhile, too, particularly Carpenter's Hall, where the First Continental Congress met) in the park is Christ Church, where the likes of George Washington, Benjamin Franklin (that other local author, recall) and Betsy Ross (the designer of the first American flag) worshipped; and its separate cemetery is where Franklin and his wife Deborah are buried, graves you can conveniently view from the street. It is primarily known for history, and contains even the baptismal font in which local founder William Penn was christened. Outside the NHP is another church, Old Saint Mary's, also noted for history. Believe it or not, even thought it was Catholic, George Washington and John Adams frequented it as well. Episcopalian Saint Peter's Church is also located downtown, where four signers of the Declaration of Independence attended services. Not mentioned by AAA are two more historic Catholic churches: Old Saint Joseph's, run by the Jesuits, and Old Saint Augustine's (are you noticing a theme here?), still run by the Augustinians, where my first spiritual director was at one time stationed, and where in those years I used to visit him (he was my old Latin teacher from high school). I remember hitting all the Catholic churches on one grade-school class trip.

I would be remiss if I failed to mention the current Catholic cathedral, that of Saint Peter and Paul, even thought it is not even alluded-to by AAA. There are no windows on the first floor, because construction was started in 1843, at the time of the anti-Catholic nativist Know Nothing riots (when many Catholic Irish and Germans were immigrating). These good Americans were known for vandalizing churches and other Catholic buildings, so the workers literally threw stones from the ground toward the walls, to see how high they would need to put the small windows they eventually installed near the top. It is quite ornate (one Italian-American seminarian in my class described it once as "Early *Gavone*"), and is certainly worth a look-see from the street. Of related interest is the National Shrine of Saint John Neumann (NOI-man), Philadelphia's fourth bishop and an officially canonized saint, in an old church, the stained glass windows of which portray his life, and the altar of which displays his remains. He is the person most responsible, along with New York convert Saint Elizabeth Ann Seton, for expanding Catholic education in our country.

Yes, history is alive in this city, but that's not all that is alive. Can any museum be said to be more alive than the Franklin Institute, on Benjamin Franklin Parkway, which I visited several times as a boy, and even once as an adult? After all, it houses, among other things, the largest heart in the world, one through which you can literally walk, as countless grade school students have done on class trips (*CW) lo, these many years. Another physical icon of the place is a 20-foot-tall metal statue of Franklin himself, the man who first harnessed electricity by flying a kite in a thunderstorm. He would be pleased with what science has done since then, given the number and variety of the exhibits – many hands-on – which await you there, as well as an IMAX theater and a planetarium. (My animal-loving, Ph.D. cousin used to work there.)

The best-known museum in town, thanks to Philadelphia native Sylvester Stallone (whom I met at a book signing in 1979 in downtown Philly at the now-defunct B. Dalton's, a positive experience), is the Philadelphia Museum of Art. Indeed, it has more to recommend itself than the fact that, in *Rocky*, Stallone ran up the steps. The building itself is essentially several Parthenons cobbled together, and boasts not only a nice view of the Schuylkill River, with or without sculls, but a magnificent view of downtown (that view from behind Rocky's back toward City Hall in the film was real, and deserved to be viewed). And yes, there is a bronze statue of Rocky outside (the one unveiled in *Rocky III*). What's inside the museum is worth seeing too. (Actually, AAA rightly states that it ranks among the world's major art museums.) Featured within is a large collection of local *Wunderkind* painter Thomas Eakins [we even had one of his efforts at the seminary, in the eponymous Eakins Room, along with a pair of official papal slippers]. I have visited there several times over the years, but what is new is that the collection has spilled over into the old Fidelity Mutual Insurance Company [Philly, like New Haven, Connecticut, is an insurance city], now called the Ruth and Raymond G. Perelman Building, connected by a free shuttle to the main building. You name the style, and it's in one of the two structures. (My mother and I visited one year when my parents were in from the West Coast, and we missed a retrospective on Man Ray by one day. The press were being taken through, and we could peek into the first gallery; but even though we whined to the management of the distance involved, they still didn't let us in. The one item I still remember from that furtive glance was a wooden chess set, which I saw decades later at a small but interesting museum in New Jersey.)

Another museum, on a much smaller scale but considerably older, and which for some reason I have yet to see, is the Pennsylvania Academy of the Fine Arts. More so in the past than today, since that place has been usurped by New York City (that doesn't sound too negative, does it?), Philadelphia was the artistic capital of the nation. Step back into history by passing through these doors, for you will recognize many of the names represented therein. Nonetheless, it is still a working school, so that some of the displays are quite contemporary. It may not be the MoMA (Museum of Modern Art, in NYC), but you will get a taste of the present and future to balance a generous serving of the past.

Right across the city line, in Merion Station, used to be the Barnes Foundation, near where I used to attend school, Saint Joseph's University (this museum has since been relocated to center city). It is a relatively small collection, but it contains many big names from Impressionism and Post Impressionism, plus a number of other media and cultures. (As a bonus for you time-travelers, there used to be an arboretum surrounding the building.) The problem is that you really need to make advanced reservations, since the hours are quite limited. The $15 you spend to get in, plus the $15 for parking, you will no doubt consider money well-spent, if you can get them to take it.

Speaking of money: you may wonder where it comes from, not in a theoretical but in a practical sense. That answer can be found in the United States Mint, in the historic part of the city. Here you will discover how money has been produced over the years, and can even see coins and currency being designed, the dimes and quarters that will rattle around in your pocket tomorrow. (Warning: you can't get in with a camera or even a cell phone.) I was going to tell you as well about the Franklin Mint, way out in the exurbs, which produced specialty coins, and which you have probably seen advertising anything from collector's plates to first editions of books, but I can't find it anywhere in AAA or the Rand-McNally. [Aha! The Internet reveals that, through several changes of ownership, the museum is currently closed, unfortunately, although they just hosted the American Numismatic Association's World's Fair of Money in Philadelphia proper in August of 2012, so there may be hope of the attraction reopening.])

As implied above, Chicago is not the only city to have nice municipal parks. Most noteworthy in the City of Brotherly Love is Fairmount Park, with which I have one negative association: it was the scene of cross-country meets for the Catholic League in the metropolitan area. I ran cross for a year, and essentially hated every minute of it, although in the last race of the season, the Catholic League Championship, I ran my best time ever, at least going out on a high note. However, even in spite of those associations, I recommend a day in this enclave. Still, don't take my word for it; check AAA, whose entry for this acreage runs on to three pages. One reason is the historic houses, some of them quite large, and each open for the modest price of $5 (less for children), with Strawberry Mansion simply having the most colorful name. It is also the site of the Philadelphia Zoo, the oldest such entity in the country, and one of the few zoological parks in a major American city not to receive a GEM (since I have only seen this collection on class trips as a boy, I'll reserve comment). Finally, it encompasses two significant museums. One is the afore-mentioned Philadelphia Museum of Art. The other is the Rodin Museum, with a casting of *The Thinker* outside in front. It is much smaller, of course, being a specialty museum. However, it can boast the most Rodin pieces of any venue outside Paris, well over 100 (and they even speak English and take American money [the workers, not the pieces]). It is surrounded by pleasant gardens.

Let's not overlook City Hall. That deceptively-tall structure (by law it used to be the highest building in center city) has been called the greatest example of Baroque architecture in the world, and is surmounted by a 37-foot statue of William Penn. You can actually walk around, not only Billy Penn's feet (as he is affectionately called), but his hat as well, although, with the change in law about skyscrapers, the view may not be so commanding as when I lived there. Guided tours are also offered. In the shadow of this edifice is the impressive Masonic Temple, which offers guided tours as well, revealing its interior architectural diversity. East from there is the old section of the city, including the NHP, as well as sections known as Franklin Court, Washington Square and Society Hill, which areas underwent a renascence when I was still living there. It is pleasant just to walk around; or you can head farther down to the Delaware River, and Penn's Landing, for things nautical, especially at the Independence Seaport Museum, which includes an old ship and a submarine in addition to a landlubber museum. In that (*CW) neck of the woods you will find the Betsy Ross House. Recall that her (*CW) claim to fame is designing the first US flag, although the restored house is of greater interest in showing what a typical dwelling looked like at the end of the 18th century. Not far away is Elfreth's Alley, a narrow lane that has the papers to prove that it is the oldest inhabited street in the country, with costumed actors wandering through, waiting just for YOU to talk to (but don't knock on the doors, since regular people like you and me actually live there, and enjoy their privacy).

Depending on the time of year, you could attend a professional sporting contest, be it with the Phillies, the Eagles, the 76ers or the Flyers (although your best bet for seats on short notice would be baseball). I recall attending the game at which Pete Rose tied the National League record for consecutive games with a hit (44), although we did not see it, since we were still buying our tickets when we heard the crowd go wild from outside, indicating that he had done it on his first at-bat as lead-off hitter. Then there are the numerous sports represented at the many local colleges. Since I went to Saint Joe's, I was well aware of certain traditions in basketball. One was that, if any two Big Five teams met (Saint Joseph's, La Salle, Penn, Temple, and Villanova, our current [in 2016] national champion, three coincidentally being Catholic schools, grouped together for the sake of basketball), they always for some reason (size?) played at Penn's venue, the Palestra. Then, at such contests, when the first team scored the first field goal (free throws didn't count), the crowd would throw streamers onto the floor, and the players would need to wait until they were cleared off by the crew. (While you're on Penn's campus, check out the University of Pennsylvania Museum of Archaeology and Anthropology, a title that is almost longer than the laconic description given by AAA. Still, since they assign it a GEM, I am sure it is worth seeing.)

At a non-Big Five game, when Saint Joe's played Drexel, our mascot, the Hawk (at the time a fraternity brother) started "flying" across the floor during a time-out, and the Drexel Dragon gave him a shoulder block that sent him to the floor, and then to the sidelines, a very unsportsmanlike thing to do. It's obviously why *they* weren't in the Big Five, even though they were founded by a prominent Catholic family (albeit a secular school), one of whose daughters is officially canonized, Saint Katharine Drexel. The suburb I lived in, Drexel Hill, was likewise named after them; and my high school, Monsignor Bonner, was on land formerly owned by them, along with our sister school, Archbishop Prendergast, or Prendie.

Katharine Drexel was a remarkable woman. Though born into privilege, she learned as a girl that she needed to share what she had with the less-fortunate. She eventually founded her own order of sisters to work with African Americans and Native Americans (she is highly revered in the American Southwest, where I had seen devotional pictures of her even before she was canonized), back before anybody was working with these two groups. She was given an annual allowance from her father's will, which she used to fund her religious order and charitable work, and God made sure the order would be funded for some time, since she lived to be 95. The mother house for the congregation she founded (the Sisters of the Blessed Sacrament), the location of her shrine, is visible from I-95, in Bensalem, in the Greater Northeast, so why not make a quick stop? Her remains are preserved there as well. (Newsflash: the shrine may be closing for financial reasons, with her remains being transferred to the cathedral, so call ahead first.)

If your tastes are more classical than athletic, there is always the Philadelphia Orchestra (if it isn't bankrupt by then), one of the so-called Big Five orchestras of yesteryear (Boston, New York, Philadelphia, Cleveland and Chicago), not to be confused with that grouping of local colleges of the same name. I have heard the Philadelphia Orchestra live three times, twice for Handel's *Messiah*, at the venerable Academy of Music (they now perform at the Kimmel Center for the Performing Arts), and once on the steps of the Art Museum, for a special Fourth of July concert. I took dates to both *Messiah* shows: the first dumped me after one date (although she sent a nice card for my ordination), but the second and I were friends for a long time, even after her subsequent marriage to some other lucky guy. The concert on the Fourth was simply a prelude to why everyone was there: to hear Smokey Robinson. He was great. In the summer, the Philadelphia Orchestra offers concerts at Penn's Landing, on the Delaware River (recall) downtown. You may also find classical music at the Mann Center for the Performing Arts in Fairmount Park, where I heard (*CW) none other than Luciano Pavarotti sing the tenor role in the opera, *Tosca*. And let's not forget the Pennsylvania Ballet or the Opera Company of Philadelphia.

If your tastes are eclectic, a mix of the above two categories (aesthetic and athletic), you might want to hit the Art Museum early in the morning and watch the scullers row down below on the Schuylkill River. Another recommendation: take your vehicle along the West River Drive after dark and enjoy all the different boathouses of the

Top City #3 – Philadelphia: The Cradle Of Liberty (And Of An Author Or Two)

professional rowing clubs, lit up in white along their edges as if for Christmas (we call it Boathouse Row). Then, for different tastes altogether, there is the Mummers Museum, towards South Philly, on, not Second Street, but Two Street, which will introduce you to the music and costumes with which Philadelphians welcome the New Year.

How about something more macabre? Edgar Allan Poe spent six prolific years of his short life in Philadelphia, and one of the houses he occupied is a National Historic Site. My aforementioned friends and I stopped there before heading downtown the day we visited the Liberty Bell. There is a visitor center, after which you can tour the actual building. (Die-hard fans will not eschew the two-hour drive down to Baltimore to visit his final resting place, which, interestingly enough, is in the patio of a Protestant church residence.) Want to move beyond mere words? Then stop by the Mutter Museum (the U in Mutter is umlauted), about which my cousin has published a book. It is two floors of actual anatomical artifacts that will make the nationally-touring exhibit "Bodies" (which I saw at the Convention Center in Albuquerque, New Mexico, on the spur of the moment: it was professionally done, making the invisible visible; and in Chicago's Museum of Science and Industry, seemingly a permanent installation) look tame by comparison. Among the many displays there is an exhibit on Abraham Lincoln and John Wilkes Booth; the tallest skeleton in North America; and a cast of the original Siamese Twins, Eng and Chang Bunker.

OK, let's change the mood here. What we need is a stroll outdoors, under a blue sky and a shining sun. And in the Philadelphia area, what better place is there to do so than in Longwood Gardens, on the edge of the suburbs, in Kennett Square, which touts itself as the Mushroom Capital of the World, although Longwood Gardens does not, to my knowledge, offer any fungus displays. What they do offer is one of the best-known collections of flora in the country (to complement the Philadelphia Flower Show, the largest annual event of its kind in the land, at the new Pennsylvania Convention Center downtown [in 2016 its theme was based on the 100th anniversary of the National Park Service, the main reason I attended]). I mean, how could you even begin to imagine 11,000 plant species? Fortunately, you don't need to imagine it: just come out, open your eyes, and enjoy. Further, being closer to Wilmington, Delaware than it is to Philadelphia, you won't be too surprised to find that the garden property was once a du Pont estate; and the old house now contains displays on the history of the raising of plants on the property. Also under roof are greenhouses filled with flowering plants all winter (since the day we went was raining [so much for the blue sky and the shining sun], I got to know these structures pretty well).

While you're out that far, drive over to Chadds Ford to see some human-made beauty, in the Brandywine River Museum (no, you will not see displays there about the Mississippi, the Missouri and the Monongahela). Philadelphia has plenty of art, but her best-known area artist makes his home *here*, as did his father, and as does his son. I am referring, of course, to the Wyeth family. Patriarch N. C. Wyeth was perhaps best-known as a book illustrator, although he moved the family name into prominence. Several of his children (*CW) followed in his footsteps, including the best-known of them, Andrew, whose work is particularly featured at this museum. He tends to employ tempera (I initially had "tempura," which is also generally edible) rather than oils, and uses a muted palette, so that his paintings are unmistakable. Still, he can diversify his work, as the Helga portraits demonstrate. I once had the good fortune to be traveling in New England, and stopped one evening at the Currier Museum of Art in Manchester, New Hampshire, where I found an entire exhibition dedicated to him. I mean, why leave Philadelphia? The last I heard, Andrew was working well into his eighties. His son Jamie is carrying on the family tradition. Then, while you're in town, head over to the Brandywine Battlefield Park, and learn about this early defeat of the Americans by the British in the Revolutionary War (Boo!).

In the chapter on Chicago, I mentioned a few authors' houses I have visited over the years. One that is right in my backyard, and which I just learned about, is The Pearl S. Buck House, in Perkasie, north of the city. She is best-known for her novel about China, *The Good Earth*, which we all read in high school, and this building contains the desk and typewriter on which she composed it. However, she was awarded her Nobel Prize, not for her fiction, but for the two biographies of her missionary parents (which is how she learned first-hand about the Far East). There is also Chinese artwork, a favorite of mine, as in the Freer Museum in DC, apparently and appropriately on display as well. I'm going to need to get there soon so I'll have another literary name to drop.

Before I leave this wonderful city and its environs, I must mention (*CW) a bone I have to pick with it. That cartilage-container concerns something called the Lights of Liberty, a AAA GEM. The L of L is a summer, after-dark show that highlights some of the historic buildings in downtown Philly. As I understand it from talking to the people involved on the phone, you walk from site to site, watching lights play off these structures while listening to a continual audio program via a headset. This attraction did not exist when I was a boy, so when I heard about it I was excited. That was in 2004, when the price was still a very patriotic $17.76 (it later became a seditious $21.50). When I was in the city with my high-school buddy and his wife, I suggested that the Lights might be the way to bring our touring day to a close. The problem was that my friend had bad rheumatoid arthritis, and did not feel up for even more walking, to be followed by a two-hour drive home, understandably. Oh well. A couple of years later I was back in the area, visiting my then-spiritual director, and thought that one day I could take it in. For once I was smart and called first, to be informed that because of the heavy rain the day before, the ground was too muddy to move the heavy light-producing machines into position (is that an oxymoron?). Rats! I was told that I could still do the tour with the audio part, but without the lights. Humph! I mean, it's not called the *Sounds* of Liberty, but the *Lights* of Liberty. Oh well again. So in 2010, the Year of Fifty States, I thought that (*CW) the third time might be the charm. However, another phone call informed me that it would not be opening until August (this was July 24). Darn. But I was soon back in the neighborhood again, determined to see this production. I phoned, and was told NO for a fourth time; in fact, the entire program was being refurbished, and would not be (*CW) up and running again until 2011. Oh well once more and finally. Am I ever going to see the Lights of Liberty? (*CW) heaven only knows. We'll need to discover what the future brings (I had no plans to be in the City of Brotherly Love in 2011, believe it or not). To be fair, it was hardly Philadelphia's fault that my classmate got tired, that it rained, or that they wanted to make the experience even better, so I don't hold it against them, really. With or without the Lights of Liberty, Philadelphia is worth seeing. But if you do plan to see the Lights, take my advice and call first. [I checked the Internet in May of 2014, to learn that the show is currently morphing into cutting-edge, state-of-the-art digital 3-D, so that I know neither when it will be open or what it will cost (I am not making this up!).] The rest of the sights, however, should be open and ready to welcome you.

CHAPTER 11

A LANE CHANGE: OR, DELIVERANCE FROM BANJOES

I noticed something recently (i.e., in 2006), one of those panels around your license plate that often contain the name of the car dealer where the vehicle was purchased. Some people get them custom-made as an alternative to bumper stickers. One year my sister gave several of them as gifts for Christmas to members of the family, such as my brother getting "Beethoven is the best." Her own was, "Ave Maria, Ora Pro Nobis," which is Latin for "Hail, Mary, pray for us" (the Latin must run in the family). I for some reason didn't get one. Maybe she thought I was too fussy to put somebody else's message on my car, or she couldn't think of anything she thought I'd like. I trust I got something else that year.

Anyway, the one I espied on a car at a parking lot was, "Get over it: it was only a lane change." I suppose that that one tells us something about the driving style of its owner, although perhaps that one was a gift, too; who knows? But I had an experience on one of my travels where that message would have (*CW) fallen upon deaf ears.

This was back in August of 1991, when I was returning from my brother's wedding in LA. That day I had toured Mesa Verde National Park in far southwestern Colorado, snug against the Ute Mountain Indian Reservation and not all that far from Four Corners. I had wanted to see it for years, since it was one of the parks chosen in the

National Parks postage series from 1934. I collected stamps as a boy, as you have no doubt inferred by now; who knows how philately has influenced my desire to see other places (such as the Hermitage of Andrew Jackson, George Washington's Mount Vernon, and Thomas Jefferson's Monticello, all of which appeared on stamps as well)?

Now Mesa Verde National Park is mainly of historical interest. This is not to say that its canyons are not pretty. But it *is* to say that the main reason for its existence as a National Park is not any natural beauty that it may contain, but rather something man-made: a small metropolis of cliff dwellings. These hundreds of units go back hundreds of years, and were inhabited in several eras, until finally being deserted after a prolonged drought. You get to view them from cliff overlooks, and learn more about them from the visitor center or on a guided tour, but they are off-limits to entry, given their fragile nature. Even now archaeologists have left some portions of the extensive ruins untouched, in anticipation of better methods of excavation being developed in the future.

I had dutifully seen the ruins and was heading out from the Park. It was at this point that the beauty highlight struck me, since in the west the late-afternoon sun was producing, along with water in the atmosphere, a double rainbow, perhaps the first one that I had ever seen. It was a pleasant way to end the day. But the day was not over yet, he wrote ominously.

Now I had started the day in Canyonlands National Park in wide-open southeastern Utah, where I had spent the night. Mesa Verde is in the middle of another nowhere, so my *touring* day was at this point over. The job now was to get on the road and put some miles behind me before hitting the sack, in anticipation of visiting Rocky Mountain National Park the next day in northeastern Colorado. All I needed to do was fill-up on gas, and then cruise for several hours due east on US-160. (As I write this I realize that that decision meant that I approached the Rocky Mountains in the dark. Talk about wasted natural beauty. How benighted.)

There is no town of any size on US-160 for 200 miles in that direction, with the exception of Durango, about 30 miles east of the Park. I drove along the main drag there, found a suitable gas station (i.e., one selling a brand I had heard of) and filled my tank, with a

A Lane Change: Or, Deliverance From Banjoes

nice cold soda procured for the road to boot. Then back onto US-160, which is four lanes while passing through town. I recall changing lanes from left to right (using my turn signal as usual), then getting back into the left lane, and soon heading out of town.

Now once I'm out of this settlement there's nothing. I mean, I'm driving through the San Juan National Forest, and then the Rio Grande National Forest. And it's not an interstate, so no one's on the road either. Just the way I like it (except for the undoubted absence of radio). It's evening, and sunset is not far away.

All of a sudden I see a pick-up truck driving awfully fast in my rear-view mirror. I wasn't (*CW) dragging my own feet, of course, but this guy was really speeding. He barreled down upon me, then swung wide into the oncoming lane to pass (illegally, as it happens). As he did so, his friend in the passenger seat gave me the finger out the window. They sped ahead of me briefly, but then turned off the two-lane highway to the right and stopped.

At this point my heart was in my mouth. Having them flip me the bird was unpleasant, but if I were driving in New York City at rush hour it wouldn't surprise me. But getting it here …

Yes, strains of "Dueling Banjoes" from the movie *Deliverance* were passing through my head at this point. But as my car's momentum carried me past where that pick-up sat, I glanced into my rear-view mirror again, to see the vehicle make a U-turn and head back toward town. I was greatly relieved, as you can imagine, although for some time I continued to inspect my mirror to see if my buddies were planning on paying a follow-up visit.

I figure I was an hour out of town, but it's hard to say. All I can surmise is that some local didn't like the fact that some guy from Pennsylvania cut him off (in *his* mind) while changing lanes back in Durango. And the best bet on a Saturday night in that town, apparently, was chasing this foreigner an hour until you get to offer him a digital salute.

To me it was a normal, courteous lane change, but to them, apparently, it was an affront. I'm happy that they were satisfied to suggest to me the anatomically impossible, because out there (*CW) in the middle of nowhere I was at their mercy. I don't recall precisely where I slept that night, but I'm sure it was far from Durango.

I've been through Durango at least once in recent years, and stopped at that same gas station for a fill-up. Nothing untoward has occurred since that one dusky evening in 1991, but I can't think of Durango and US-160 without calling that episode to mind. And I doubt that having that message around my license plate that I noticed in a parking lot in 2006 would have done me any good that day.

CHAPTER 12

TOP CITY #2 – SEATTLE: THE TOWN ON THE SOUND

Once again it just so happens that one of my five favorite American cities has a strong connection with music, so that the last word in the title can be seen to refer both to Puget Sound, on which it is physically located, and musical sounds, like the Philly Sound, or the Delta Blues in Memphis and Chicago. Long before grunge made itself synonymous with this city, the likes of Jimi Hendrix were sending it into musical immortality, himself on the heels of the Seattle sound that made "Louie, Louie" a must-play for every garage band doing gigs in the area. However, it was not music that drew me to the metropolitan area. In fact, my first time there was quite forgettable, in that I simply passed through it on the way home from Olympic National Park on I-5. However, my former disc jockey brother put the bug in my ear years later to get to know the place a little better than that, and so I took the bait, and was reeled-in, (*CW) hook, line and sinker. I spent the better part of a week in the area, seeing much, and pledging to myself to return to see the rest, which I did several years later.

I must start with what has become the icon of the city since the 1962 World's Fair: the Space Needle. It towers above the buildings, built on an eminence and rising high over that. They offer a special ticket that enables you to take one of the three primary-colored elevators up to the observation deck. I first did so after dark, and was greeted with the city in lights beside the loomingly-dark Sound. The next day I used the other ticket (both together cost slightly more than one alone), and got to fill-in the blanks between the erstwhile night-lights in the sunshine. The restaurant just below the deck revolves, but proved a little too rich for my blood, so that I satisfied myself up there with a large hot Seattle-born Starbucks beverage while I talked to my brother on the phone, commending his good taste in cities.

There was another sound nearby as well, or, rather, lots of them in one attraction: the Experience Music Project that lies at the base of the Space Needle and looks from the top like it was designed by an architect on the same sort of hallucinogens that Jimi regularly ingested. This phenomenal music potpourri was the brainchild of one Hendrix fan who wanted to put his passion on public display. It morphed into a showcase for the Seattle Sound, and the rest of rock music, and presents not only museum-like displays, but also its own restaurant (where you can dine without paying the overall entrance fee); a venue for concerts that otherwise shows extended music videos on a huge screen; a room where budding young (or not-so-young) musicians can record their own demos; and even (at least back then) a museum dedicated to science fiction (I have no idea why; but Why not?).

If all that is not enough on one parcel of land, the same site also features a small science museum connected with a large IMAX theater. Thus, you can buy your ticket for the desired show (they feature more than one, and conveniently run them into the evening), waltz through exhibits of planets and other space stuff, ride up to see the lights below, and then take-in a high-tech, informative and enjoyable show. If that were all there was in Seattle, it would be worth the drive through.

However, there is a great deal more. Now I admit that (at least before the age of the GPS) it is not an easy environment to navigate. I am not here referring to the weather, since, while generally cloudy and often rainy, my own experience is that it has few good-old-fashioned day-long downpours. Rather, I mean how the city is laid-out. It finds itself squeezed between the aforementioned Sound, and cliffs that soon begin rising toward the Cascade Mountains to

Top City #2 — Seattle: The Town On The Sound

the east. Thus, the town slopes down rather drastically from east to west, so that it can be tricky getting from one road to what looks on the map like an adjacent one, since the declivity is too extreme to drive down without a Hummer. Boston has its aforementioned driving challenges, and Seattle has its own as well. However, nestled in every part of town is something worth the effort it takes to find it, with downtown being the mother lode.

So let's start with downtown. One slice of that part of the city is one of the area's best-known attractions to outsiders, and doesn't even charge a fee for entering it: the Pike Street Market. It extends for blocks, with shop after shop, and type of shop after type of shop, proceeding (*CW) as far as the eye can see. The atmosphere is pleasant: bustling but not invasive, giving you a sense of excitement rather than annoyance with the other people there, fellow travelers who have found the epicenter of that part of the world. Of course, the true bull's eye is the internationally-known fish market, where the catch is fresh, plentiful and relatively cheap, and the fishmongers as efficient as they are enthralling. You could easily pay good money in a Vegas casino for a show less-entertaining than they are. So whether you want lunch, souvenirs or artsy stuff, you will run out of money before you run out of options here.

While we're for the most part out-of-doors, let's stay there for now. The old section of the city contains some attractive architecture, giving a small flavor of what the place would have felt like a century or so ago. Near the center is a small bust of the eponymous Chief Seattle, next to a much larger totem pole reproduction, indigenous to the northwest. (For a lot more such art of this branch of Native America, walk over to the Seattle Art Museum, or SAM, where tons of such artifacts vie with European paintings.) Now if you know where to look (i.e., a particular tavern), you can link-up with the Underground Seattle Tour. I had heard about these folks for years, as they guide you through the city-under-the-city, a rare phenomenon in North America (apart from subway and sewer systems), and was not disappointed in what I discovered. Frankly, while what you see is interesting, what you hear comprises the lion's share of the experience. The woman who led my tour (two assemblages left at the same time, given the number of tourists) was hilarious, as entertaining in her own way as the fishmongers earlier. She had her facts straight and her script internalized; and the way she presents her words had me guffawing practically the whole time. It's probably the best show in town, a true must-hear. (I need to add that I took a certain pride in the fact that I was often the only one laughing at her sometimes-subtle jokes because of her dry delivery.) And it is much less-expensive than the Teatro Zinzanni, one of the very few local sights I have not experienced, given the price tag (the Underground Tour, even including a nice lunch at the bar, would have been a mere fraction of what this other dinner-theater costs). All this, and exercise, too. It would be on my short list of things to do in this distinctive city.

    Another offbeat experience (meaning off the beaten track) lies surrounded by the Sound, on an island. It is another sort of dinner theater, featuring both local Native American cuisine and entertainment. However, it is really not entertainment in the conventional sense of the word, since the dances that the Indians perform are not simply an outward show, but an inward expression of their cultural attitude toward the rest of the universe. You take a boat out to Tillicum Island, where you are greeted by a tribal official, who points you toward the evening's appetizer: small steamed clams in their own juice. You eat them seated on long, stout tree trunks, and then crush the shells into the ground, itself comprised of the shells left by generations of former feasters. You can also peruse the totem poles, and perhaps even find one in the making on its side. Eventually you move into the large building for dinner, the entrée of which is fresh salmon cooked the indigenous way: pierced by tree-branches carved into large forks, and staked over a hot coal fire. When this local delicacy was served, my salivary glands hurt, it tasted so good. I have eaten salmon all my life, but never like this. Of course, there are other fixings to augment the seafood. You sit at long tables, so that I found myself with a German couple, older seasoned travelers, with whom I shared a pleasant conversation (which, of course, included lots of geographic name-dropping). By the end of the masticating, the show, or, rather, presentation, begins, with enough musical dance pieces to fill an hour, although the time flew by for me. It was staged professionally, complete with lighting, sound and props (including fire and a movable platform within a hole in the center of the stage).

The costumes were museum-quality (I had seen similar ones that afternoon in the SAM), especially the button-cloaks and the various sorts of masks, some with that signature alligator-look that would excite any University of Florida fan. Afterward I bought a loaf of their delicious bread in the gift shop, where nice art reproductions were also available, then headed out to walk the grounds until the boat's whistle summoned us back. The two black-tailed deer I saw just before departing added a pleasant coda to the overall experience.

I really can't conclude this chapter without giving a taste of the wider area. In the interest of space, I will pass over nearby Tacoma and Olympia, and focus on what could be described as Seattle's suburbs. Allow me to start with an unlikely stop, especially for a guy: a doll exhibit. However, this particular one resembled a museum. I have seen one other one in the USA, in South Dakota, which was a series of dioramas that essentially represented the maximum number of figures one could squeeze into the allotted space. Here, while the total number of dolls was fewer, their quality and presentation were a quantum leap higher. Indeed, their gift shop itself could in fairness charge admission for the items available to view. It is telling that this attraction netted a worldwide award for the best museum of its kind within five years of its opening. Since I am willing to visit anything done well, I would recommend it (if it is still open, since as of 2014, both this one and the other in SD were not listed in AAA: pity).

So let's swing to the other end of the touring spectrum: airplanes. Seattle is known internationally for its place in this industry, so that two of the sights ought not to come as a surprise to anyone. One is the Museum of Flight, chock full of various aircraft: not the biggest such venue that I have ever seen, but worth the visit, if only to soak-in some local ambience. The other is an actual Boeing factory, where, at the time I took their free tour, they were assembling the then-new 777s, or Triple-Sevens. Imagine looking from a walkway down onto a factory floor where full-size jets are being moved around by terrestrial tugboats, and you will arrive at some idea of just how big this inside space is.

To the far north is Deception Pass State Park, aptly named (by a certain Captain George Vancouver), at least as far as I found it quite difficult to find that morning (although the unmistakable sighting of an adult bald eagle in flight helped ease my frustration a tad). There is a bridge across it. You can't park on it the span; but, after leaving your car at either end, you can walk to the center and soak-in a killer view in either direction (I was fortunate: it was clear that day, with blue sky over bluer water). On the way back toward town, I stopped at a sort of living history farm called Hovander Homestead. Too bad the central house was closed for the season still, although the critters were out and about as the volunteers readied the fauna for the expected hordes of visitors two weeks hence.

The geographic antipode of Deception Pass lies to the southeast of the city: an animal facility that features creatures (sorry) native to that part of the country, maintained in settings as close to natural as possible, and aptly named the Northwest Trek Wildlife Park in Eatonville. The collection was not large, given its scope and focus. Still, the environments, I found, were done very well, offering an overall atmosphere of welcome into another world, where we are the guests, the visitors, the outsiders. For the more conventional, there is a local zoological garden in another corner of town, the Woodland Park Zoo, also well-done, where I spent more time than I budgeted, placing me on catch-up mode for the rest of that day. Nearby is yet another sort of attraction: the Hiram M. Chittenden Locks. It was constructed by the Army Corps of Engineers, explaining the flag flying overhead with a castle featured on it (there is a small museum dedicated to the building of it on the way-in past small but nicely-landscaped gardens). The distinctive aspect of this sight is that you get to observe the locks in operation, as boats pass from the river to the lower Sound (slower but preferable to the rapids option). We have all learned about how this sort of thing works in grade school. Still, actually observing that amount of water rising and falling can prove hypnotic. All sizes of boats float through, as long as they can fit and get tied to the wall; and the service is free to all sailors. The fact that they tended to employ the mentally-challenged as the cleaning staff constituted an added feather in their collective cap.

Still another niche of town houses an entity connected with the SAM: the Seattle Asian Art Museum, or SAAM (confused? so were many others, apparently, which moved them to rename it simply the Asian Art Museum). It is in a difficult-to-find corner of the city, on high ground to the east, situated in a small park, pleasant surroundings for the sort of venue housing art in various media that I tend to find relaxing and meditative. I visited on the one night of the week that it was open late, so I was able to spend a good hour there at the end of the touring day, exploring the galleries, and occasionally stopping for a few minutes in front of a piece that grabbed my fancy. In the Smithsonian I have been known to spend 20 minutes in front of one Japanese screen.

A handful of GEMs added later can be mentioned together. They are not dramatic like some of the earlier ones, but are still worth a look-see if you are already in town. Two acknowledge the significant contributions of Asian Americans to the city. First is the Wing Luke Museum, named for the first Asian member of city council, which relates history, contains art and artifacts, and discusses specific temporary topics. I recommend taking the tour, since it allows access to parts of the old buildings generally off-limits to tourists. Second there is a small garden right on the Sound, the Olympic Sculpture Park, so that you can enjoy plants, stone and metal figures, and a swath of water (benches are provided for that purpose, since the sea has always proven contemplative for me, and, apparently, others as well). Finally, the Washington Park arboretum offers yet another way of appreciating aspects of nature in this general environment, containing its own sub-GEM, as it were, the Seattle Japanese Garden, right on the water. While this formal garden is not large, it is nicely maintained, and abuts a much longer walk along the Sound, where one can view waterfowl and the stuff they like to hide in.

(I was touring the Joslyn Art Museum in Omaha in 2015, and descried the unmistakable hand of glass virtuoso Dale Chihuly. When I commented on the fact to a young couple behind me, the man instantly agreed, adding that he was from Seattle, and asking if I had seen the Chihuly Gardens and Glass. I replied that I had, with the Bridge of Glass, but later realized that the Bridge, created by him, is in nearby Tacoma. Actually, this attraction in Seattle is so new it did not exist the last time I was in town. Given that I love Chihuly's work, and love Seattle, and love the Meijer Gardens in Grand Rapids, Michigan, where there is also a sculpture garden peppered with his work, I diverged slightly from my path from P-A to Las Vegas for my Dad's birthday in 2016 to see it. It proved to be located conveniently in the Seattle Center, right under the Space Needle, so that it was an easy in/out. While pricey, the attraction proved hypnotic in the expected quality of the individual pieces, as well as the creative themed displays in each large room, not to mention the enclosed gardens. I was in glass nirvana.

As it happened, since the EMP was the last thing I visited on that first integral stay, the last entity I noticed as I made to leave the city for points south was the omnipresent Space Needle. I waved goodbye to it, the symbolic guardian angel of the city, and drove away, knowing that I had made a new friend in the Pacific Northwest. And, while I don't quite remember, I was probably humming something by Pearl Jam as I headed right on I-5 to SoCal and my family.

CHAPTER 13

TR NP: BADLANDS AND BISON

They may have displayed Woodrow Wilson's picture in all the National Parks in 1991 when I first visited Theodore Roosevelt National Park (TR NP), for the 75th anniversary of the founding of the National Park Service (NPS) in 1916, but the real inspiration behind that federal entity was my favorite president, Theodore Roosevelt. The NPS impetus began under him, although the actual legislation was not finalized until two presidents later. Thus, I am happy that he has a National Park named after him (the only president with such a distinction), since it was where he lived one summer in his younger days, far from his native New York State, in then-wild North Dakota.

This was not my first brush with TR, as he liked to be called. In 1985 my Pittsburgher priest friend and I climbed Mount Katahdin, the highest point in Maine. Well, on a subsequent cross-country trip I found myself at my brother's place when he was reading a biography of young TR. (*CW) Son of a gun, wasn't he the guy who blazed the trail up Mount Katahdin? *Que uomo!*

My first experience of Theodore Roosevelt National Park was brief but memorable. In 1990 my brother and I drove cross-country together. He didn't have enough vacation time to go both ways, so I drove back alone. One morning I was in Glacier National Park in Montana, and really enjoyed how deserted the place was at dawn, and how beautiful. I could appreciate the stunning mountains while I drove without needing to watch out for a thousand other drivers with the same idea. Then I pushed myself to be able to get to TR NP by evening, where I camped for the night.

What is memorable for me is that just at sunset I climbed a small hill at an overlook, and had the experience of seeing the sun and the full moon in the sky at the same time, for which you need not only the right day each month, but also two unobstructed horizons. On such days the moon is in the far east just making its appearance before the sun dips below the western horizon. I was struck by how they seemed to be gazing at each-other for that moment. On the rise I felt like I was on top of the world, watching what is rarely able to be seen in most topographies. The feeling of somehow being in God's presence during those few minutes has stayed with me, and brought to my mind Psalm 8, about God creating the moon and the stars. I knew I would need to return some day when I was in less of a hurry.

That day was to come two years later.

I myself have several times lived in another state than my native Pennsylvania, once for 3½ months in a monastery in Vermont in 1993. I took a month's discernment retreat there in the fall of 1992, the same year that my oldest nephew was baptized. For some reason I took a plane out rather than drove for that family visit, as mentioned above, and still remember flying home and looking down onto all that space, wishing that I was passing through it in my car. Then when I got back, at a clerical social, another priest, the one saying that he was about to finish his packing for his annual drive out to Yellowstone to fish, lit my *Wanderlust* fuse. Subsequently, my pastor said that I could certainly take another vacation that summer, especially in light of entering a monastery some time after.

I decided to re-engage two National Parks I had simply driven through before. One was Zion National Park, one of the first I visited, since it happened to be along the road that that same priest friend and I were taking north to Yellowstone from the Grand Canyon in 1986. I was very impressed by all the granite, as you will recall; and now I was fulfilling my vow to return again to do some non-technical rock climbing.

But back to TR NP. Notice how the trip is unlike my usual jaunts, since I was taking my time and enjoying the places I visited at greater length than usual. I put-down stakes at the Cottonwood Campground in the Park (this is all in what they call the South Unit; I spent a day in the smaller North Unit in 2010, and once again saw bison peppered throughout [but that's getting ahead of myself]). In the aforementioned biography, there is an entry in Roosevelt's journal stating how sometimes in the afternoon he and his friend would sit on the porch of the cabin and almost allow themselves to be lulled to sleep by the sound of the wind in the cottonwoods. That is a distinctive noise, I was to discover, helping to bring to life the Debbie Reynolds song of years ago, "I hear the cottonwoods whispering above / Tammy, Tammy, Tammy's in love."

The campground was my base of operations, and was of course fun in itself. I do what is called car camping, as opposed to backpacking, since I have never carried anything on my posterior for a night's stay somewhere in the woods. That's the way to get to some remote and beautiful places in this country, but up to now I have not done so, don't ask me why, since I had all the right equipment, thanks to my friend's urgings. But it's still a departure from the normal routine to heat dinner over a small butane container in a mess kit, and later roll into a sleeping bag in the tent for the night. Given my long drives, or hikes, I always managed to drop off to sleep right away and stay asleep until morning.

Well, almost always. On one of the two nights here in the tent I was asleep, but then suddenly awakened by a loud howl. I've heard a wolf make its trademark sound in a zoo presentation, and it did not seem all that loud. Coyotes, like dogs, can also make a lot of noise that way, so it was probably one or the other. The next morning a fellow camper explained how he had been awake at the time, and heard something hit the water of the stream that wound on by the campsite right before the howl, and was surprised that a coyote was hunting a deer (indicating that it was probably a wolf). In any case, I can tell you, nothing quite sounds like a howl when you are in a light tent rather than in a building. I did get back to sleep pretty soon, but I knew more than ever that I was in the wild.

The heart of this leg of the trip came on the day between the two nights camping. I decided to go hiking on a particular trail, hoping to find bison. The people at the visitor center don't know where the bison, or, if you prefer, buffalo, are, except as reported by hikers who happen to see them here or there. (Buffalo are strictly speaking an Old World animal, as with Cape buffalo in southern Africa and water buffalo in Asia, two species that could not be more different in their approach to humans.) Well, I found them, all right. They were in a box canyon, and I was able to climb up the back of one of the sides (of the canyon, not of the animals) and look down upon them. I counted about 30, of all ages. Well, *that* was cool, I thought, and continued on my way.

I finished the one-way hiking trail at the second parking lot and began retracing my steps to the first, where my car was. Surprise, surprise! The clan of bison I had viewed in the canyon had apparently gotten tired of being boxed in, and so decided to spill out onto the trail. So as I got to the canyon, there they were, moseying up the thin sliver of dusty dirt toward the distant first parking lot.

They were clearly in no hurry. They'd walk, then stop, maybe eat something growing on the ground, then walk a little more. They were in absolutely no rush, they had all day, they were in their home (they could probably teach me something about travel). At first I was excited, and got imprudently close to a huge bull, perhaps 10 feet away at most, keeping only a small bush between him and myself. I knew how ill-advised this maneuver was, since I had been to Yellowstone and learned a thing or two about bison in the past. You see, they're big and slow-looking, but they can actually outrun a horse over a short distance. There are not only warnings in Yellowstone about not approaching bison, but a count of gorings (that's right, gorings, as in blood) kept in the one center for the season, mute testimony about how the moods these gentle, pet-able-looking beasts can suddenly change. (When my brother and I drove through Yellowstone, we passed a bison on the road, and then noticed a jogger on the same road, heading in its direction. Whoops.)

Prudence and a healthy fear began to reassert themselves over me as I realized (*CW) the pickle I was in. About half of the bison (I now counted 35, bulls, cows and calves) were already on the trail, while the other half were exiting the canyon. Thus, I perceived that I could not safely continue along that rustic road just yet. The thing was, they were moving so slowly that it could be hours before they'd be finally gone. What to do?

TR NP: Badlands And Bison

I decided to head back to the second parking lot and try to hop a ride back to the first. On my way I encountered a young mother and her son (perhaps 9 or 10), coming from the direction of the second lot. I felt compelled to describe to her what awaited them on the trail, but they continued anyway, as no doubt I would have done (weren't we looking for bison in the first place?). When I arrived at the lot there was one car with any occupants, and it was just about to exit the area. I ran and caught it, and this retired couple kindly agreed to drive me back to the first lot. In that lot I saw a man with an RV who seemed to be waiting for something, so I asked him if he were expecting his wife and son to come via the trail. He said that he was, so I explained the way things stood, and suggested that he might want to drive around to the second parking lot to pick up his party, which he did (hopefully finding them there safe and stoked). (I notice I've been using that word a lot.)

I've seen bison a small number of times, both in the wild (usually on government land) and in captivity (there's a herd kept on US-30 not far from Bedford, Pennsylvania, a town that also maintains elk and caribou on another nearby farm). Even though in Oregon in 2010 I saw over 200 such beasts in the Hells Canyon National Recreational Area, this is *the* time I've seen them. There was something primal about getting that close to them without being in a car. (True, you can tend to do the same around Old Faithful in Yellowstone; still, there are lots of other folks around, including rangers. Here I was the only one on two legs.) I can still see that huge bull looking at me, then continuing on his way. He could easily have been spooked (that's why I kept the bush between us) and charged. But he didn't, and (*CW) I've lived to tell the tale, thanks to my guardian angel.

And this is precisely the sorts of thing that awaits those who take the trouble to visit National Parks and other places where wild animals can live in safety.

As a footnote, I must tell you about my milk. On this trip I was using milk for daily protein, buying a quart in the evening, drinking a pint then, and then the other pint the next morning before driving away into the day. Well, in TR NP, for some reason, I didn't drink the second pint in the morning, so that it remained in my car the whole day (and it was hot, yes, even in North Dakota). Nor did I drink it that second evening. No, I didn't attempt to drink it until the second morning. I can still feel that container, which I raised to my lips. There was an initial trickle of milk, but for a second or two nothing more. Then my face got hit with a solid wall of something that the milk had turned into. See what we take for granted with refrigeration?

So I invite you to come to the wild, where conveniences like refrigerators are replaced with furry critters. And really, how many ways can you talk about yet another week at the shore to your friends and make it sound interesting? But go to a National Park and, like Bilbo Baggins, have an adventure, and you won't need to think about making the vacation sound interesting: just tell them what happened in plain language, and you'll get *them* wishing they had taken the road less traveled, not to yet another theme park, but to Where the Wild Things Are.

CHAPTER 14

TOP CITY #1 – WASHINGTON, DC: A CAPITAL CITY

If its place at the head of favorite cities does not clue you in, let me be graphic: I Love DC. After all, everything along the National Mall is free, and the Metro takes you anywhere else you want to go, cleanly and safely. So where do you begin in the city that has more AAA GEMs than any other (I just counted 45, not including the greater metropolitan area; New York, many times its size in population, comes in second nationally at 27). I say, go to the center of everything: the National Mall, which, incredibly, is not a GEM in its own right. No, this is not a collection of stores trying to compete with the Mall of America near the Twin Cities. Rather, it comprises a large tract of land around which some of most memorable parts of DC have gathered. It weighs in at over two miles long all told, and a good three hundred yards wide, with lots of green grass (or brown grass in the summer). It's nice and even for joggers (I know, hills are better for conditioning, but I like flat). It has several streets crisscrossing it, but that invasion is minor compared to the sense of peace that can flood you as you simply sit down and *be* there. Or crunch down the gravel walkways, watching the trees that line the Mall in their seasonal array. I have seen these towering plants in all four quadrants of the calendar, and have watched while the buildings disappear behind the arboreal verdure, only to re-emerge after the fall. There are benches all along it, and in its own way it provides a set of oases from frenetic Washington. It's such a huge space, that sound gets muffled, even of the soccer games that get played there; and traffic is far enough away, not to mention slow, as to be practically silent. Even without the Smithsonian, the Mall is worth the walk. But how much better is that stroll when it can take you to any number of museums and monuments!

One highlight of the year is the spring cherry blossom event, near the Jefferson Memorial, a little off the official Mall, but part of it just the same, as far as I am concerned. I have been fortunate enough to see these trees once in full bloom, and it is as impressive as you have heard. I love flowering trees in general, so in the East in April I am in (*CW) hog heaven (oink). The word gets out locally, and even regionally; and then the paths that are generally deserted in that part of the Mall become clogged with nature lovers, all walking the same direction, around and around again and again, waving to the people on blankets on the grass with picnic lunches and bottles of wine, kind of like the Hollywood Bowl on a summer evening. (I might add that the trees themselves are transformed in the fall, as I had the good fortune to see in 2012, from green to a brownish yellow, a beautiful pair of arms along the water surrounding the Jefferson Memorial. The bonus here is that the leaves will last longer in this state than the blossoms, and that there is no crowd to compete with, since this is one of DC's best-kept secrets. [Don't tell anyone. Or, rather, tell everyone.])

These trees are located mere blocks from the United States Holocaust Memorial Museum, which, like the trees, is practically on the National Mall. I am proud to be a charter member of this institution, which shows the growth, seeming triumph, and ultimate demise of the Nazi movement. There are small exhibits on the first floor, which I had visited before on a day when I did not have that much time. Of particular note here is the Hall of Remembering, with a surrounding solemnity matching a religious sanctuary. In 2010, however, I headed to DC for the express purpose of taking the full tour, which is comprised of the top three floors. They tell you that it takes three solid hours to see everything, but the day I was there it required all of four. My favorite part of the tour was a two-sided wall with the names of righteous Gentiles who risked their lives to save Jews during that time. A number gave their lives in their efforts to save others. Among those who survived, when interviewed years later, there is a common refrain: "I didn't do anything special. I was simply doing what any decent person would do." But if all the decent people in Europe did something positive, Hitler would never have happened. This museum does not stay focused on the past, however. It was here, during my initial visit several years before, that I first heard of the genocide of the Darfur region of Sudan. In an exhibit entitled, "Not on Our Watch," they documented what was happening in that isolated part of the world, especially to Christians, and what could be done to try to stop it. This is why I believe that this museum is key: it reminds us of the evil that needs our attention in the present day. The only way we will deserve to enjoy all these wonderful monuments and museums is by continuing to work for freedom, to fight for freedom, and, if necessary, even to die for freedom; for it is only in working for the freedom of others (Americans and non-Americans alike) that we can maintain our own. And as if to underscore that very message, admission to this museum is always free.

OK, so much for the homily. Remember, it's an occupational hazard. Instead, allow me to emphasize what a national showcase we have in and around the perimeter of the National Mall. It's not only a place where Americans can come to receive an adrenaline shot of patriotism. It's also a place to which we can invite international visitors, to show them what has become of the experiment in democracy that we started back in the 18th century. When I stand in the middle of the Mall and look, either toward the Capitol building to the east, or the Washington Monument to the west, I feel proud to be an American, and proud that this is what we have to show to foreign guests when they vacation here. And (*CW) to top it all off, just about everything, like the Holocaust Museum – the monuments, the Smithsonian museums, the National Gallery of Art – is all free.

What I am about to say will no doubt surprise you. I am going to start with a sight that I have *not* visited, but would like to: the White House. Yes, can you believe it? I've never been there. Oh, I've seen it dozens of times from the outside, from general touring, to March for Life rallies on the Ellipse in front, to a huge detailed reproduction, inside and out, of it, at this writing currently residing in the Ronald Reagan Presidential Library in Simi Valley, California. So why haven't I ever gotten inside? You guessed it: you need to notify them ahead of time, and I never know what I'm going to do a day in advance. Well, I did get close to entering it once. It was back in high school, and we were on a class trip to Washington. We were waiting in line at the start of the day, when a local Communist started talking to us about the evil government (this was in the early seventies). He even predicted that music would come out of the speakers located among the bushes (no, not those Bushes) soon, and, son of a gun, he was right, as we heard a band start playing "Hail to the Chief." But then the line refused to move, and we eventually left without getting in. I don't know what the dealbreaker was that day, but now you need about a month's notice, so that backgrounds can be checked, as I understand it. Perhaps one of the teachers had not done his homework; or perhaps they were full for the day; or perhaps there was a crisis inside. Since then it has remained one of those things on my bucket list. But the way I travel, with very little notice even to myself, when will it ever work out for me? So, what am I saying? If you ever get there, let me know how it was.

So, have I actually seen anything? Let's start with the monuments. The one that literally towers above the others, the one that divides the National Mall in half, and the one that I take for my personal icon of my favorite city, is the only one that is officially named a monument rather than a memorial: the Washington Monument. I was more successful on a grade-school class trip to DC than with the White House, in that I actually made it up to the top. There are 898 steps to get to there, but the view is phenomenal. Of course there is an elevator to take you up, the same elevator that takes you back to the bottom. I heard years ago that, in the decades even before that, you were allowed to walk *up* the stairs; but by the time of that class trip, you were required to take the elevator up, although you could still walk down. I recall hitting the steps with a classmate and counting them as we descended, as the elevator in the middle continually moved between top and bottom. The steps got wider, of course, as the monument expanded on the way down. That was not the surprise. The surprise was how warm it got as we continued earthward. I thought warm air was supposed to rise. (So much for science class.) Anyway, we made it safely to the bottom, with my step count being 10 off. (So much for math class.) I mused that I could have touched the bottom and then quickly begun walking back up without the guard noticing; but while I was not *too* tired after that adventure, I didn't think I had it in me to do the reverse trip. (Now, at age 60, the thought of walking *down* fills me with dismay. I'm glad I did it when I could. I'm not sure if you are even allowed to walk down now.)

I recommend everyone going to the top of the Monument at least once. It gives you the panoramic view of DC that the Space Needle does for Seattle, the Empire State Buildings does for NYC, the Willis Tower (OK, the former Sears Tower) does for Chicago, and the San Jacinto Monument does for the Houston environs. You view the Mall, and the city, and the water, and can sense what you want to visit once you get back to ground level. It can also be described as the heart of the city of Washington, a man for whom I have the highest respect and filial affection. So why have I only been up once? Since by the time I'm near it, the tickets for the day are already gone. (There are a limited number of free tickets, first come, first served. The only reason I got up even once is because a teacher took care of such details, one who in this case had done her homework.) Maybe next time I'll arrive early. (By way of note: the far side of the Mall, with all the memorials, is called West Potomac Park, and is appropriately GEMmed.)

There is another great view of DC, or at least of the monuments (a term that is used generically to describe what are more properly called memorials). It is from the back porch of the formerly-named Custiss-Lee Mansion, in Arlington National Cemetery, which is now called Arlington House, the Robert E. Lee Memorial (Robert E. Lee married a Custiss). Martha Washington's maiden name was Dandridge (as a girl she was known as Patsy), but she married Daniel Parke Custiss, who died and left her a widow (Department of Redundancy Department), and whom George Washington later married. In any case, walk the bridge across the Potomac into Arlington and climb to the back porch: you will see the major monuments and the White House displayed for you as if they were planned with that perspective in mind. For those of you with cameras (and that probably includes all of you), it is the best photo-op in the city.

The Lincoln Memorial is my next-favorite monument. I like the classic shape of the building (check the back of the five-dollar bill, until they change it in 2020); there is a great statue of Lincoln, by Daniel Chester French (also on the back of the fiver); his two best-known speeches are carved into the stone inside: the Gettysburg Address (yeah Pennsylvania) and the Second Inaugural Address; there are 36 Doric columns, one for each state at the time of his death; and the 50 states' names are carved around the outside top in the order in which they were admitted into the Union. All that for zero dollars. And walking up the steps is cool, too (although there is an elevator for the physically-challenged).

(Now sometimes my description of a memorial might not make it sound like it deserves a AAA GEM rating, since it doesn't contain all that much stuff. However, here as elsewhere, less is more; and the care with which these monuments have been designed produces a sense of awe and excitement that you are on the one place on earth called, say, the Lincoln Memorial. As often as I've been back here, I've never gotten tired of it, and have always experienced the thrill that you feel when the National Anthem is sung before a baseball game.)

There are two war memorials nearby, one on either side. Stage left is the Vietnam Veterans Memorial, popularly known as The Wall. This black structure, with the names of every American who died in that war inscribed (there is a book that lists where each individual name is found, since they are not alphabetical), has for many, especially veterans of that war, become a sort of national icon, standing as it does in its stark, dark simplicity. It is not flashy, but it is not unusual to see some people who stop and pay their respects silently weeping. There is also a statue of three comrades, which, vets explained after its dedication, was inaccurate, since the one soldier would not have draped an ammo belt over his shoulder with the bullet heads pointing toward his neck, since the points would have rubbed and caused bleeding. Whoops. Another statue grouping pays respect to nurses. It reminds us of how our lives and the lives of the Vietnamese people have become intertwined. Even if you don't know anyone who died in 'Nam, the Wall can be an eloquent testament to a portion of our recent history.

On the other side of the Lincoln Memorial is the relatively new Korean War Veteran's Memorial. This is named by some the forgotten war (I refuse to call it a conflict), and it is true that no peace treaty has yet been signed. Like the FDR Memorial, it uses space rather than a building as its focus, presenting a platoon of 19 soldiers walking warily and wearily forward into the unknown. When I first viewed it I thought of my father who served in the army during Korea, even though he did not see combat.

Closer to the Washington Monument is the even newer National World War II Memorial. In order to maintain the visual openness of the Mall, but also be near the other monuments, a compromise was struck: it is next to the Washington Monument, but is actually built below ground level, although out of doors, covering 7.4 acres. It is very well done, with my favorite part being the pillars that individually commemorate the states and territories, plus the District of Columbia, at the time of the war. It also uses water well, always a plus for me. (Did I mention the long reflecting pools between the Washington Monument and the Lincoln Memorial?) It is important to recognize the brave deeds of those who went before us, so that we too can rise to the occasion, if it ever becomes necessary, to become America's newest Greatest Generation.

A little off to the side, so that you need to walk around the Potomac River Tidal Basin (or swim), is the Jefferson Memorial. This round, classical building contains, predictably, a standing statue of Thomas Jefferson, in bronze. As with the Lincoln, FDR and MLK memorials, there are samples of Jefferson's writings on the walls. On Independence Day of 2001 I sought shelter here from a cloudburst that delayed but did not dampen the Navy Band concert (complete with cannons and bells for Tchaikovsky's *1812 Overture*).

Continuing to perambulate around the tidal basin will land you at the Franklin Delano Roosevelt Memorial, the newcomer to the presidential monuments. When I first heard about it I was not impressed, since it does not use a building to house a large statue, but rather sprawls outdoors in historical fashion. However, I tried to keep an open mind; and once I visited it, my misgivings were removed. Who decreed anyway, that a memorial needs to be comprised of one large building? This way we have a view of his life, and a larger-than-life-sized statue of him at the end anyway, along with his dog, Fala. A controversial addition was made, shortly before I saw it, of a life-sized bronze of FDR in his personally-designed wheelchair, which image I think is very appropriate, and hopefully gives strength to others who suffer challenging disabilities in their lives. Not surprisingly, a statue of Eleanor Roosevelt graces the site as well. I even discovered a piece by George Segal, one of my favorite sculptors, on the Depression. Throughout, the architect provided an excellent use of water, and at the time I saw it some of it was frozen, which added its own dimension to the experience.

It pays to surf the net. I was on a national news website, and got wind of an even newer memorial being dedicated in 2011, not to a president, but to the Rev. Dr. Martin Luther King, Jr., the civil rights hero and martyr. I saw it a year later (when I also discovered the cherry tree autumnal leaves), and was impressed with the creative pink-granite carving (the color shows up better in the light of the setting sun, apparently), purposely the same height as the Lincoln and Jefferson statues in their respective monuments nearby (it was placed in such proximity, given the connection of these two men with civil rights in their own day). I arrived just as a callow young park ranger was beginning a short presentation (he could not answer my question afterward, explaining that it was only his third day on this assignment). As implied above, there are quotations from his speeches and writings along a sloping wall on either side of the main structure. It is right on the shore of the tidal basin.

So let's talk about the Smithsonian, where I could spend every weekend for the next year. It is comprised of over a dozen museums, a couple of which are actually underground so as not to interrupt the view. (One is the National Museum of African Art, with three subterranean floors, probably the best attraction of its kind in the country. In the same isolated neighborhood is the Arthur M. Sackler Gallery, a sort of physical twin to the other, with its own focus on Asian art.) The Castle, as it is now called, is the original Smithsonian building, back when it was the only one. It is an institutional icon, and a sort of nerve center of the complex, a place for orienting yourself to the overall Mall, containing as it does samples from the other museums, restrooms, and a large gift shop.

Perhaps the best-known is the Natural History Museum, a favorite of school trips, especially with its wooly mammoth, which is simply the largest of the land animals presented in interesting natural dioramas; and the Hope Diamond, amid a stunning collection of jewels. I was in the IMAX theater as recently as 2005, but forget what I saw (duh). Nevertheless, my memories of this place go back to grade school, and it is the very sort of museum to make a strong impression on the young, although it remains of interest for adults as well. I wondered where that 45-foot right-whale went, but was relieved to know that they simply moved it to an ocean exhibit (the critter even has a name: Phoenix).

Then again, the most famous could be the Museum of American History, Behring Center, with the actual Old Glory that flew over Fort McHenry in nearby Baltimore, and inspired the penning of the National Anthem by Francis Scott Key (one of the bridges between the District and Virginia is named for him), being repaired as you watch. This structure tends to be another perennial favorite of school groups, although it held my attention as well the last time I was there.

Then yet again, it may be the National Air and Space Museum, technically the most visited museum of any kind in the world, which contains such national relics as the Wright Brothers' *Flyer*, Charles Lindberg's *Spirit of Saint Louis*, and the Apollo XI command module. (Indeed, most of the hardware is housed off-site, in the [also free] Steven F. Udvar-Hazy Center, in Chantilly, Virginia, including the space shuttle *Discovery*.) You can even take a simulated ride in a jet. (Curiously, it offers three women's rooms and one men's room for your convenience. I suspect it used to have two and two. I suppose that it is good that someone has done something to shorten the lines in women's rest rooms. As always, it's cutting edge.)

Nearby is the Hirshhorn Museum, with a good deal of contemporary sculpture, along with some paintings from a similar period (there are circular hallways, with the sculpture in the aisles and the paintings in the outside rooms, the inside wall having windows to the courtyard). It is oval-shaped, and reminds me a little of the Guggenheim in New York City. It also presents a sculpture garden outside, with contributions from such masters of the medium as Auguste Rodin, Henry Moore and Claes Odenburg. It is not enclosed, so it is available before and after hours, unlike the similar garden at the National Gallery of Art (NGA) across the Mall, which is fenced in, but which has a changing fountain. If I am anywhere nearby on the Mall, I will invariably walk through here one more time, if only to see Rodin's *Burghers of Calais* (yum).

I particularly love the Freer Gallery, also a repository for Asian art, with different rooms dedicated to various countries. They have some beautiful Japanese screens that, as mentioned above, I could just sit and look at for minutes at a time. There are a few occidental paintings as well, including one of my all-time favorites, Winged Figure Seated upon a Rock, by Abbott Handerson Thayer (no, he was not a monk, since he used his daughter as the model, who looks bored). It also houses (by appointment only) a piece of a codex containing a non-canonical complementary ending to the Gospel According to Mark, called the Freer Logion, of obvious interest for Biblical scholars. In the center of everything is a nice courtyard, so that there, in the middle of Washington, you can sit and relax, observe the garden, and listen to the fountain, my single favorite Mall oasis. No matter where else I fare on the Mall, I always try to stop there for a few minutes of meditation.

The newest member of the Smithsonian family is the National Museum of the American Indian, or NMAI. The building itself is curved, like the Hirshhorn and unlike the more classical buildings in the area. The bulk of this museum's collection, which I am told is quite extensive, is in New York City, in Lower Manhattan (for some unfathomable reason) for storage (with some also in Virginia), in a facility that is nonetheless open to the public. What the museum exhibits in DC is just a smattering of what they own, and it is displayed nicely (although I would like to have seen more of it: more is better, right?). There is also a restaurant therein, the Mitsitam Café (the name is Delaware for "Let's eat," [*CW] my general sentiments exactly), which specializes in Native American recipes, so that you can finally get that buffalo chili you've been wondering about all these years.

Right next to that structure is the National Botanical Garden, always occasioning a pleasant stroll through the flora for me. It was renovated in the 2000 decade, and provides another quiet oasis in the Mall area. And the fauna at the National Zoo? In a separate part of the city, a healthy walk from the Metro, but one of the few zoos in America with giant pandas (and probably the only such one that is free, although they charge for parking). I was there in 2001, and remember it as a quaint zoological garden, not all that big, but certainly a bargain for the money.

So why haven't I mentioned the National Gallery of Art, or NGA? A number of people, like myself at one time, assume that, since the NGA is on the National Mall, and is comprised of two buildings of museums, and since it too is free, it must be part of the Smithsonian. That assumption is incorrect. It was Pennsylvanian Andrew W. Mellon who donated the original grant for it, and he stipulated that it always be free. There are two edifices, with the West Building housing more traditional art, and the East Building focusing on newer pieces. The WB is imperial, containing oils and sculpture, from ancient to modern, the sort of items you see in art books, with familiar names next to them. I have made friends with several of the pieces, and like to visit them when I am in the area, such as Salvador Dali's *Last Supper* (it used to hang in a stairwell, but they moved it to the basement to allow access by the physically-challenged). The EB looks more contemporary, appropriately, and houses pieces closer to our time, although they will occasionally sponsor exhibits of more traditional masters (I recall such a show of Corot's work there). I find the basement to be one of my oases along the Mall. A friend I went with once said he didn't warm up to these 20th-century pieces, being a West Building kind of guy, but I find them refreshing and at times contemplative. (He didn't really think these modern pieces were art. One huge painting was simply a mono-colored canvas with one line across it, and I told him, OK, I'll give you that one.) Between these two buildings above ground are magnolias that bloom prettily in the spring. Below ground is a café in the hallway that unites the two buildings, with a fountain falling down from ground level above, another place to shut out some of the DC noise while refortifying yourself for several more hours of touring. The extensive gift shop is also located there (these two entities, alas, are not free). Something else that is free, however, is the foreign film series on weekends in the East Building, which I have attended often. Where else would I have heard of people like trendy Iranian director Abbas Kiarostami?

So now you are at the other end of the Mall, in the shadow of the United States Capitol, with the largest dome in the country (Pennsylvania's capitol has the second-largest, by the way). It is one of my most favorite buildings anywhere, sitting as it does on that hill and dominating that side of the Mall, practically sparkling in white. I haven't been in it lately, but it's a little easier to get in there than into, say, the White House. (You can take a guided tour, or obtain passes from your Congresspersons for the two chambers. In high school we used to collect the passes from any senate office that would give them to us.) Of particular interest to me, in addition to the House and Senate chambers, is the National Statuary Hall. Each state at some point was allowed to choose two of its citizens to be represented by statues in the Capitol. Many but not all of them are in that hall, with others scattered throughout the building (there is a list of locations for those interested in seeing [*CW] favorite sons or daughters). I take pride in the fact that, of these hundred statues, four are Catholic priests: Saint Damien de Veuster, the Hawaii leper priest; Saint Junipero Serra, the California missionary; Father Eusebio Kino, an early Jesuit active in Arizona; and Father Jacques Marquette, who helped to map and missionize Wisconsin and Michigan (he represents the Badger State). There is even a Catholic nun, Mother Joseph, for Washington State, along with eight other women, including Sacagawea, for North Dakota, and Helen Keller, from Alabama. In fact, I just love this impressive edifice, especially when the white is backed by an azure blue sky (Department of Redundancy Department). I used to get off the Metro at Union Station, touch the large replica of the Liberty Bell outside (once a Philadelphian ...), and walk to the Mall while looking at that beautiful structure. It sickened me to think that, but for the bravery of the passengers aboard Flight 93 above Shanksville, PA, that plane could have crashed into this national symbol. I may not always agree with what goes on inside it, or even agree *that* anything much goes on inside it, but it's nice to think of 100 Senators and 435 Representatives working to make life in the USA that much better.

(The two Pennsylvanians represented are Robert Fulton, inventor of the steamboat; and John Peter Gabriel Muhlenberg, revolutionary patriot, army general, US Senator, and yet another religious type, being also an Anglican cleric [although he served a Lutheran parish]. So why not Philadelphian Ben Franklin? Because he gets his own statue just by being himself.)

In back of the Capitol, from the Mall's perspective, is the Supreme Court Building, which also allows for tours and seating. A little down the road is where every author wants to be represented – the Library of Congress – with two of the three buildings open for self-guided tours. Of particular interest is the Thomas Jefferson Building, not only for its architecture, but for its rotating exhibits. Congresspersons and Senators are housed in nearby buildings, and are always happy to receive visits from their constituents.

Now I hope you've noticed that everything I've mentioned as being on the National Mall is free. Zip. Zero. Nada. I also hope you notice that 23 enumerated items were AAA GEMs. That's more than some states. Is DC a happenin' town or what?

So let's go to another spot that's free, at least to walk around in: Union Station, which, regrettably, is not a GEM. It's a handy place to grab the Metro, as well as Amtrak trains departing from the city. It is a restored train station from an era when the railroad was king. It now contains tons of restaurants in the giant food court (the biggest I've ever seen, by far) in the basement, with sit-down bistros upstairs (in one of which eateries I had my first soup in a bread bowl). There are also specialty shops, such as one selling Godiva chocolates, and, of course, as implied above, real live trains.

Across the street is the National Postal Museum, another free extension of the Smithsonian. Remember all those rare specimens you saw as a kid pictured in your stamp album, especially those first two issues, the five-cent Washington and ten-cent Franklin, which you knew you would never own; or the Columbian Exposition of 1893; and the rest? They're not only all there, but there are full sheets of them. You simply need to pull their protected holders out from the wall to look at a fortune in philately. The rest of the museum is nice, too. Further, it may be the only place in DC where you can buy postage stamps on a Sunday (well, not those stamps).

While I was in high school I toured the John F. Kennedy Center for the Performing Arts, a quasi-presidential memorial, or you might say a functional memorial. It was a week-long educational program, at the height of Watergate, packed with exposure to the many aspects of national government, an excellent package called Close-Up. The Center offers free (free again) tours during the day, and various performances in the evening (not free). You can even walk up onto the roof to get a view of the Potomac and surrounding area.

There's another place in DC that has a nice view from the roof, if you are (incoming Cliché, Redundancy and Alliteration Warning) brazenly bold as brass enough to go up there. I am referring to the Organization of American States (OAS) Building (referring not to US states, but to countries in our Western Hemisphere), not far from the White House. I visited there in 2005, and wondered why the place had been awarded a GEM: there just didn't seem to be that much there. Perhaps if I had taken a guided tour (also free), I would have seen and understood more. I did like the tropical patio with its indoor vegetation, including trees. Well, as I looked for more things to justify my visit, I headed upstairs, and finally discovered a door that led up some more stairs to the roof. At this point I was looking at the tops of the trees at eye level, and could view the surrounding area fairly well. I doubted that the workers would have been happy to find me there, so I soon withdrew, feeling that perhaps with the impromptu roof tour included, the place deserved its GEM.

A block to the north is the Daughters of the American Revolution (DAR) Museum. Though not a GEM, it is free, and contains a number of period rooms according to many of the states of the Union. If you're in the neighborhood, stop in for half an hour. Another block to the north is the Corcoran Gallery of Art, a fine museum and a GEM. I have been there in the past for special exhibitions. The permanent collection is worth the stop, but it's (obviously) better to visit when they have a special exhibit in addition to it. Sorry, folks: this one charges admission. Three more blocks to the north is the Renwick Gallery. I was only there (it is not a GEM) because the Smithsonian American Art Museum (another SAAM, seemingly, which is a GEM) was undergoing renovations and so was exhibiting in the Renwick. I was very happy to find a couple of more pieces by my friend, Abbott

Handerson Thayer. (Where the Renwick collection was exhibiting at this time I have no idea.)

Jumping to where the Smithsonian American Art Museum is located, is another site that was being renovated in 2005: the National Portrait Gallery. I've walked by it on the outside, but the insides remained unknown to me (although I could make a pretty shrewd guess as to what was housed there) until my 2012 autumnal visit. I hadn't planned on stopping, but by making a wrong turn looking for something else, I cruised right past it, noticed that it was open late, and made a mental note to return. I was happy I did, since the refurbished galleries are very well presented, with more space between paintings than the time I had seen it about a decade before, in another venue. (Yes, this is another one of my déjà vu experiences. I began to get an inkling after a while, and knew I would know for sure if I encountered a particular oil of John Adams, which the friend I had seen it with before commented on, saying that, at his advanced age, "his eyes are still liquid." Subsequently seeing that painting removed all doubt.) There were some American masters represented, not surprisingly, in a museum of such stature. The backbone of the attraction was one of only two complete collections of portraits of American presidents in existence (the other being in the White House, which paintings I am sure I shall never see). Several of the recent ones were creative, like the unconventional official portrait of the former and current governor of California, Gerry Brown Jr. in the capitol in Sacramento.

Then, on the other end of the quadrangle building is the SAAM, with its own high caliber of offerings. The personal apogee for me was encountering my friend Abbott Handerson Thayer, with several paintings of his children used as models for various subjects, including his daughter Gladys, as a young woman, the same model who posed as the Winged Figure mentioned above. Many heavy hitters are represented, from John Singleton Copley and Gilbert Stuart through Winslow Homer and Albert Bierstadt to Georgia O'Keeffe and Pennsylvanians Mary Cassatt and Andy Warhol. Indeed, my other favorite American painter, Edward Hopper, has a piece that was featured on the lighted marquee outside as an ad for the museum. However, don't miss the expansive atrium between the two entities, itself quite attractive, where they were getting ready for a banquet the evening I was there (no, it wasn't in my honor, since even I did not know I was coming). My visit ended on a high note, with the gift shop featuring a map of the USA in back of the cash register made entirely of 50 license plates cut into the shapes of the states represented. The helpful and friendly sixty-something woman even gave me the name and web site of David Bowman, who sells them on-line at www.designerturnpike.com, before directing me to the closest exit in that confusing building to my car, parked for free, and for an unlimited time, in front of the National Archives building, it being Veterans Day, no accident in my planning.

In the same neighborhood is the International Spy Museum. Now this place is very commercial, to the tune of $25 for a combined ticket, but by now you're probably *looking* for a place that will take your money. It is a GEM, and I found that it deserved it the day I visited because of an extensive special exhibit they featured in addition to their permanent galleries. You see, if an entity is a GEM, I'll go, even if, in this instance, the subject may be off the beaten track for most people. Finally, in that same neighborhood, is Ford's Theater National Historic Site. I was impressed by the presentation given in the theater itself on the murder of Abraham Lincoln by an excellent speaker (which John Wilkes Booth was as well), one of the park rangers. He made the period and event seem recent and real. The basement houses a museum connected with the assassination. Across the street is the Peterson House, in which Lincoln eventually died the next morning (the infamous April 15). They are both free (although the theater still presents shows many evenings).

It is most interesting to me that AAA designated three functioning churches in DC as GEMs. I've never seen that number before in any city (just getting one is rare enough; New York has two). One of these three is on the campus of the Catholic University of America: the Basilica of the National Shrine of the Immaculate Conception, which I've seen several times, including for Christmas Midnight Mass, when I got there early and poked around in all the corners, upstairs and down. While not a cathedral, this is probably the most important Catholic church in the country, and its size and interior design rise to the occasion, using a good deal of mosaic decoration.

Bob and Dolores Hope (both were Catholics) even bankrolled one of the side chapels, as long as they dedicated it, appropriately, to Our Lady of Hope. (Within walking distance but technically not on campus is the Pope John Paul II Cultural Center [now renamed the Saint John Paul II National Shrine], promoted to a GEM now that it is completed. It is an oasis of prayer and education sponsored by the Knights of Columbus.) The second church is the Washington National Cathedral, which is Episcopalian, and which I saw as a high school student. AAA relates that it is the sixth largest cathedral in the world. Important national dignitaries have lain in state there, as well as in the Capitol rotunda. The third church is Saint Matthew's Cathedral, the main edifice of the local Catholic archdiocese, which I finally got into in 2005. All three churches are worth the visit. On a final religious note, the Franciscans inhabit a monastery, which features a sort of catacombs containing models of early church scenes, called Mount Saint Sepulchre, The Holy Land of America. It may not be Jerusalem, but it's safer and easier, and all the people speak English. However, they don't take American dollars (since it's free). It's good to know that religion is well-represented in our nation's capital. We don't want any church, even the Catholic Church, *running* the capital, but it's good to know that they are there, inside the Beltway, keeping a heavenly eye on earthly things.

Out in the NW section (it is important to know which quadrant of the city you are looking for in DC) is the Hillwood Museum and Gardens, which I also visited in 2005. It is essentially the private collection of Post cereal heiress Marjorie Merriweather Post (the same people after whom the Merriweather Post Pavilion, a music venue in Maryland, is named), and focuses on Russian and French three-dimensional art. Of particular note are the Faberge eggs. Of special interest to me was the icon room, which displays religious objects (OK, so they're not three-dimensional).

So what about some non-GEMs? One is called the National Aquarium, as distinct from the much larger National Aquarium in Baltimore (that's its full name). It can make that claim, I suppose, small as it is, since it is not only located in the nation's capital, but in the basement of a federal building, the Department of Commerce (don't ask me why). You're not going to get a dolphin show here, *a la* Baltimore. However, for a change of pace, or to get away from the hot summer sun (as I did in that same July of 2005), a trip underground to view various sea creatures can be a refreshing and meditative experience. And $5 isn't going to bankrupt anyone.

Another is a must-see, even though it does not contain a great deal. I am speaking of the National Archives, north of the Mall, the building that houses nothing less than the US Constitution, the Bill of Rights, and the Declaration of Independence. Admittedly, it's hard to see them, given the special glass used to keep light damage to a minimum. Still, our nation is based on those three documents. As a bonus, and for no reason that I can understand (not that I'm complaining), the site also houses the Magna Charta, the foundational English document from 1215 (perhaps there is more than one), written by a Catholic cardinal. There are a handful of other activities offered there as well. If it were up to me, I would give it a GEM, in spite of that opaque special glass (and I'm otherwise against GEM inflation).

The Old Post Office Pavilion is an impressive structure to see. However, it is even more impressive to see *from*, since its towers offer an outstanding view of downtown DC (even better than the roof of the OAS building; and its legal). Once the national postal headquarters, the inside has been transformed into a number of restaurants and shops in order to maintain its attractive building shell.

The Phillips Collection is a small museum in a large house near DuPont Circle that occasionally houses special exhibitions (I've been to at least one of these) in addition to its permanent collection. It also offers regular concerts (mi mi mi MIIII).

I haven't even begun to discuss nearby Virginia. From Arlington National Cemetery (a walk across the handsome Arlington Memorial Bridge from the District [as the locals call DC]) and the Pentagon, to Mount Vernon (George and Martha Washington's home) and Wolf Trap (the national park for the performing arts), a trove of treasure (is that a cliché?) awaits. From an art gallery called the Torpedo Factory Art Center (this is not a misprint), another example of taking an old building and maintaining its appearance by using it for something other than its original purpose, to a nearby old edifice whose identity escapes me now, but where a friend and I received a short tour, but which then drew us into a staid period dance with costumed actors (well, actresses) as well (I was hesitant, but my dance partner would not take No for an answer [not my usual experience with women in my younger days, believe me]). I wish I could remember where it was. It was another way of experiencing history in an historic town. (Finally, I had no idea at the time that there was a Frank Lloyd Wright house within the city's confines. As AAA explains, it is the Pope-Leighey House, on the Woodlawn Plantation, a Usonian structure [meaning that it is, like Festivus, for the rest of us], and typically with furniture he designed himself. Oh well.)

Finally, allow me to direct your attention back into the District, to the Folger Shakespeare Library, near the Library of Congress. These are the people who publish those paperback editions of the Bard's plays, often used in high school classes. I don't know what it's normally like, but I had the good fortune to happen upon it for Shakespeare's birthday, April 23, one year. It's like a Renaissance festival then (and even that day is free), and includes the chance to recite a Shakespearian text from the stage of one of the theaters inside. I wanted to declaim *Sonnet 29* ("When in Disgrace in Fortune and Men's Eyes"), but they only had photocopied pages available from the plays. What to do? I quickly hoofed it to the other end of the building, to a gift shop, to borrow a copy of the *Sonnets*, but they would not let me take the book until I left a $20 deposit (I already owned it and so did not need to buy another one). Then the walk back, where I was told that they were just finishing up for that hour. "But," I pleaded, "it's only 14 lines." True enough, I was told by the young woman, and soon I found myself on stage, playing to an almost-packed house. It was great. I knew the piece well enough so that I only needed to glance at the book occasionally. My homiletic training and experience gave me a sense of presence in front of a crowd, and I made continual eye contact. I was very happy with where I placed all the stresses and pauses; and as I finished, the audience, which had been listening to people stumble through soliloquies until now and responding with polite, muted clapping, broke into enthusiastic applause, with at least one person shouting, "Bravo!" I had nailed it, and it felt good to get that response from the gallery, I, who had never spoken a line in a play in my life. Then I went and got my Andy back. May you have an experience somewhere in DC that in some way parallels that moment for me at the Folger.

Beyond these GEMs and selected non-GEMs, there is still much worth seeing. And then there is the very atmosphere of the District, with statues and fountains everywhere. I think you can see that not even an entire week could do the city justice, or even perhaps merely the Smithsonian. But a week spent here will be richly rewarded. It's great to live in a country where we can actually see our government at work. Pardon my religiosity, but I think that a secular pilgrimage once in your life to this grand city would be time well-spent. And I recommend an "I [heart] D C" t-shirt from one of the many sidewalk vendors for the plane ride home. I mean, after all, you've got to spend your money on something.

CHAPTER 15

THE CROSS-COUNTRY DRIVE FROM HECK: SNOW, TORNADOES AND ICY HOT

In 2000 I decided to take an approved sabbatical of sorts from active priestly ministry, and so move out to the Southwest, near family in Los Angeles and Las Vegas, but not in either of those arid, crowded areas. Thus, I planted myself for a time in northern Arizona. However, I eventually discerned that I was in fact being called by God back to my diocese, and so I made the necessary preparations to return east. Such was the occasion of the most challenging, and, really, only consistently negative cross-country experience I have ever had. (The one in 2015, during which I blew a tire in the morning in Utah, and hit a deer in the evening in Wyoming, was fine up to that day, and will need to await a sequel.) So, on to the tale:

I did drive out to see siblings in SoCal one last time on **Saturday**. I was expected to be home nine days hence, and so, while not being in a real hurry, at the same time I did not have the luxury of dragging my feet as I drove. Thus, I took I-8 out from the San Diego area on **Sunday**, in order to see Organ Pipe Cactus National Monument in southwestern Arizona, which drive actually took me to the Mexican border (and the signs advertising temporary car insurance for travel into our southern neighbor).

From there I headed to Pirtleville, outside Douglas, AZ, a border town, where my Arizona priest-friend was then stationed as pastor. I had visited there before; but now, in the dark, I forgot which dwelling on the same block was the rectory, or priest house. I decided to check in the more recognizable church first, and so walked through the back door. I could not find a light switch, and so was in almost complete darkness. Providentially, there was a vigil light candle burning in the sanctuary, next to the then-invisible tabernacle, where the consecrated hosts from mass are kept. We Catholics believe that that is the Real Body of Christ, and so we show these sacred species high honor. Part of our practice is to genuflect upon entering a church where the Blessed Sacrament, as we call it, is kept, and so I did this instinctively, turning to the right and going down on one knee in the direction of the light.

Or at least attempting to. You need to understand that that sort of candle is generally surrounded by a dark red sheath of glass, so that there is no real light to see anything else by, even the tabernacle, which I simply assumed was there. And that was when the Big Surprise occurred. Basically, I did not feel any floor underneath me, and so continued moving downward until my hip hit against something hard, which stopped my fall. That contact really hurt, and I could now feel two shafts, one on either side of me, which I used to push myself back up to standing. Then I limped out of the door and back to my car to retrieve a flashlight and investigate exactly what had happened.

When I returned (*CW) I could hardly believe my eyes, since the wooden floor in the sanctuary – the front section of the church – was missing, except for the joists on which the floor had rested. I could see directly down into the stone basement floor between them. And that is exactly where I should have landed, since walking in through the back door put me parallel with the joists, guaranteeing that I would have fallen between them and down. Remarkably, there was not the slightest barrier around this potential disaster, and I later gently took my friend to task for leaving an accident ready to happen, with an unlocked door through which any kid could have unsuspectingly and impulsively darted.

But because of the vigil light next to the tabernacle, I turned my body to the right, and so did not fall straight through the joists, but rather banged my left hip against one of them. It left a nice bruise, but very well could have saved my life, and certainly saved me from serious harm. As it happened, when I finally found the rectory, he bought me some Icy Hot to put on the spot, and the next day I simply didn't drive.

That was the plan, anyway, for **Monday**. I guess I was literally dragging my feet at this point (or at least my one foot), but rather than leave the next day as originally intended, I stayed to enjoy some local sights with him, who did all the driving (as if seeing these items would be a sacrifice for me). I needed to sit at a certain angle in the back seat of his car for that hip not to hurt, which by now sported a nasty black-and-blue mark. Still, it didn't give me much pain, and hardly restricted my mobility.

We first traveled up to Tombstone, "the town too tough to die," where we hit the usual sights on its main drag. What was disconcerting about the visit, however, was that it was freezing. There I was, practically in Mexico in early November, and I needed a coat. However, that was just the warm-up (so to speak). When we next drove, down in direction but up in elevation, to the Coronado National Monument, literally right on the border at the end of an unpaved road up a mountain, it was actually snowing.

Snowing! Well, the good news was that I had plenty of weight in the car, with all the stuff I didn't mail back to Pennsylvania. Further, it was a stick shift, albeit with rear-wheel drive. But OK, let's not panic: this is a mountain, after all, and I won't be driving through mountains, since I'll be passing south of the Rockies when I cross the Continental Divide in New Mexico on I-10. No, there's plenty of time to freak out later. And anyway, I had my hip to occupy my thoughts, since I did have the width of the continent to traverse with a stick shift, and not much time to do it. Would it be able to take the strain?

Well, that inaugurated this cross-country drive from heck. By the next morning I needed to scrape ice off my windshield, but nothing had fallen overnight, at least anything that stuck. There was word of snow to the east, but I discovered that the roads here were dry. And my left hip? With the grace of God, and the Icy Hot, that joint was doing OK, even with a stick shift. The weather was now clear, and things were looking up.

There were a couple of other things I had wanted to see (some people never learn), given that they were sort of on my way in New Mexico. One was White Sands National Monument. There the sand blows around so much that they need snow plows to keep the roads through the sand open, with the white stuff looking like snow piled up along the sides, a disconcerting feeling for a Pennsylvanian. I didn't like that reminder of snow, but it was cool (so to speak) to see all that granulated silica.

Next was a sight in Alamogordo, the New Mexico Museum of Space History. It's actually on state route 2001 (like the science fiction film), a rare such designation with four digits, and really only a novelty here. (Texas uses them, obviously related to its size; Louisiana does as well, for some reason; and I have encountered them in at least one other state.) My clear recollection here, however, is not about the museum, but rather that as I drove up the short NM-2001, there were snow flurries falling. I stayed anyway, but with one eye on the windows the whole time. The attraction was quite interesting, but I did not give it the time that it deserved, certainly not staying for the IMAX planetarium show. By the time I bailed out and emerged, I knew I was not going to be able to visit the third planned sight of the day, the famous UFO museum in Roswell. The problem? Snow had already closed the stretch of US-70 that cut through the mountains between the two locations. I could have tried US-82, but the presence of a ski area on the map did not bode well for my safe passage. Even Alamogordo rested at 4341 feet of elevation.

Thus, my plan morphed into heading due south, and so (*CW) I was off like a shot toward the Mexican border (the co-theme of the trip so far, along with the snow, the two phenomena in my mind tending to be mutually exclusive), to El Paso, where I would pick-up I-10 again, and-so head east as far south as possible. The road south to there, US-54, was straight and flat, moving through a wide valley, which was good, since the flurries continued. My car thermometer registered mid-thirties, and I thanked the Lord every time it went up a degree.

It was actually snowing when I arrived at Sun City, El Paso, a stone's throw from *caliente* Mexico. It was election day in the US, and so must have been a **Tuesday** (I used this reference to figure out the rest of the days on this trip). Still, since it was late afternoon and still a little sunny in one part of the sky, I could not resist stopping at Chamizal National Memorial, pretty much in the downtown area, almost at the river. It is a monument to friendship between the USA and Mexico commemorating the peaceful resolution of a long-standing border dispute. (As you can see, I was still in denial about the snow.) Then I was out of town and heading east.

Of course I had local radio on, and heard that there was a big snowstorm in Texas. I tried to estimate whether, when I arrived at the fork where I-20 begins, about 150 miles east of El Paso, it would be better to take I-20, or to stay with I-10, since both head east, just at different latitudes. True, I-10 is farther south; but by the time I got to the fork, it seemed to me, based on the radio, that that was where the greater chance for snow lay. I picked I-20, procured gas at Kent (where the middle-aged woman who took my money wasn't sure about the snow), and (*CW) hit the road.

Well, I managed to catch the storm. Indeed, the farther east I drove, the deeper the snow grew. One small town sported a sign advertising a motel approved by AAA; and when soon afterward I was down to the third of five gears and still sliding a little, I decided to turn around on the interstate and head back to that motel. I had thought for a moment of simply stopping and sleeping in the car, but I quickly dismissed that brainstorm, given how cold it was out, given that my hip was still on the mend, given that another driver could lose control and hit me, and given that the car was full of stuff. Thus, instead of driving far into the night, which was the plan to make up for lost time for that day in Arizona, I actually broke down (metaphorically speaking) and paid for a room.

And broke-down is exactly how the room looked. I rang the bell and clearly got the man out of bed, being that it was by now after 1:00 a.m. Still, that was part of his job, I figured. It wasn't that I was too drunk to drive home in July or something. I disturb motel operators so infrequently anyway. He handed me a key, and out I went to find the unit. It was a basic no-frills room, with a bed, a TV and a bathroom.

The shower head was even off, but that was of little concern to me as I sank into the luxury of a warm queen-size. As I drifted to sleep, the thought of the election that day played second fiddle in my head to how the roads would look later that morning.

Now I forget what town this was. Odessa perhaps (home of the Presidential Museum,. I would learn on another trip). In any case, it was small, and had exactly what I needed for the night, with no hassles. The next morning, **Wednesday**, I saw that the snow was already melting, so I gave the sun some time to perform its magic, and then dared to return to the interstate in late morning, shaven but unshowered (I never thought to take a bath, so I really must have been tired). At most the lanes were wet. By the time I got to Dallas, the snow was no longer even an issue. I was home free.

Or so I thought. Oh, the temperature continued to rise as I entered Louisiana, but that was the problem: it rose too fast and too far. I had left frigid air in Arizona and west Texas, and found balmy air in east Texas and farther in that direction. It was nice while it lasted, but by evening things had changed drastically. At one point in Louisiana there was a story on NPR, and when I started losing the station, I stopped to hear the last half hour of the piece, resting in preparation for a long night of driving. Little did I realize what awaited.

I don't know, but I may have caught up with the snowstorm again, although now at an inflated temperature. In any case, I hit a front that indicated severe storm activity. I don't remember when the rain started, but it eventually began falling hard. As each city passed, the temperature rose: Dallas, Shreveport, Jackson, Montgomery. And by the time I got into Alabama, the radio was issuing tornado warnings. Great.

Now I've done a lot of driving in the past five days, although I have also had more sleep than originally planned. Still, by now I was feeling tired, and could see that I was following the heels of a storm that was not going anywhere fast. There is a physical drain from driving in bad weather, such as snow or torrential rain, and once again I found myself in it. It was in the 70s, so I did not fear freezing-up roads. No, I could barely see the road at times, so large and hard were the drops falling from the sky. And traffic on I-20 was, shall we say, robust, so that I needed to be concerned about other drivers as well, drivers I could barely see.

I tried as best I could to follow the map when it came to tornado sightings. I was happy that I had a Deluxe Edition of the Rand-McNally Road Atlas, since it would stay open, as now at the Alabama pages (yes, I was actually attempting to read a map as I drove through this torrent). I soon came to realize that I was following the one tornado as it crept east. It was moving at about 45, and I was moving at about 55, so I asked myself why I was in such a hurry to catch it? I had unwittingly but fortunately given the thing a lead when I stopped back in Louisiana to hear that NPR radio show; and now I saw that that brief rest did me good in more ways than one.

I lowered my speed, which was a good idea with the rain and traffic anyway. There was a part of me that simply wanted to break through to the good weather (wherever *that* was) on the other side; but I knew that I was moving east, not west, and so running *with* the storm. Indeed, the tornado seemed to be following the line of I-20. I kept driving, hour after hour, making for Atlanta so I could be past that city by the next morning's rush hour. Then, somewhere in the meantime, the tornado zigged north as I zagged east, and so suddenly I was out of danger. I jumped onto I-85 and stopped at the first rest stop northeast of the city for some sleep, with a crowded car and a bad hip. It was heaven (or at least a heavenly answer to prayer).

I needed to keep moving, given my appointment schedule, so that morning, **Thursday**, (*CW) I was off and running at Hialeah (or thereabouts). The radio now explained that there were tornado watches for North Carolina, through which I'd be passing; but I knew that a watch simply meant that conditions were ripe for a tornado, unlike a warning, when a funnel cloud has actually been sighted. Thankfully, nothing ever materialized around where I was driving (my mother's prayers were obviously working). I continued moving northeast through the two Carolinas and into Virginia. It was a long day of driving, since there was a cumulative draining effect of everything I had come-through up to then.

That evening I remember entering Pennsylvania from Maryland in dense fog, another result of unseasonably warm weather, so much so that I felt I was in an alternative existence. I've been so tired at times driving in the past that even familiar roads appeared unfamiliar. Add the fog to the tired, and I felt like I was in a tunnel, with taillights in front of me and headlights in back of me, and nothing on the sides. It was hypnotic. On and on, mile after mile on I-70 and then onto the legendary Pennsylvania Turnpike, with the four lanes of two-way traffic in close proximity, separated only by a metal barrier.

I eventually arrived at my destination, the rectory of a local priest friend of mine, where I had mailed my book boxes. Because of my unremitting driving, and so the good time I made, I was now able to stay there for the weekend before reporting for duty. **Friday** night into **Saturday** I crashed, **Sunday** I packed, and **Monday** I headed to where I was to begin afresh, in a simply wonderful state of mind and body.

As a footnote to this tonic trip: I needed to travel to our nation's capital soon thereafter, which I did in December. I uncharacteristically arranged to take the train to DC from my friend's rectory in the tiny hamlet of New Baltimore, PA. He would drive me down to Cumberland, MD, an old railroad town, where I would pick up the train on the line from Chicago to Washington.

Well, it was snowing, not only in DC and not only in New Baltimore, but especially from Chicago east along the train's route. I called Amtrak, and was told that the train was delayed. Well, it certainly was delayed. He finally drove me through the fallen snow to Cumberland that afternoon, the run several hours late already. The choo-choo didn't pick up any time after that, and so I eventually found myself in Union Station in DC a full *nine hours* late. It was already past the time to be picked-up by anyone from the church place I would be staying, so I was told to take a cab and they would reimburse me later. No problem.

I walked out front, where DC's replica of the Liberty Bell (rah!) stands by the Christopher Columbus fountain, to the taxi stand, which I foolishly took as a good omen. I soon had my things and myself ensconced in a cab being driven by, of course, a man with a thick foreign accent. He tended to speak about our government in negative terms, at least when he was awake. That's right, because, at the end of this very long day, I found myself under the care of a drunken cabbie, one who would nod off to sleep at red lights. Then he would

The Cross-Country Drive From Heck: Snow, Tornadoes And Icy Hot

wake up, and quickly forward we would lunge. I tried to encourage him in conversation, not that I felt like talking, but just to keep him awake, but it did little good at the stop lights. Finally and suddenly I recognized the side street to turn onto, and told him. We were on a road that had three lanes of traffic either way, and were in the center lane. What did he do but make an immediate right turn onto the side street. If another car had been in the right lane it would have clobbered me. I was very happy soon to be free of him, and perhaps I made a mistake not to report him later, but my only thought was to get settled for the night. The trip from heck was officially over with this coda. But if nothing else, it acted as a chiaroscuro, a shadow to highlight how nice all my many other trips have been. How have I fared on my average trek? Better than I deserve.

The lesson? Something that I have tried to tell myself at other times when stuck on the ice on some dark evening on the roads of central Pennsylvania in winter: that at some point tonight, you will probably be in bed, and this stretch of dicey driving will be a memory. Of course, I would hope that that bed would not be in the ICU section of some nearby hospital. Here I am, writing this, with all the challenges of my life so far in the past, including that trying cross-country drive from heck. May I remember it when I am similarly tempted to think that the road is dark and there is no light yet shining at the end of it. As Saint Paul says, If God is for me, who can be against me? And thanks again, Mom, for those prayers.

CHAPTER 16

THE BEST IDEA AMERICA EVER HAD: OUR NATIONAL PARK SYSTEM

Wallace Stegner has described the American National Park system as The Best Idea We Ever Had. Admittedly, I would tend to place the Declaration of Independence, the Constitution, and the Bill of Rights ahead of it on the American Best Ideas List. Still, it certainly deserves to be in the Top Five, for I do agree with his basic intuition that this was and is a great concept, inspiring the conservation of natural beauty not only in our country and but throughout the greater world as well. So let's see what the National Park Service (NPS) has to offer.

I don't quite know precisely when I decided to visit every full National Park in the contiguous 48 states, but that seed was probably planted in August of 1978, when Bro and I took the afore-mentioned road trip to New England and the Canadian Maritime Provinces. On that excursion, recall, we briefly visited Acadia National Park in Maine, the only National Park in New England. It still took a few years to get bitten by the bug. However, in 1985 it began to put out shoots (to mix the metaphor). You see, I was now ordained, with a car and a regular salary, out of school forever. Since my family moved to California during my seminary years, and I still lived in Pennsylvania, it was natural for me to drive every 12 months to LA

(Los Angeles, not Louisiana, although at times passing through that LA *en route*), or, in the local lingo, SoCal. I have by now traversed the continent probably 40 times, and at some point I decided that if I'm driving through this beautiful country, I might as well stop to see points of interest between the coasts.

But what to see? This was in the days before I used AAA's tour books as my multi-volume travel bible. As mentioned above, all I had was a current Rand-McNally Road Atlas. But in addition to showing cities and the roads that connect them, this excellent collection of cartography included every full National Park on the national map in the front of the book. They were listed on top, and outlined in purple, so it was easy to see where they were, and how to get to each one. The more of them I visited, the more I wondered what was keeping me from seeing them all, a musing that one day evolved into a plan: I had visited quite a few, so I might as well experience the rest.

At that point I started traveling to the remainders systematically. I was in no hurry, or I could have done it all on one annual monthly vacation (the way I drive, anyway: I have seen four of the National Parks in southern Utah in one day, for instance, back when I used to tour like that [egad!]). On each trip from now on, I would take a different route, and in the process cross a couple more Parks off my list. Over time the NPS added a few more, but for a while I stayed current with these augmentations to the system through buying a new Rand-McNally. A handful of times I had already been to a new National Park when it was a mere National Memorial (specifically, Joshua Tree National Park in California; Great Sand Dunes National Park and Black Canyon of the Gunnison National Park, both in Colorado (those Centennial State senators seem to be doing their job as far as conservation goes); and Death Valley National Park, in both California and Nevada), so that I counted it as already having been seen. Otherwise, it meant (*CW) setting my sights on the newbies on the next trip (such as Cuyahoga Valley National Park in Ohio, which had been promoted from the status of a National Recreational Area). Thus, over time I managed, as of 2004, to get to every continental National Park (apart from Alaska [and, by implication, Hawaii], given how it is difficult to drive to these places), except one.

This one was difficult to drive to as well, being due west of Key West in Florida: an interloper called Dry Tortugas National Park. However, I bided my time until March of 2004, and a post-monastery trip with my sister, from SoCal to FLA. Thus, by Easter of that year I could accurately claim that I had been in every National Park in the 48 contiguous states.

Or so I thought. I must not have been dealing with a 2004 Rand-McNally Road Atlas for that trip, since another National Park had been added in 2003, one that I had not previously seen in its former life as a National Monument: Congaree National Park in South Carolina. Indeed, I did not become aware of this addition until 2010, once again with a current Rand-McNally, and so was unwittingly lying to people with my National Park brag (as if anyone ever listened). That year I finally addressed that lacuna by visiting Congaree, making me truly current for the first time (until they hopefully create another one somewhere I haven't been to yet). Indeed, that was a banner year, the Year of Fifty States, since I also visited the two National Parks in Hawaii, the National Park in the US Virgin Islands, and three of the eight National Parks in Alaska, bring my grand total up to 52 of the 58 total full National Parks in the NPS. (Since then they added another I had already visited in its former life, Pinnacles National Park in California, so that I have made it to 53 of 59 as of this printing.)

At this point, however, I need to come clean and admit to a certain, well, not exactly cheating, but a cutting of corners, in a way that defeats the purpose of the National Parks in the first place. You see, in my effort to cross every National Park off my list, I would on occasion just skirt a Park. How? Well, for instance, Isle Royale National Park lies in Lake Superior, requiring a boat trip at a boat price. You can buy an NPS annual pass (the last one I bought was in 2010, for $80; for seniors the price tag drops considerably), and get into any entity in the NPS system for free for a year, quite a bargain if you plan to do any serious traveling, such as touring the more expensive western Parks. However, some Parks have added fees for things like boat crossings, and I have traditionally been a cheapskate. Further, such crossings take time; and usually on these trips I was covering hundreds of miles a day driving, apart from time spent visiting anything. So, given these two factors, I would sometimes get to the visitor center of the Park (which for Isle Royale was on the shore of the Great Lake), check it out, and then leave, with (*CW) another notch on my holster, but with the whole purpose of the Park overlooked, and thereby defeated. I am embarrassed by this fact, and am happy to assert that it happened only a handful of times.

It was in 2010 that my travel conscience finally got to me, moving me to revisit several of the National Parks to which I had previously (*CW) given the cold shoulder, and so spend at least a day there. Because, with rare exceptions, I never spent more than a day in any National Park. I always resented (before buying the NPS passport) that the bigger, western Parks would charge, say, $20 per vehicle, and then add that the ticket was good for a week. Were I planning a week's stay in, say, Yellowstone, that would be a bargain, even with the added per-night fees for camping (which used to be a lot cheaper, as in Shoshone National Forest, to the east, in 1986). However, I was usually planning a drive-through on the hard-surface roads, with perhaps a stop for some hiking. Highway robbery. Still, it's going to a good cause, I told myself. There's my cheapness coming out again. Some habits of mind die hard.

But what again are the other Parks that didn't even get the drive-through? One not far from Isle Royale is Voyageurs National Park in Minnesota. How nice to be canoed by modern-day voyageurs in the evening, listening to the old French trader songs under the stars. Nope: too much time. Maybe someday. And how about Los Angeles' own Park, Channel Island? My mother, my sister and I got as far as the visitor center before realizing that you needed to climb from a boat deck to the dock on one of the islands up eight feet of rails, a little beyond my mother's range of mobility. Then too, there is Great Smokey Mountain National Park in Tennessee and North Carolina, which I hit at dusk on a foggy day, thus driving all the way through it on the highway but seeing nothing. (It was the first night of a cross-country drive, and soon after exiting the Park I pulled over and slept while the recent rain passed. It was off-highway travel in nowheres-ville, and I marvel that I found my way in the dark, on a Sunday night after a full day of church services, without a GPS. I had planned to arrive at the Park during the day, but underestimated the length of time it would require to travel there.) Capitol Reef National Park is a wilderness Park, where you need to go inside with a backpack to see anything. It is bisected by UT-24, and I considered that pass-by enough exposure. And how about North Cascades National Park in Washington State? It is also a true wilderness Park, since you need to hike into it and out from it: no internal roads. However, at the end of 28 miles of unpaved gravel is one trail head, and my sedan and I made that jaunt one afternoon until I crossed where a brown NPS sign welcomed me into the Park itself. I had no time to do any hiking, but nonetheless considered that effort something of an accomplishment. On the hour-plus drive back to civilization, I noticed a woman whose vehicle had skidded off the washboard road-surface into a large, steep ditch, but who assured me that help was already coming. Finally, Biscayne National Park near Miami was not taking the glass-bottom boats out that day since there had recently been a storm, which made the water too murky to see anything. Pity, since that day I was actually willing to take the time, shell out the extra few bucks, and do the park right.

So the time had arrived to address this (*CW) skeleton in my closet. I had the time, and the inclination, and so decided to fill in some of the gaps in my travels in the USA (and a little in Canada, and a tad in Mexico) as the final preparation for sitting down and finishing this book. Thus, on one trip I actually visited two of these Parks that are near each-other. One was Isle Royale National Park, which is technically part of Michigan but which I accessed from Minnesota, which shore is actually closer. As the French name implies, it is an island, and is almost totally wilderness. In fact, there are no vehicles or even bicycles allowed on the island, except for one truck they use to move large items around. I paid the money for the boat to take me across, where I was able to do some hiking, although I did not see any of the grey wolves for which they are known (which some people would consider a good thing). There are also moose there, although I missed seeing a mother and baby feeding in the water by mere minutes. (Others in the group saw them, and for some time, but I was sitting facing the other way, enjoying the verdure, and nobody said anything to me. There is something to be said for awareness.) There is a visitor center on the island, which sells camping supplies for the folks who stay overnight. For the less-adventurous (like me in my old age), there is a nature trail, on which lies a famous (among people who care about such things) Controlled Environment. By that phrase I mean that they have fenced-in and covered a small part of the forest, so that animals that eat plants can't get in, and over the years compare the growth on either side of the metal mesh. It is quite obvious which side the animals are on, since the protected side has more, and bigger, plants and trees.

The other such stop that trip was Voyageur's National Park, which is squarely in the Gopher State, along the boundary waters with Canada. Quickly: the good news was that I was able to take a daytime boat ride for a handful of hours. The bad news was that it was not one of the nights for the traditional voyageurs experience that I described above, which is what I had my heart set on, so I needed to leave it at that (it gives me a good reason to return). The boat tour zoomed us around the lakes for about three hours. We saw a bald eagle, no moose, and lots of beautiful blue and green. Oh, and who were the voyageurs (accent on the last syllable)? Men, usually French, who carted heavy loads (each one carried two 90-pound parcels) from site to site when the boats needed to be portaged over land around rapids.) They would canoe for many miles, in the warmer parts of the year, effecting trade between the fur trappers in the Canadian interior and a civilization that wanted beaver pelts. You can find a lot more about them in nearby (sort of) Grand Portage National Monument. If even that's not enough for you, take a drive into Ontario, Canada, to nearby (sort of) Thunder Bay, where Fort William offers the tourist more things than can be done in an entire day.

There is also Biscayne, one of the three National Parks in southern Florida. I had just disembarked from a Caribbean cruise on a Sunday, Fathers Day. Thus, I occupied myself at Biscayne, where I thought I'd (*CW) take another stab at the glass-bottom boat tour. The bad news was that the water was again murky. The good news was that they were still taking out the snorkeling boat to the reef, so I decided (*CW) to go with the flow, literally, and have an adventure underwater. As had happened in Dry Tortugas, I just couldn't get the hang of snorkeling, and was one of several people sick in the boat at one point, moving the captain to comment dryly that he should take down the scuba flag and hoist a red cross flag, since it had become a hospital ship.

I was able (*CW) to kill two birds with one stone (or, to use the more politically-correct version, feed two birds with one seed) in visiting the North Carolina-Tennessee state line, the location of Great Smokey Mountains National Park. By seeing the Park in the daytime, I ki- , OK, I fed one bird. The other? That Park is also the sight of Clingman's Dome, the highest point in Tennessee. In fact, the road goes all the way to the summit, as another road does in neighboring North Carolina for its own highest point, Mount Mitchell, in the aptly-named Mount Mitchell State Park, where I saw layers of blue mountain ridges in the distance on the way up on another excursion, a stunning sight. These two separate visits remind me of another possible list I could make my own: seeing the highest points in each state. I would need to go state by state to jog my memory, but I have seen at least 10, which puts me one-fifth of the way there. The problem is that they are not always on public land, so that at best you may be able to see them in the distance. (Just what I need: another travel obsession.)

The last of the five (of the seven to which I had [*CW] given short shrift over the years) I visited was, ironically, the closest to my family: Channel Island, right off the coast from Los Angeles, recall. I decided to jump into my car one Sunday and drive out there without competing with rush-hour traffic. I had called ahead to make a reservation, although the passenger load was light that exceptionally overcast day. For more irony, since the one hiking island was off-limits because of some work they were doing to the dock, I took the excursion that involved circumscribing the island without actually landing, meaning that my mother could have taken that plan if we had known about it (*CW) lo, these many years ago (assuming they offered that option back then). So what was the point? The scads of sea lions that (*CW) call the island home. I have a soft spot in my heart for natural beauty, but also another for wildlife, and that day that particular ventricle won-out. Mother Nature threw-in not one but two types of dolphin pods (*CW) for good measure.

And the two wilderness Parks? That will need to be the job of another year, when I'm in better shape, buy some new camping gear, and find someone else who wants to enjoy that sort of vacation (besides my Guardian Angel). I do like camping, if I can find like-minded people to do it with. It's just that I rarely if ever give myself permission to spend any length of time in one spot, since AAA still has books full of things I haven't seen yet (well, a few things).

Now, to move from personal history to national history: the first National Park was Yellowstone, established by an act of Congress (as all full National Parks need to be; National Monuments, by contrast, can be authorized simply by the President's signature) in 1872. However, the National Park Service was not formed until 1916 (there were 35 separate unorganized entities before then, according to an article in *National Geographic*). That enactment occurred under President Woodrow Wilson, a former college professor who had probably never seen the inside of a tent in his life, ironically, although the idea politically came from one of his predecessors, conservationist president Teddy Roosevelt. He did get the Antiquities Act passed in 1906, which allowed the president to create National Monuments, which he subsequently did a number of times. However, Congress just wasn't ready to create the NPS yet. I felt bad in 1991, when the Park Service was celebrating its 75th anniversary, that I was at the visitor center of Theodore Roosevelt National Park in North Dakota, of all places, and noticed a poster that showed the face of Wilson rather than outdoorsman TR (as Roosevelt liked to be called). Oh well. I'm sure he doesn't care now.

There are hundreds of entities in the NPS, including not only full-fledged National Parks (such as Yellowstone NP, in Wyoming, Idaho and Montana), but also National Preserves (such as Mojave NPres in California), National Memorials (such as Flight 93 NMem in Pennsylvania), National Monuments (such as Canyon de Chelly NMon in Arizona), National Historic Sites (such as Tuskegee Airmen NHS in Alabama), National Battlefields (such as Cowpens NB in South Carolina), National Seashores (such as Cape Hatteras NS in North Carolina), National Lakeshores (such as Sleeping Bear Dunes NL in Michigan), National Recreational Areas (such as Lake Mead NRA in Nevada and Arizona), National Wildlife Refuges (such as Aransas NWR in Texas), National Rivers (such as Buffalo NR in Arkansas), National Scenic Trails (such as Appalachian NST, along the eastern part of the USA), Parkways (such as the Blue Ridge PKWY in the southeast of the country) and the like. They are pieces of land (and sometimes water [I'm not aware of any in the air yet, although the cable cars in San Francisco constitute, according to AAA, a uniquely mobile National Historic Site]) that have been set aside from general use and development, telling us in the present that these sites need to be preserved for the future. The locations are not chosen indiscriminately, of course, but rather are carefully selected to represent significant national importance, be it of beauty, history, or wildlife. Thus, you find beauty in Glacier National Park, Montana, history in Pompey's Pillar National Historic Site in the same state, and wildlife in Yellowstone National Park, partly in Montana, a truly happenin' state, obviously (and yes, these categories do at times obviously overlap).

Over a quarter of a century, I have visited a number of these entities, including, as implied above, every continental National Park outside Alaska. Thus, I have a pretty good idea of what to expect in these places, and what to recommend. And that rec? My experience has convinced me that, from my first adult encounter with the NPS, Hopewell Furnace National Historic Park, in Pennsylvania, which I saw with my then-girlfriend (we eventually parted amicably), to now: if it is connected with the NPS, it is worth seeing. The rest is details, details with which the rest of this chapter will be concerned. Of course, those details are the reasons to go exploring in the first place, since, as it were, (Improved Cliché Warning) the angel is in the details.

Some states, like Alaska, California, Utah, Colorado, Washington, Arizona and Florida, have multiple full National Parks, while certain other states, especially in the eastern part of the country, have none. (That fact gave me an early prejudice, so that I would often say that there was nothing east of the Mississippi worth seeing. I even took exception that there was no full National Park in Pennsylvania. As mentioned above, it took AAA's excellent travel books, and a little reflection, to convince me otherwise.) Still, it is not good to be a full-Park snob, since the lesser sights are almost in every case worth visiting, too, and exist in every state. There is even a National Park, as mentioned above, in the US Virgin Islands, and American Samoa, with other entities in Puerto Rico and Guam

Thus, in one sense, the national park cells are all over the country, and are all worth visiting. So why discuss them specifically? To give you a sense of the particulars, so that you can choose, from among hundreds, which ones you want to see first. I considered offering a sort of Top Five list here, but have moved in a different direction. One reason is that I will mention many of my favorites in the chapter on states. Another is that, in this case, my favorites list, like my list of favorite Beatles songs, or my favorite books in the Bible, is always changing. Thus, I have chosen to present entities (I seem to like that word) in the NPS that I do not discuss elsewhere (I may include a park that I mention but do not really discuss), a sort of NPS smorgasbord. After you read it, you're free to sample as little or as much as you like. But once you buy your annual pass, you might as well get your money's worth from it. (Oh, that annual pass covers not just one individual but the entire vehicle, making it an even better bargain for groups.)

So let's start with a park I have just mentioned but did not discuss: Hopewell Furnace National Historic Site. It was one of the first pieces of the NPS that I ever visited. I did it, as I mentioned above, with my then-college-girlfriend, who had experienced it before and who recommended it (it was not far from where she lived at the time). For that reason, it has nostalgic value for me. Two memories of it (besides being with her) stick in my mind. One was that it was built, at least the wooden sections, with mortice-and-tenon fastening, which means that two holes are drilled in two pieces of wood, but not evenly, and that a peg is then inserted into the two holes, pulling the two pieces of wood together tightly because of the discrepancy in the drilling. Clever. The other memory was that, because the iron furnace (made of stone) burned so hot, it was rarely allowed to go out, perhaps once every few months for cleaning, since it took too long and required too much energy to start it up again; so that it operated with three shifts, around the clock. For a history buff like me, this was good stuff.

What about the very first NPS entity (there it is again) I ever saw, as a grade-schooler? That would be Independence National Historic

Site, in downtown Philadelphia. It includes at least 19 sub-locations, not all of which I visited on class trips. (Imagine: getting onto a bus, riding less than an hour, and seeing *Independence Hall* or *the Liberty Bell*! How cool was that!) However, I did see some of the better-known spots during those years, back when the afore-mentioned Liberty Bell was still housed in Independence Hall (hey, two for one: that's cheating!) rather than currently, its own little pavilion a block away. This entity (I'm sorry) is not only part of my personal nostalgia, but part of our national nostalgia as well, concerned as it is with our struggle for independence from Britain. It would take several days to see everything, and that would not include other interesting sights in downtown Philly. In later years my mother used to take us down there, especially during the Bicentennial in 1976 (did I really need to say that? well, for our foreign readers), to see things like the tall ships in the Delaware River. With apologies to Boston, there is probably no more historical square acreage in the realm.

Speaking of furnaces and forges, another early visit for me, this time with the Boy Scouts, was Valley Forge National Historic Park. I bring it up in this context, since, when I was dating this young woman, I would literally drive through Valley Forge, even underneath the arch, to get from my place to hers. Ah, history ...

To show that I have nothing against Boston, I will mention the Saugus Iron Works National Historic Site (yes, believe it or not: another patriotic furnace). AAA also mentions the existence of Boston National Historical Park, which no doubt is similar to Independence National Historic Park in Philadelphia, i.e., being a geographic location with multiple sites of interest. One mentioned by both AAA and Rand-McNally is Dorchester Heights National Historic Site, which commemorates the fact that George Washington drove the redcoats from Boston, appropriately, on Saint Patrick's Day, 1776 (the fact that my Irish ancestors didn't begin to arrive until the 1840s is beside the point; my Italian grandfather came through that same harbor in 1916). There is a white marble tower to mark the spot.

Let's get out of this Pennsylvania/Massachusetts revolutionary rut and head south, to a park that holds some recent nostalgia for me (is that an oxymoron?), Congaree National Park in South Carolina. Why is it nostalgic (I'm suddenly using that word a lot, too) for me? As I mention above, because it was the most recent National Park I visited for the first time, meaning that I had now seen all the full continental National Parks outside Alaska (are you bored yet with hearing this factoid?). It is rather small, but protects important growths of trees, including state and national champions as far as size is concerned for several species. It is actually a cypress forest, and features a boardwalk set up (not always clearly) so that you can follow a walking tour of this type of woodland. They also provide a creative, non-technical mosquito meter, with several possible settings, going from Clear through Mild and Moderate and Severe and Ruthless to War, something I have seen nowhere else. I was fortunate, since even though it was set at Moderate the day I was there, they just weren't biting as long as I kept moving (hard to do when reading the stationary descriptions on a walking tour, admittedly). To be fair, I would not make Congaree your first choice; but if you're in the Carolinas, why not? It is a full National Park, after all. Just remember to bring plenty of Deet.

Staying along the East Coast (where I used to think there was nothing worth seeing), there lies Shenandoah National Park in Virginia. The main drag through it, the Skyline Drive, a segment of the Blue Ridge Parkway, takes you, not surprisingly, along the ridge of the mountains, while the Park unfolds on either side below. I would recommend seeing this Park in the fall, when that potentially-boring (?!) all-green scene turns into (*CW) a riot of colors that draws people for tours just to enjoy the leaves. Then, when you've finished with the Park, you can keep driving south along the Parkway, through the rest of Virginia into North Carolina, where you can, as it were, watch the leaves in the act of changing all over again (I mean, is that even allowed?).

Moving into Georgia, you can discover a couple of national sites not far from each-other, but pretty far from everything else. One is Andersonville National Historic Site, the location of a notorious Confederate prison camp during the Civil War. It became synonymous with horrible living conditions and a high mortality rate, and has been preserved as a reminder of how bad things can become, with a view to not repeating the same atrocities in the present and future. One exhibit in the visitor center discusses some other such (dare I say it?) entities in human history. (To be fair, there was another such camp, in the north, in Alton, Illinois, that was considered just as bad, but it is not included in the NPS, since it was conveniently demolished at the end of the war.)

About 45 minutes away, in Plains, lies Jimmy Carter National Historic Site. It is a blessing that it is far from most anyplace, since the character of Plains as a small town has so far been preserved. You can visit the farm on which President Carter grew up, the school that he attended (now a museum), and the house where he and Mrs. Carter now reside. In fact, you can even drive to the Baptist church where the former first-couple not only worship, but where President Carter continues to teach a weekly Bible study when he is home. I even saw his summer class schedule posted on the glass door of one of the stores in town, since these lessons are open to the public. Too bad I wasn't there on a Sunday.

On the subject of religion, you can visit Father Marquette National Memorial, just across the Mackinac Bridge in Michigan's Upper Peninsula. Father Jacques Marquette, as you might guess, was a Catholic priest and Jesuit missionary who was important in the settlement of that state. The memorial was, you will recall, damaged by lightning in the recent past, and they have been having a hard time procuring money to replace it with new indoor facilities (there are currently outdoor exhibits). Nevertheless, it is worth the visit if you are doing the Mackinac tour, since he was one of the first Europeans to visit that part of the country.

In neighboring Ohio is another relatively new National Park, Cuyahoga Valley, south of Cleveland. As is typical with National Parks in the east, its focus is not so much on impressive rock formations and mountains as it is on forest area (like, for instance, the afore-mentioned Shenandoah NP, and Great Smoky Mountains National Park [I know, I know, this park has mountains in it, but they are still all covered with trees, with no tree-line]). It is one of the last National Parks I have visited, and houses the gift shop where I bought two of my three books on the NPS. My gut feeling is that, unless you plan to do some canoeing, this too is a good place to visit primarily in autumn.

If you really want to go east, there is one more National Park *really* to the east: on Saint John in the Virgin Islands. I took an Eastern Caribbean (I put the primary accent on the third syllable, just in case you were wondering) cruise just to get to it (well, partly, anyway). The cruise ship stopped at Saint Thomas, so I needed to take a tour boat over to Saint John. There were two packages offered, and you couldn't do both of them on the same day, so I needed to choose. One sounded better historically, but did not explicitly mention the Park by name. The other mentioned the Park explicitly, although it was mostly an eco-hike followed by beach time. It did not occur to me to get clarification, believe it or not, since I was doing this in the AAA office, and did not want to get locked out of both tours by waiting until cruise time, so I chose the eco-tour. It was nice, as far as it went, although the guide kept repeating herself (HA!). This female mentor, who graduated the University of Chicago ([*CW] no mean feat), pointed out a number of flora on our hike, which I appreciated. She also talked me into eating a termite from a nest in a tree if she did it first (she correctly predicted that it would taste like wood [as opposed to chicken]): obviously a sucker for a pretty face. Then the ocean (sea?) felt like bathwater, which is the way I like it (and it was one of my only two times to swim in the surf on the cruise, so it was truly an integral part of the overall experience). Still, when we got back to the ship and someone who had taken the other tour related how much of the island he saw (it turns out the Park is over half the area of the small key), I felt a little jealous. So which one do I recommend? Take them both on successive days, then wait two weeks until the ship comes back that way again.

One further category of eastern parks involves military sites. Now, you would expect an entity (I must have some sort of a syndrome) with the name Chickamauga and Chattanooga National Military Park to be in Tennessee; and it is, sort of, although *most* of it in fact lies in neighboring Georgia. This park, according to AAA, has the distinction of being the oldest park of its kind in the NPS. I recall seeing its visitor center, with its multimedia presentation, museum, and grounds (for some reason, outside cannons stick in my mind, a common accoutrement in such places). However, I was hoping to visit a couple of other sights that day (how unusual), and so did not linger to see the Electric Map and Museum, the Craven House, or Point Park. Re-reading their AAA descriptions, it would seem to me that this park has more to do than most like it (many present no more than a visitor center and a site car tour, which is fine, as far as it goes), and deserved more quality attention from me.

Another military site, which I really enjoyed, since it had to do with the Revolutionary War, is Cowpens National Battlefield, in South Carolina. The visitor center, predictably, offers a video presentation, along with a helpful electric map, some relevant art, and artifacts; but for some reason this site, like another Revolutionary War location – this one in Pennsylvania, Fort Necessity National Battlefield – really grabbed my attention. It may lack the bells and whistles of a Gettysburg, and a Chickamauga and Chattanooga, but it teaches us about a war when we Americans were all cheering for the same side (well, except those traitorous Loyalists).

So there is stuff to see east of the Father of Waters. How about to the west? Let's go about as far west as you can in this country (if you don't count American Samoa): Haleakala National Park, on the island of Maui in Hawaii. There is an active volcano there, way up in the mountains, which meant that my visit was cold and blustery (I am not referring to my interaction with the others on the tour), unlike the typical image of the Aloha State. In fact, even though I wore a windbreaker, it was not enough to keep my teeth from chattering, and it was threadbare anyway, so I bought a functional souvenir, a heavier jacket with the Park information on front, announcing to everyone I meet what a big travel snob I am. The only real problem (the cold was an annoyance, not a problem) is that it costs real money to gad about from island to island (Hawaii Volcanoes National Park is on yet another solitary location), so that what it really costs to see the Park is hardly reflected in the entrance fee (and I had an annual park pass that year anyway).

My one regret (apart from pecuniary considerations) about visiting Hawaii is that I was not able to squeeze-in a trip to the island of Molokai. Some of you may already know that there was a large leper colony there in years past (well, some old-time residents still live there), before Hanson's disease, as it is now called, was properly understood. A Belgian priest, Saint Damien de Veuster, worked there among the inmates (it was segregated from the rest of the island) until he himself caught the illness from which he ultimately died. His work was then carried-on under the direction of another saint, Franciscan sister Marianne Cope. There is now an NPS site, Kalaupapa National Historic Park, which preserves that ground for future remembrance. Other visitors have informed me that it is hard to get to it even today. It is most revealing that, of the two statues from Hawaii in the US Capitol, one is of this foreign priest, so much did the insular people of Hawaii admire him.

By the way, Saint Junipero Serra is the fourth Catholic priest honored in the US Capitol by a statue, this one representing California. If you want to know more about him and other Franciscan missionaries, you can visit one of the 21 missions in California, including one that is in the NPS, Sonoma National Historic Park. Another one, not in the NPS but still on federal land, is Mission San Antonio de Padua, sitting on the Hunter Liggett Military Reservation in central California. You need to show photo ID to get onto the site, of course, but if you say you're going to the mission, and don't look like an ax murderer, they'll let you on with no problem.

North of California, in Washington State, and the highest point therein, is Mount Rainier, which is also in an eponymous National Park. The problem with that mountain is the same as with Mount McKinley in Alaska: it produces its own weather. The day I made the trip, I was driving under a (*CW) clear blue sky as I approached the eminence. However, it was wrapped in mist, so that I could only see the base. Undeterred, I drove up the mound as far as you can go, and soon entered a thick fog. The high point of my trip (so to speak), then, was not the majestic peak seen at a distance (it is not in a range, but by itself), nor was it the (*CW) commanding view of the surrounding countryside. No, it was seeing a mule deer hop over and start eating bugs off my car grill. (Yes, this was the day I discovered that mule deer don't walk, but hop, and almost started laughing.) (Years later, waking up at a rest stop to the east, I could see this solitary mount, several dozens of miles away at that point, in the clear matutinal air with the morning sun glancing off it, a breathtaking sight.)

Further south in the same state is Mount Saint Helen's National Volcanic Monument. It used to be a taller mountain, but the eruption in 1980 blew over 1000 feet off the top and caused havoc for some distance around. Things have remained relatively quiet since then, and over the past 30 years several areas of interest have been built in the present-day park. I recall a talk by a ranger on the shore of Spirit Lake, who stressed that, even though the eruption produced a lot of pumice, which might be handy in your home bathtub, it was illegal to remove even a leaf or a blade of grass from an NPS entity (well, not her words). It wasn't the point of the talk, but drove that particular message home for me from then on (not that I had a collection of such absconded items from before then).

Another Park noted for elevation is aptly-named Rocky Mountain National Park, northwest of Denver, Colorado. It straddles the Continental Divide, and so contains some pretty high peaks. In fact, I am not surprised that the squiggly line they call a road on the map announces that it is closed in winter. Lots of Alpine beauty, right? The problem was, that was back in my fast-moving days. Thus, I drove around the whole interior of the park, not stopping to gaze at the scenery, but rushing, trying to pass the slowpokes in front of me, so that I could make good time and so get to the next thang. So what was the point? To say that I was there? Don't let this happen to you! If you're going to see something, really see it. You may see fewer things, but you'll enjoy them a lot more (and so will the people driving in front of you). And you'd be surprised how few people really care where you've been, except as a springboard to telling you about where *they've* been; which, admittedly, can be interesting to travel novices, and to the thoroughly secure.

Now, moving on to mountains of another sort: I am aware of several places in the US with honest-to-goodness sand dunes in the interior of the country. One is the aforementioned entity (I couldn't resist), Great Sand Dunes National Park in Colorado. Another is the aforementioned White Sands National Monument, in southern New Mexico near Alamogordo. It was somewhat eerie driving through the latter, since it is one stretch of nothing but sand dunes. They also let you walk anywhere, since you can't really get hurt falling on the sand, which perambulating is fun until your legs get prematurely tired and your shoes fill with the white stuff (well, the *other* white stuff). Finally, along Lake Michigan in the state of Michigan (that statement only appears redundant) is Sleeping Bear Dunes National Lakeshore. I stopped here one evening and started climbing to the top. The more I climbed, the farther the top receded into the distance, until I eventually (*CW) threw in the towel and headed back down. (For the sake of completeness, allow me to mention two more dunes that are not in the NPS. One is in southeastern California, just coming in from Arizona on I-8: Imperial Sand Dunes Recreational Area, which is federal land but controlled by the BLM, or Bureau of Land Management [the NPS and the BLM are apparently in a perpetual feud]. There is another smaller non-NPS one [notice how I didn't write "entity"?] in southeast California, along CA-78 not far from Death Valley National Park, where people are invited to bring their four-wheelers, not to mention the dunes in the Park itself [without the ATVs, which are not allowed in National Parks, but are permitted in Mojave National Preserve, one of the two reasons that it is not as full National Park {the other? they permit hunting}].)

Of course, there are sand dunes along our national shores. One of note, since it is in the NPS (an NPS entity, as it were), is Oregon Dunes National Recreational Area. I have driven past it several times, but usually (for some reason) at night, always heading Somewhere Else. I'm sure it looks better in daylight. (And I don't even *want* to know about Seven Devils State Recreational Site to the south.) Speaking of the evil preternatural, there are dunes by Kill Devil Hills in North Carolina, at Wright Brothers National Memorial. After doing the tour, I went hiking out toward the water, but then had no way of knowing which way, in all that pathless whiteness, led me back to my car. I missed it by well over a mile and needed in my fatigue to thumb a ride back to it. If you want sand in your shoes for the next month, these are the places to go.

Back up the Oregon coast near the top is part of the multifaceted Lewis and Clark National Historical Park, specifically the Fort Clatsop segment. It was there that the Corps of Discovery wintered their second year out. It takes its name from the local Native tribe that befriended them. Camping there that winter was not a whole lot of fun, since, the entire time they stayed, it rained or was overcast all but about a week (welcome to the Pacific Northwest). The current experience of the fort should be for you much more positive, since there are costumed actors who bring the recreated structure to life. Then, if you're energetic, you can go west on the ocean trail and then south from that point to where they evaporated seawater to make salt for the trip back. Maybe you'll even be as thrilled as Sacagawea was to see the Big Water for the first time. (I mean, what's the point of traveling and experiencing New Things if you don't get thrilled when you see them? [a lesson I could clearly have benefited from in Rocky Mountain National Park].)

Just across the Washington state line is the Lewis and Clark Interpretive Center. While in another state, it is still part of the same National Historic Park. The two-storey structure had recently been refurbished when I saw it, and I found it GEM-worthy, with its various exhibits concerning the Corps of Discovery. It makes a good interpretive complement to the fort.

Back along the Columbia River in Washington, across the state line from Portland, in the American Vancouver (confused yet?) is Fort Vancouver National Historic Site. The day I was there it was pouring rain (again, welcome to the Pacific Northwet [sic]). Still, it did not dampen (sorry) my spirits, as I walked from building to building under an umbrella to snag a sense of the history of the place. The fur trade was active in the area in the mid-19th century, for which the fort was founded. You can view the enlisted men's barracks, as well as the large officers' houses. What I did not know at the time is that there are two campuses of the overall site (Vancouver National Historic Reserve), and that there is a section devoted to Native American history, and another to the Corps of Discovery, two areas of particular interest to me. I hope the weather is better when you see it, but don't bet on it.

A number of years ago I was driving through southwestern Colorado and noticed a brown sign for Bent's Old Fort National Historic Site near La Junta. Having never been directed wrongly up to then by such signage, I stopped and checked it out. It is not a GEM, but deserves to be. The entire structure has been reconstructed, with its interior buildings, all of which contain something of historical interest, as explained by costumed docents. I recall, for instance, first learning about the importance of beaver pelts for trade in those days, and actually saw and touched some in the trading post. It was also here that I started thinking differently about Native Americans. Before, I saw them all as being interested in living as non-technologically as possible, whereas the guide explained that they were as interested in having the latest technological items as everybody else, as evidenced in their quick adoption of things like horses and rifles, as well as iron kettles and Venetian glass beads. In other words, they were just like me (a frightening thought, for them).

Native American history of another sort awaited me much more recently in Oklahoma, in the Washita Battlefield National Historic Site (and don't ask me how to pronounce it). Two famous Americans were involved in that conflict, which massacred Indian men, women and children: George Armstrong Custer, who led the attack; and Chief Joseph, who survived it. Both of them later met their destinies in Montana. Chief Joseph, whose pacifism may possibly be dated to the Washita battle, was later to lead his Nez Perce tribe in Montana almost to the Canadian border to escape capture by the US army, but was nabbed within a handful of miles of his goal. The poster of him I used to own shows an actual photograph taken shortly after capture, in full feathered regalia, with the saddest look on his face that I have ever seen. (There is a Nez Perce National Historical Park, also in Montana, with the Bear Paw Battlefield in the north, and the Canyon Creek Battlefield, in the south, which I recently noticed on the map, which probably gives more information about this leader.) And what happened to Custer? That question is answered, as my other sister and I discovered in 1993, at Little Bighorn Battlefield National Monument, where he and all of his men, ironically, met their end in a massacre of another sort, at the hands of Chief Sitting Bull and the Lakota, or western Sioux.

While we're in Montana, let's look at the less contentious Pompey's Pillar National Monument. It is a natural tower of rock near the Yellowstone River that affords a great view of the waterway's valley. However, its importance lies in human history as well. William Clark, of Lewis and Clark fame, nicknamed Jean Batiste Charbonneau, Sacagawea's baby boy, Pomp, no one is quite sure why. When the Corps of Discovery happened upon this tower, Clark named it Pompey's Pillar, after the Roman city, but really after the boy, whom he later adopted and educated. The pillar is historically important because it preserves the single known surviving piece of physical evidence that the Corps left behind: the name of Clark, carved into the rock, along with the date: July 25, 1806. It is preserved behind a plastic shield, and a set of steps (lots of steps) enables you to climb up and both see this historic graffito (it is monitored by closed-circuit TV so that no more graffiti appear), and then go to the very top and view the surrounding country.

To the east, in neighboring South Dakota, in Wind Cave National Park in the Black Hills, you will espy something that I have seen only in this cave, although I have been to a number of these underground wonderlands around the country: boxwork. Boxwork is just that: rock formations that resemble square boxes with inscribed Xs. In fact, as the ranger explained to me and my brother in 1991, there is not only more boxwork in Wind Cave than in any other known cave in the world: there is in fact more boxwork in Wind Cave than in *every other* known cave in the world put together. So why is it named Wind Cave? The guide demonstrated the answer to that query by placing his Smokey-the-Bear hat over a hole at the entrance and letting go, at which point we saw the lid fly up into the air. Windy. (Directly to the west is Jewel Cave National Monument, which for some reason, even with my several trips to the Black Hills, and my love of the NPS, and my interest in caves, I have never seen. Is it wet, and so slowly producing formations? Is it windy like its neighbor? Is there more boxwork there? Which of us will discover the answers to these questions first?)

(And though it's a lowly *state* park, allow me to mention Itasca State Park, since it is both east and west of the Mississippi. How? By containing the headwaters of that river. Thus, if you go there, you can walk across that mighty body in one stride. Go for it. [And, while we're on the subject, the source of the Missouri River lies in another such (wait for it) entity, the aptly-named Missouri Headwaters State Park, near the aptly-named town of Three Forks, in western Montana.])

So how should *you* approach the National Park Service? I recommend starting where you live, trying to find the closest NPS (OK, one last time) entities to you. That can be done easily by logging onto the www.NPS.gov website. Then, after getting that taste of nature and history, allow your sense of wonder to take over. Think of places around the country that you have always wanted to see, or places you have recently heard of that sound interesting, especially during this centenary year of the NPS, and design a vacation around them. So it might be Yellowstone and Glacier; or Yosemite, Sequoia and King's Canyon; or Carlsbad Caverns and Guadalupe Mountains; or Shenandoah, Congaree and Great Smoky Mountains. If it's going to be a multi-park trip of a lifetime, make sure you buy an annual pass at the first park you visit, since especially those western Park costs can add up quickly. If you have a family, think how much money you're saving by driving in one car rather than flying everyone there, and then renting a vehicle. If you don't, talk several of your friends into signing on. The federal government may not get everything right, but the NPS just about always does, so get out there and try to prove me wrong. You'll be glad you did, and couldn't.

For the photographs accompanying this book, I have utilized snapshots from my latest cross-country drive (in June and July of 2016, for my Dad's 87th birthday). Rather than attempt to assemble a comprehensive visual record of travel in America, I have chosen simply to provide a tasty slice of what our nation has to offer in that department, as well as an example of some of the items that one might see on one such typical excursion. For that reason, the collection is not meant to be complete in itself (which would have required actual research work on my part), but simply one of a thousand possible ways to experience our continent. Believe it or not, I bought my very first camera for this drive, and so do not have cardboard boxes brimming with such visual evidence of my travels. I think, then, that this small, focused assemblage will appear less intimidating than a much larger compilation of all the big names, and so will highlight my contentions that not only is such a project possible for anyone, but that there is no one right way to do it. Let the adventure begin!

I present these picture subjects in the order in which I visited them this past summer:

Forest History Center, Grand Rapids, Minnesota – This tall log loader (they display a smaller one of a different design) is one of several rustic but effective recreated pieces of equipment on display here.

Forest History Center, Grand Rapids, Minnesota – This actual cooking wannigan, which was employed on the annual spring log drives in this area, rests in the nearby river, and is accessible after the excellent tour of the rebuilt logger camp led by informative and entertaining costumed docents.

Mississippi River, Grand Rapids, Minnesota – The headwaters of this major national thoroughfare are not far from here, where the gathering currents spill over a dam in the center of town.

Blue Moose Bar and Grill, East Grand Rapids, Minnesota – My priest-classmate and I drove across the Red River (the lesser-known cousin of the one in Texas) from neighboring Grand Forks, North Dakota for dinner at the Blue Moose Bar and Grill, to enjoy good food and pleasant company in their relaxing ambience.

Cabala's, East Grand Forks, Minnesota – On the way out of the above-mentioned eatery, we drove by this adjacent sporting and camping store, where I snapped a photo of these two full-size bronze moose bulls going at it with their impressive antlers.

Geographic Center of North America, Rugby, North Dakota – This stone obelisk marks the center of our continent, and provides an out-of-the way photo op.

North Dakota Lewis and Clark Interpretive Center, Washburn, North Dakota – Articulate guides walk you through this reproduction of Fort Mandan, where the Corps of Discovery wintered in 1804-05, which itself is quite similar (not surprisingly) to the related though distant exhibit of Fort Clatsop, where the party wintered on the Oregon coast a year later.

North Dakota Lewis and Clark Interpretive Center, Washburn, North Dakota – The two Captains of the expedition discuss their plans to winter in the area with Black Cat, one of the most influential of the local Mandan chiefs.

State Capitol Campus, Bismarck, North Dakota – This bronze statue of Sacagawea carrying her infant son Pomp reminds the visitor that this young Shoshone woman was instrumental to the success of the Corps of Discovery expedition.

State Capitol, Bismarck, North Dakota – This tall structure is one of several skyscraper-like state houses around the country.

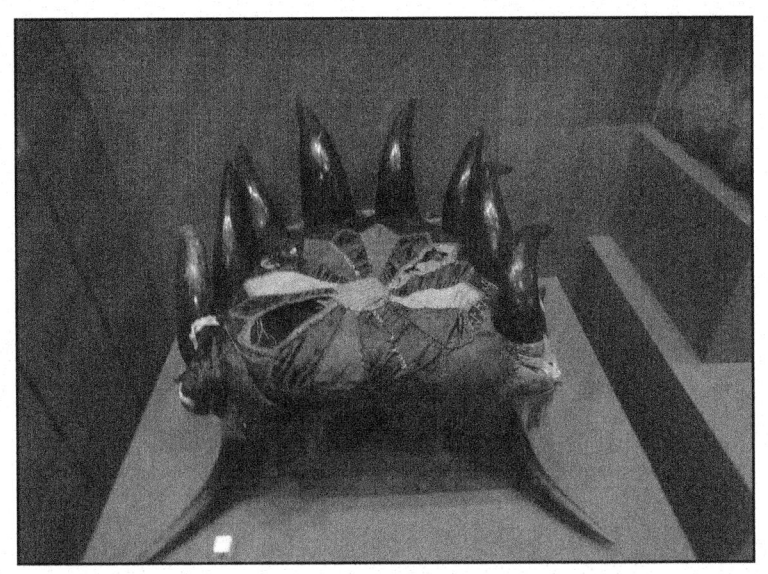

North Dakota Heritage Center, Bismarck, North Dakota – This recently-refurbished state museum contains the first bison-horn chair I have ever seen, a complement to the several steer-horn chairs I have encountered around the country.

North Dakota Heritage Center, Bismarck, North Dakota – This display case of Native American artifacts is just one part of their exhibited collection of such items, an important aspect of the state's past, and present.

North Dakota Heritage Center, Bismarck, North Dakota – What good is a state museum if you don't get to see a dinosaur skeleton, or at least one of an Ice Age North American mastodon?

Theodore Roosevelt National Park, North Dakota – This is the scene of the most fun I've ever had with a herd of bison. The terrain is ruggedly beautiful.

Cathedral of Saint Helena, Helena, Montana – Seeing this majestic edifice in the morning light was one of the spiritual highlights of this trip. (It is open most of the day, and at least as impressive on the inside.)

Curecanti National Recreational Area, Colorado – This structure (the Cimarron Dam) lies at the end of a scenic gorge, in a federal entity that follows the Gunnison River for a considerable distance (including the breathtaking Blue Mesa Reservoir), offering a number of camping facilities for those who enjoy outdoor activities.

Royal Gorge, Canon City, Colorado – The flags of the fifty states fly proudly in the crosswind along this bridge (with pedestrian-only traffic from 7:00 to 10:00 A.M., which allows you to look down to the canyon floor between some of the wooden slats).

Royal Gorge, Canon City, Colorado – While no diminutive photo could do the sight of this gorgeous canyon justice, 1100 feet below the wooden vehicular bridge that traverses it here, I thought the humor of the sign thereon would produce a chuckle or two. (By the way, the N in the name of the location sports an invisible tilda over itself.)

Cheyenne Frontier Days Old West Museum, Cheyenne, Wyoming – The emblematic bucking bronco and rider image of this state is an appropriate outdoor accouterment for this history museum, with a nearby bronze, life-sized twin, of another cowboy riding a bull.

Cheyenne Frontier Days Old West Museum, Cheyenne, Wyoming – This creative and humorous bronze fountain reminds us not to take either good roads or good water for granted on our travels.

Cheyenne Frontier Days Old West Museum, Cheyenne, Wyoming – Yes, this is indeed myself sitting in a photo op carriage inside the museum, thanks to the kindness of one of the workers there. (And yes, that hat is really mine, for hot, sunny days.)

Chimney Rock, Nebraska – This sight offered many travelers on the Oregon Trail hope that, if they arrived there by the Fourth of July, they had a good chance of traversing the Rocky Mountains before the late-fall snows set in.

Courthouse and Jail Rocks, Nebraska – These silent rock icons, as it were, while not so famous today as Chimney Rock, are still visible for a great distance, and almost as striking as their better-known neighbor.

Carhenge, Alliance, Nebraska – This imitation of ancient Stonehenge in England is constructed of actual old cars uniformly painted, and was dedicated on the day of the Summer Solstice in 1987.

Carhenge, Alliance, Nebraska – Would you believe that this classic traversed the entire Oregon Trail in the 1840s?

Corn Palace, Mitchell, South Dakota – The current year's mosaic theme for this unique structure was "Rock of Ages," accounting for the presence of larger-than-life corn-cob representations of musical legends like Elvis and Willy Nelson on the facades.

Corn Palace, Mitchell, South Dakota – One of the many local citizens ready to welcome you to this unique piece of Americana.

Spam Museum, Austin, Minnesota – This distinctive venue was recommended to me by a parishioner before I left, and proved a happy (and tasty) mixture of information and fun.

Nelson Dewey State Park, Cassville, Wisconsin – This mansion of Wisconsin's first governor sits on the bank of the Mississippi River, and is open for guided tours.

Stonefield Historic Site, Cassville, Wisconsin – One of thousands of surviving covered wooden bridges in our country (be they in Madison County or elsewhere), whose roofs helped protect not only travelers from risky crosswinds, but the structures themselves from cumulative weather damage.

CHAPTER 17

50x5: FIVE RECOMMENDED SIGHTS IN EACH STATE

I have presented the idea in this book that, no matter where you live, there is something interesting nearby. True, some places have a higher concentration of such potential travel goals than others, such as, for example, Washington, DC. Still, not every interesting thing in the country needs to be a AAA GEM. If you pay attention to local signs and local conversation, and scour travel books, you will uncover something worth visiting in your neighborhood, some place to take your friends from out of town. In this chapter, I apply this principle to each individual state, presenting five of what I consider to be particularly interesting sights in each one, hoping that they will be of interest to you as well. (Please note that these are not necessarily what I consider the best items in each state [although I think they often are], since sometimes I pick them according to geographic distribution, or according to topical diversity.) Thus, no matter what state you inhabit, a short or medium (for me) drive will take you to a top pick. They are not ranked, but listed in alphabetical order.

[Well, sort of. You see, this chapter started with three picks from each state; but after the list was completed and being revised, I decided to add an honorable mention category as well. Why? Since some places, while small or out of the way, might still be of interest to the general reader. For others, it was the fact that, in a populous state, I had unintentionally ignored a large metropolitan region, like the Bay Area of California. Then too, there are sights I have not seen yet that might be of interest to you, but which are not that well known. Finally, I went through and categorized the entire original list, and tried to add types of sights that were under-represented (like ships, for instance). Then, when I couldn't decide on certain states between two, I decided to add a second honorable mention category, bringing each state's total to five. Don't feel bad if you don't get to all of them in one year (smirk). I've been doing this sort of thing for over three decades, and there are still a handful on the list, as I point out in the descriptions, that even I have not managed to breeze on through yet. At the suggestion of a friend, I include the entry for Washington, DC as well.]

Alabama

Bellingrath Gardens and Home (Theodore) – The word order is intentional, since the gardens existed before the house did. Eventually the Bellingrath couple decided to move out to the grounds on which they had lavished so much care. Even out of season, the gardens are attractive because of such things as diverse types of grasses. They also use the movement of water well to add sight and sound. I was particularly impressed with the extensive Asia Garden. The house itself is a showpiece, and contains (along with a nearby building) Bessie's collections of furniture and porcelain. (While I was waiting for my house tour, I watched the adjacent river while brown pelicans dive-bombed into it for shallow-swimming fish.) Walter made his fortune in Coca-Cola, so the staff weren't too impressed with my unintentionally-worn Pepsi shirt [after all, they make Diet Mountain Dew].)

Birmingham Museum of Art (Birmingham) – I may not have picked the best day to view this collection, since the environmental system was on the blink, which meant that some sensitive pieces needed to be moved off-exhibit for the day. However, what was still on display made the stop well-worthwhile. One area that was not affected, of course, was the attractive sculpture garden. Another welcome surprise was some Dale Chihuly glass. Other highlights for me included collections as diverse as Native American art and Beeson

Wedgwood, not to mention the Japanese kimonos. (And while you're in this steel town, make sure you visit the huge iconic statue of the Roman god Vulcan, visible day and night, with its adjacent tower for viewing both structure and city.)

Carver Museum (Tuskegee) – At this destination, located in the Tuskegee National Historical Site, you will not only come to appreciate how brilliant and hard-working George Washington Carver was, but also get a sense of his personal humility, as if over all those years he was just doing his job, Ma'am. He is best known for goober peas, but is in fact responsible for ground-breaking research into a number of natural products. Anyone who loves peanuts (peanut butter is one of my staples) should visit two places in the country: the Jimmy Carter Home National Historical Site in Plains, GA, and here.

[Honorable Mention: Ave Maria Grotto (Cullman) – Ave Maria means Hail, Mary in Latin, so I'm once again tipping my Catholic hand here. Brother Joseph of Saint Bernard Abbey produced a number of miniatures of famous world buildings on a four-acre plot over five decades, some religious, some secular. I've only seen one other non-professional attempt at something like this in the country, and it wasn't even close to what they have here. What I don't understand is why AAA removed the GEM status from it since I saw it (although I'm trying not to take it personally).]

[Second Honorable Mention: The American Village (Montevallo) – Who says make-believe is only for children? The day I was here I had a delightful one-on-one thirty-minute conversation with George Washington (it was a slow day). Being a native of the City of Brotherly Love, I found this colonial enclave charming. There are several famous American buildings reconstructed here, with others in the works. In the edifice modeled on Mount Vernon, see a full-size reproduction of the Houdin statue of George Washington that stands in the Virginia state house. Stroll through the Liberty Bell Garden (although, unlike on the original, they spell "Pennsylvania" with a double-n) and read all the amendments to the US Constitution, guaranteeing our freedom. Inside one building, relive American history through small dioramas. It's a true feel-good place for Americans and others who cherish liberty. A bonus was the very friendly staff (but what else would you expect in the gracious South?).]

Alaska

Denali National Park – I would say that the tallest point in North America, Mount McKinley, is a must-see, but two out of three days you can't see it because of mist. Still, if you get as far as Alaska you owe it to yourself at least to make the attempt. You can't drive to the mountain, but you can take a shuttle bus past the 14.8-mile paved-road point and considerably farther. I happened to be there on a foggy day, but that's just the roll of the dice. It gives me a reason to go back. (Actually, so do the five National Parks I did not get to see last time: the Last Frontier is hard to tackle.)

Glacier Bay National Park – The visitor center can only be reached by water. However, on the cruise ship, the rangers came to us. It is about 65 miles up the channel before you get to the end, and its two rather different glaciers. If you go at the right time of year (i.e., spring), you will probably see humpbacked whales as well (not to mention the surrounding mountains still covered with snow).

Kenai Fjords National Park – Apart from seasickness on a fast motorboat, this stop was, as it were, a moving experience. You get driven across the water to an actual glacier that is falling into the ocean (if you're lucky you'll get to see the sheet calve, or drop some ice in). The time I was there, we got so close that the boat was completely surrounded by such cubes. On the way there and back, much wildlife was in evidence as well, including mountain goats and bald eagles.

[Honorable Mention: White Pass and Yukon Route (Skagway) – There must be something to do in Alaska outside of a National Park! This sight involves a train ride up to White Pass, which was used by Klondike gold prospectors. The day I showed-up in May, the ground on the coast was clear, but an hour and a half later, the snow alongside the tracks was almost as tall as the top of the train cars. There is some pretty scenery along the way, with accompanying commentary, and even a free snack.]

[Second Honorable Mention: Riverboat Discovery (Fairbanks) – I enjoyed this leisurely cruise down a couple of Alaska's rivers, where the guides pointed out, among other things, the house of a former Alaska governor, and the boat he used for campaigning. The excursion includes a stop at a mock Chena Native American village, to observe such things as fish smoking. The most exciting moments were across from a sled dog compound. The animals knew they were about to be harnessed up, and were excited. You have not lived until you hear the happy simultaneous barking of three dozen motivated canines.]

Arizona

Arizona State Museum (Tucson) – This is the only state museum of which I am aware that sits on a college campus (the University of Arizona). The focus of this sight is the native people who have lived in this state (and nearby northern Mexico) over the centuries, and is a happy fusion of carefully-gathered information (not surprising for a college) with carefully-preserved artifacts, some ancient (like centuries-old pottery), some new (like Navajo weavings).

Desert Botanical Garden (Phoenix) – My grandfather taught me to love cacti, so you can imagine how happy I was to discover 145 acres of them and related species nestled in Papago Park. The day I toured it, I could not at first imagine why I was literally the only visitor there, until it occurred to me that it was the height of summer. Be smart and go in the cooler spring, when you can catch the wildflower-blooming-season as well.

Grand Canyon National Park – If you have only enough time to visit one attraction in the entire country, this is the one to pick. The south rim is the easiest to get to, but the effort you expend to get to any of the three will be amply rewarded. (The west rim, developed by a Native American tribe [the Hualapai], does not fall within the National Park, and so is pricey. True, you can't climb down to the Colorado from there, but you do get to walk onto a clear, high-tech glass floor and look straight down several thousand feet to the canyon floor, an experience you won't soon forget.)

[Honorable Mention: Mission San Xavier del Bac (Tucson) – Not all the missions were along the California coast! This impressive white edifice, which looks like none of the missions in the

Golden State, is still a pristine, functional church after over two centuries. Come to learn its history on the video, and then marvel at the architecture.]

[Second Honorable Mention: Tombstone – My local priest friend took me here, on our way to Coronado National Memorial on the border with Mexico, where there were actually snow flurries that day. Yes, you can visit the historic OK Corral, along with other sites that go back to the day, or tell you about it. If you have ever seen the movie of the same name, one of my top ten film picks of all time, you will want to visit "the town too tough to die."]

Arkansas

Great Passion Play (Eureka Springs) – I'm going out on a limb here, since I have not attended it. Still, the AAA description reminds me of the one I have seen, in Spearfish, SD, which was very impressive. It depicts the final days in the life of Jesus on stage. In addition, the Living Bible Tour presents other Old and New Testament stories. There are also a Bible Museum, a huge Christ-of-the-Ozarks statue, and a Sacred Arts Center. I can't believe I've never been here. It is not far from Branson, Missouri.

Hot Springs National Park – This is the only National Park within an urban setting. The focus of this entity is the series of hot springs bathhouses where even today people can "take the waters." In addition, there is a visitor center, a lookout tower and a Duck Tour (by which I mean being driven around in an amphibious conveyance, which does in fact operate during the tour on land and in more conventional water).

William J. Clinton Presidential Library and Museum (Little Rock) – This museum was, for me, the most informative of all the presidential libraries, with a ton of data on a range of topics from his (their?) presidency. There is also a replica of the cabinet meeting room, and samples of gifts from foreign dignitaries.

[Honorable Mention: Petit Jean State Park (Morrilton) – I was here in the hot and humid summer, so be prepared to sweat if you walk to any of the interesting features of this park. It is a good advertisement for the Natural State, since there are facilities for just about anything you could want to do outdoors, including hiking, camping, fishing and boating.]

[Second Honorable Mention: <u>Fort Smith National Historic Site</u> (Fort Smith) – You might wonder why I would recommend a sight, the best-known aspect of which is a rebuilt gallows (a postcard of which I sent to my western-loving Dad), but this is a good place to learn about the frontier, including frontier justice. True, the fort was involved with the forced removal of Native Americans on the infamous Trail of Tears, but it is important to know the past accurately so that we do not some day unwittingly repeat its less-appealing aspects.]

California

<u>Balboa Park</u> (San Diego) – How can you argue with an attractive campus that offers you a lucky 13 museums (everything from plants to photography), and includes the world-famous San Diego Zoo? But don't miss my favorite part of this complex, the huge cactus garden, large enough to take rambling walks through.

<u>Universal Studios</u> (Los Angeles) – This theme park bills itself as the Entertainment Capital of Los Angeles. With rides of different sorts, characters such as Shrek and the gang and the Simpsons walking around, and an after-hours section of shops and restaurants, you can literally spend all day and evening there. (Sorry, you still need to go to Florida for Harry Potter and Dr. Seuss.)

<u>Yosemite National Park</u> – Just iconic *El Capitan* by itself would be worth the visit, which even appeared in one of the Star Trek movies, and on a US postage stamp. Throw in Half Dome and the Upper Falls, where I discovered snow on the last day of April, and you have a must-see. (Technically it was founded before Yellowstone, but at that time it was not yet a National Park.) Still, given its elevation, it is definitely not a four-season attraction.

[Honorable Mention: <u>SeaWorld</u> (San Diego) – How can you argue with such universally excellent offerings, be they whales, dolphins, sea lions or otters, or even an occasional Clydesdale? You can spend the entire day here and still not experience everything. Indeed, unless you are as intense as I am, you can easily expand it a full two-day excursion. (I just saw a TV commercial for a new interactive exhibit called Turtle Reef {I have a number of carved turtles in my room}, so I guess I'll need to go back and check it out.)]

[Second Honorable Mention: <u>Winchester Mystery House</u> (San Jose) – This is the famous edifice that the Winchester gun heiress kept building her entire life, which accounts for why it contains over 160 rooms. There are several tours, which, admittedly, are a little pricy; still, you are offered a good discount on the combined ticket. (If you are able to find your way out within three hours, you get $10 off your next visit–HA.)]

Colorado

<u>Downtown Aquarium</u> (Denver) – So what's an aquarium doing in the middle of the Rocky Mountains, far from shore? It, among other things, compares and contrasts two rivers, the Colorado in the US, and the Kampar in Indonesia. Then, when you arrive at the end of the exhibit, don't be surprised to find real, live Sumatran tigers, since they are native to the Kampar (and remember, among cats, tigers love to swim).

<u>Mesa Verde National Park</u> – Some of the best-preserved cliff dwellings in the country can be found here. In fact, there are actually guided tours that take you close to the buildings, after passing through rugged scenic beauty along the road within the park. The museum offers a good deal of information about the people who formerly lived there. From here it's not too far a jump to the unique Four Corners.

<u>Pike's Peak</u> – Yes, you can actually drive to the top of Pike's Peak, which affords spectacular views of the surrounding country. Be warned, however: the people who manage it take pride in the fact that there are no guide rails along the winding road that leads to the top. If you plan to get out of your car at the summit, bring something warm, since it tends to be windy and chilly year 'round. (The mother and adult daughter who were there the day I saw it were freezing in shorts and t-shirts. I forget their license plate, but it was probably some place like Florida, a state essentially devoid of cold air and mountains.)

[Honorable Mention: <u>Bent's Old Fort National Historic Site</u> (La Junta) – I visited this jewel near the beginning of my historic tourist investigations, and it really set the bar for what I would be exposed to afterward. The fort is completely reconstructed of original adobe, with various rooms inside appointed with period artifacts. Guides in costume inhabit the old place, and will tell you all about what things were like when it was a center of trade between the white man and the red man. Visit this most attractive and informative place, and then try to explain to me why it is not a GEM.]

[Second Honorable Mention: <u>Air Force Academy</u> (Colorado Springs) – Make sure you have plenty of gas before driving onto this expansive campus, since I almost ran out the day I visited. My priority, of course, was to view the Cadet Chapel, of which I had seen images previously, including on the side of a U-Haul truck. (It is appropriately shaped like a row of jet fighters.) A visitor center stands close by. Entry may be limited by a heightened security level, so call ahead to confirm accessibility.]

Connecticut

<u>Mashantucket Pequot Museum</u> (Ledyard) – If you have any interest in Native American life, I can hardly think of a better museum than this one. It is not only run by the Pequot tribe on its own land, but members of the tribe posed for the life-size dioramas inside, including a large canoe of riders, a wooly mammoth hunt, and an entire village. It's refreshing to get the Indian view about Indian history and life for a change. A large bell tower dominates the site. Then, when you're done touring, the casino awaits. (Allow me to mention for parents that the women in the dioramas are authentically clad in just loincloths.)

<u>Mark Twain House and Museum</u> (Hartford) – See where this American icon and novelist, who gave us Huck Finn and Tom Sawyer, lived during the latter part of his life, including a top-floor pool table that was often covered with the papers of his latest literary project. The guide did stress that in society he was known by his original name, Samuel Clemens. The house itself proves impressive, even apart from its historical value and the Tiffany appointments

inside. While you're there, stop next door and visit his neighbor and fellow author's house, which belonged to Harriet Beecher Stowe, who penned the influential *Uncle Tom's Cabin*.

Mystic Seaport (Mystic) – I first encountered this interesting museum concept in 1978, vacationing with my frat brother. There are not only a number of buildings connected with seafaring in this village, but three ships that can be boarded and toured. If you want to understand life at sea without leaving *terra firma* (at least for too long), this is the place for you. And if that's not enough about the sea, the Mystic Aquarium is right next door.

[Honorable Mention: Yale University (New Haven) – When Bro and I visited New England in 1978, we stopped here briefly. My goal was to spot at least one Ivy League type smoking a pipe; mission accomplished, we moved on to Amherst. I hope you stay longer than we did, particularly to visit the Yale Peabody Museum of Natural History, which I'm sure I would have loved, what with its dinosaur fossils and animal dioramas. For more recent fare, the library actually sports a Gutenberg Bible. Even if you're just passing through, walking the campus is a relaxing way to refresh yourself after several hours of driving.]

[Second Honorable Mention: Hill-Stead Museum (Farmington) – This museum may not feature the same number of paintings as the Athenaeum in nearby Hartford, but its pictures and other objects d'art are well-chosen, and housed in an attractive refurbished mansion. The gardens surrounding the structure represent a bonus, which I viewed while waiting for the place to open (I was actually running early for a change). Nearby is the Stanley-Whitman House, which was being renovated when I was there, alas (although I did get to see the rare pendant drops on the front of the building).]

Delaware

Hagley Museum (Wilmington) – The du Pont name is probably the most famous in Delaware, and this site contains both a family mansion and former gunpowder mills. A walking tour following time spent at the visitor center gives you a good sense of the history of the place. A guided experience of the house completes your visit.

Nemours Mansion and Gardens (Wilmington) – This du Pont estate is as large as anything in Newport, RI, but is much homier. There are plenty of artifacts and appointments inside, but the house, unlike those summer cottages in Rhode Island, is a home, since the actual family of Alfred I. du Pont lived here for years. Follow this visit by a walk or bus ride through the scenic gardens. (Once I saw them I stayed longer than I planned.)

State House (Dover) – This restored 1791 building is not GEMmed, but is part of the most attractive state capitol campus I have ever seen (and I've seen them all). Close to a dozen governmental buildings, all colonial red brick with white trim (what the man on the phone called Georgian Revival), stand in pleasant aesthetic contrast to the green grass and shrubbery of the site. Then right across the street is the Biggs Museum of American Art.

[Honorable Mention: Winterthur Museum and Country Estate (Wilmington) – I left this du Pont sight to the end of the day, and so was not able to take more than one tour of the huge, six-storey house and the historical American artifacts therein, or really do the gardens justice. I hope you take more time when you go, and that you make sure you catch the smaller building brimming with museum-quality soup tureens.]

[Second Honorable Mention: Biggs Museum of American Art (Dover) – This attraction is small but belongs precisely where it is, right off the colonial capitol mall. The sight specializes in vintage American furniture, with some venerable paintings to provide a pleasant contrast. You could describe both the mall and the museum as true Americana.]

District of Columbia

Holocaust Memorial Museum – This museum demonstrates why we at times need to fight wars: to oppose unadulterated evil. It can also be an uncomfortable reminder of groups in our world and even in our country who are the targets of prejudice. If you have time between flights at Dulles and want to see just one Washington sight, tell the cabbie to drop you off here (or take the Metro). As with everything else on the National Mall, it is free.

National Mall – I love just walking around here, even apart from visiting the various buildings that line it. It was designed by Pierre Charles L'Enfant, after whom one of the nearby Metro stops is named. What I can't understand is how AAA has not awarded this federal park GEM status. Come and see if you agree with them, or you agree with me; and then take in a museum or ten.

Washington Monument – George Washington is rightly considered an American legend and icon, and this structure does him justice. You can view it from many places, but come early and procure a complementary ticket to ride to the top. It will give you a (*CW) bird's eye view of the district, after which you can explore its many (*CW) nooks and crannies at your own pace.

[Honorable Mention: Freer Gallery of Art – This small but delightful Smithsonian treasure contains primarily Asian art, although there are selected American works as well. If you desire a few minutes to get away from the bustle of the city, take a seat along the enclosed floral courtyard and simply listen to the fountain (in season).]

[Second Honorable Mention: Madame Tussauds Washington DC – Here the political and non-political movers and shakers are immortalized in wax. The day I visited, the new Rihanna image had just been unveiled. It's fun to see if your favorites like George Washington and the Jonas Brothers (remember them?) have made the cut. They also explain the painstaking work that goes into each celebrity representation, from minute body measurements and individual hair placement, to (at times) procuring actual clothing from the model. (I mention this place, in case you were wondering what to do with your money in DC.)]

Florida

Everglades National Park – You can't think of south Florida without taking this wide, slow-moving river of water-through-grass into consideration. If you contract a boat ride, expect it to be slow, since the driver is trying to protect the even-slower-moving manatees (but that speed will make it more likely that you will see something interesting). The Park will provide you a great introduction, but that does not mean the end of the fun, as Big Cypress National Preserve is right next door.

Saint Augustine – This charming municipality is the oldest permanent European settlement in the United States. Most impressive is the Castillo de San Marcos National Monument, a five-sided fort that looks like it was just built. This small city, with its eight GEMs, offers quite a bit to do, including the Old City, a museum in an old Flagler hotel, a golf museum and hall of fame, and a reptile farm. It reminds me of the Black Hills of South Dakota, without the hills. (The accent, by the way, is on the first syllable.)

Walt Disney World (Lake Buena Vista) – I know, I know, it's almost a cliche. Still, can you really think of a resort anywhere in the country with more things to do, and of such high quality? With four theme parks, two water parks, the Wide World of Sports Complex, the original Downtown Disney, and a raft of hotels for all price ranges, it is the total package. People have been known to spend an entire week here (I did it in four days, staying at the French Quarter hotel, a nice room I saw very little of).

[Honorable Mention: Key West – Key West is a state of mind, a world of its own, the Conch Republic (it tried to secede from the state once, under that name, the flag of which you still espy there occasionally). It is no coincidence that there is a Margaritaville bar and restaurant there, named after a song about a similar sort of world. Unlike Saint Augustine, it only has one GEM (a tour of the island, a good start); but to me Key West has more cohesion. I go to Saint Augustine to see the GEMs, but I go to Key West simply to be in Key West again. The drive to there through the other keys is beautiful if the sun is out, with all that green water. Swimming is warm, and free. If, that is, when you go, stay on the western half of the island, which looks less like the rest of civilization, and where you can walk to everything. If you go once, it won't be the last time.]

[Second Honorable Mention: The Salvador Dali Museum (Saint Petersburg) – I have been to this museum thrice, which presents the art of one of my favorite 20th-century painters. There are a number of docents, each of whom gives a unique tour, as it were, of the art, so do yourself a favor and budget your time for at least a couple. I always liked its old location, right on the water; but have managed easily to see this particular glass as nine-tenths full, viz., the spanking new building in which to see this timeless art, especially his monumental religious subjects.]

Georgia

Fort Pulaski National Monument – Just seeing this impressive structure is worth the trip to suburban Savannah. However, there is a good deal of information available as well, including a video. An important Civil War battle was fought here, in which the powder magazine was exposed by new accurate rifled cannon fire, resulting in the surrender of the fort to avert its total destruction (luckily for us tourists).

Martin Luther King Jr. National Historical Site (Atlanta) – This site encompasses Dr. King's entire life, containing as it does his birth house, the church where he ministered (after his father and grandfather: Ebenezer Baptist), and his grave. The center provides a video and exhibits concerning his life. The day I was there the place was packed with black school children. He is one of two Georgians to have received the Nobel Peace Prize, for his nonviolent approach to racial equality, economic justice and social change. (The other? Jimmy Carter.)

Stone Mountain – This site could with reason be called the Mount Rushmore of the South, not only because Gutzon Borglum worked on it for a while, but also because it depicts three heroes of the War Between the States: Robert E. Lee, Stonewall Jackson, and Jefferson Davis. There is quite a lot to do during the day, such as an old plantation, and a cable car ascending to the top of the mountain; but stay until dark, to catch the impressive laser light show.

[Honorable Mention: Agrirama, The Georgia Museum of Agriculture & Historic Village (Tifton) – I hope your visit here is less dramatic than was mine, given that there were tornado warning sirens going off that morning. That detail kept school groups away, but not me, which meant that I pretty much had the place to myself. This way I could get into uninterrupted conversations with the costumed docents, who explained what life was like on a typical Georgian farm a century ago. There were even men squeezing cane into syrup (non-distilled), which I tasted (perhaps it's an acquired taste, but I'll take maple syrup from Vermont, thanks).]

[Second Honorable Mention: Jekyll Island Historic Landmark District Tour (Golden Isles)–This travel destination has nothing to do with Robert Louis Stevenson, but was rather a winter get-away for the super-rich of their day, making it the Newport of the South. If you want a taste of how the Rockefellers, the Vanderbilts, the Morgans and their ilk lived, take the tour, then (after experiencing the local turtle rescue center) drive north a tad to Rhode Island and compare.]

Hawaii

Hana Highway (Maui Island) – I missed this ride due to time constraints (I could not see it and Haleakala National Park on the same day), but had it recommended to me more than once while there. If it is half as nice as another GEMmed road, the Beartooth Mountain Highway from Montana to Wyoming, it is worth experiencing. Remember, the bus driver executes all the sharp curves and ups-and-downs, leaving you to marvel at the beauty of nature undisturbed. Sure, you can rent a car and drive 3½ hours each way, but do you really want to negotiate over 1200 hairpin turns yourself? (There is also a black sand beach near Hana you might want to check-out.)

Hawaii Volcanoes National Park (Hawaii Island) – This park is on the big island, and encompasses two volcanoes, with one, Kilauea, the most active in the world. You actually get to see the steam-like gas escaping; and I was told that after dark you can view red lava flowing in the distance. I took a special plane from Oahu, which wasn't cheap, but you can simply stay in the town of Hilo as your base of operations to avoid all the tourists at Waikiki.

Pearl Harbor (Oahu Island) – There are four GEMs here, making it an obvious destination. If you have all day (which I did not), you can tour a battleship, a submarine, and an air museum. However, if you only have time for one, take care to see the USS Arizona Memorial, which reminds us of the price it takes from generation to generation to keep our country free.

[Honorable Mention: Bernice Pauahi Bishop Museum (Honolulu, Oahu Island) – This place gives a good historic overview for starting your tour of the islands, with explanations on everything from the local pantheon to volcanic activity. The artifacts that most impressed me were the royal capes, made with thousands of yellow feathers (the guide assured us that the birds from which they were garnered were not harmed in the process). Then strike out from here and see as much of these enchanting islands as you can during your stay.

[Second Honorable Mention: <u>Hawaii State Capitol</u> (Honolulu, Oahu Island) – It is a shame that the bus tour of Honolulu that I took did not involve a full stop at this most distinctive building, but only a drive-by. It is modeled after a volcano, and uses water to represent the ocean that surrounds these islands. If you rent a car for a day the way I did, be sure to make this structure one of your stops.]

Idaho

<u>Craters of the Moon National Monument</u> – If you can imagine the surface of the moon, but in black, you have some idea of what is waiting for you in this park. The result of volcanic action, this stretch of ground is fun to walk on as long as you're not in a hurry, and have good ankle support.

<u>Hells Canyon National Recreation Area</u> – I have driven through part of this site, but the full loop amid this high-to-low canyon area takes several hours to negotiate. Opportunities await for jet boat tours of this magnificent formation as well, with the chance to see the canyon from a crocodile's-eye view. There is only one drawback, which some will consider a blessing: it is truly in the middle of nowhere.

<u>Museum of Idaho</u> (Idaho Falls) – This venue features a limited permanent collection, some of which concerns the Corps of Discovery mission (i.e., Lewis and Clark and York and Sacagawea), some of which concerns nuclear power (an interesting juxtaposition). However, this institution leaves a significant swath of floor space for excellent temporary shows, giving you reason to keep going back. Once I saw a NASA exhibit, another time a presentation on the evolution of dog breeds, a third on the history of the guitar, and a fourth on real pirates. What will be showing when *you* visit?

[Honorable Mention: <u>Discovery Center of Idaho</u> (Boise) – If you seek a happy mixture of fun and learning, which appeals to (*CW) kids of all ages who want a hands-on experience of science, this is the place. (By the way, the locals pronounce it BOY-see, not BOY-zee.)]

[Second Honorable Mention: <u>Sacajawea Interpretive Cultural and Educational Center</u> (Salmon) – If you find yourself in southern Idaho and would like to enjoy a scenic drive through the Bitterroot Mountains, why not head on up to the town of Salmon, and learn about the woman without whom the Corps of Discovery would not have made it out of the Rockies? As providence would have it, Lewis and Clark stumbled onto her old tribe, the Shoshone (she had been kidnapped as a girl and taken east), whose chief was now her brother, so all was well. Her presence in the boat, along with her young son Pomp, also convinced the various Native peoples they encountered that they were not a war party, so all remained well. Come and learn about one of the (*CW) unsung heroines of American history. (By the way, I prefer the Sacagawea spelling, but that's just me {my spell check accepts both}.)]

Illinois

<u>Abraham Lincoln Presidential Library and Museum</u> (Springfield) – This attraction is put together very well visually, with interesting (and in one case entertaining) dioramas, and priceless artifacts. The glasses-less 3-D effect when an historian on stage discusses Lincoln makes it hard to believe that he is only a projected image. It is a great introduction to this American icon, after which you can explore other sites in Springfield concerning him, including his tomb with the large bust by Gutzon Borglum (the Mount Rushmore guy).

<u>Field Museum</u> (Chicago) – There are so many excellent sights to see in the Windy City; still, this natural history museum is in my experience among the best of its kind in the country (some say the world). You could spend half a day there and still not see everything. Then, when you're done, the nearby Shedd Aquarium and Adler Planetarium (a short walk along Lake Michigan), and the Chicago Art Institute (a slightly longer stroll, through Grant Park) await.

Nauvoo – This small town was once the home of the Mormons, and it has been to a large extent restored. In fact, there are two Mormon groups involved, with two visitor centers and two sets of buildings to tour. After spending a day immersing yourself in this history, including seeing the outside of the rebuilt Temple, there is a pageant, a sort of passion play, presented in the evening, concerning the founding of the town, with a number of actors of all ages involved. The price? Everything is free, except for one guided tour, which is a whopping $2.

[Honorable Mention: Cahokia Mounds State Historic Site (Collinsville) – Here you need to use your imagination, since what appears now as a collection of over five dozen Indian mounds once supported a civilization of 20,000 persons, the largest pre-contact site north of the Rio Grande. To help you visualize what you are walking around, the interpretive center offers a film and several tours, plus a life-size re-created Native village. The most striking aspect of my visit, however, since I (typically) arrived there after the center was closed (the mounds were still accessible) was the largest flock of birds I have ever seen, which rolled over in wave after wave scudding west toward the nearby Mississippi.]

[Second Honorable Mention: Brookfield Zoo (Brookfield) – This is one of those zoos that believe that the animals should be more comfortable than the people. Thus, you will need to do a bit of walking to see the place's denizens in their cage-less enclosures, but this way you feel good twice: you know the animals are happy because they are not in old-style pens; and you are happy because you did not need to travel around the world to encounter them all. I was particularly impressed with the hoofed mammal section, among my favorites generally, but that's just one aspect of this excellent collection of fauna. Then, when you're done, you're (*CW) a stone's throw from everything that Chicago has to offer.]

Indiana

Children's Museum of Indianapolis (Indianapolis) – I don't tend to frequent children's museums, but this one was awarded a GEM, so I said, Why not? It turned out to be a delightful couple of hours. The staff made me feel welcome from the first, while I went from creative exhibit to creative exhibit. If you just want to have some (*CW) good old-fashioned fun (after all, the dinosaur outside announces from the start that this is definitely a cool place), no matter what your age, you can do no better than here.

Indianapolis Motor Speedway (Indianapolis) – Who has not heard of the Indianapolis 500, on Memorial Day? The venue is used the rest of the year as well, if only to give fans the chance to tour the museum and see winning cars, and driver info. They even offer the option of taking a bus tour over the huge track itself, including a six-foot strip of bricks along the finish line which commemorates the time when the arena had a track completely paved with them. The place is a must for NASCAR fans (the Brickyard 400 is run here too), but will be of interest to others as well. (The only place in the country comparable for touring is the Daytona International Speedway in Florida.)

Lincoln Boyhood National Memorial – Lincoln was born in Kentucky and worked in Illinois, but spent his youth in southern Indiana. Come see the place where young Abe learned the lessons that would serve him, and America, well in future years. The land is original to the Lincoln farm, although the buildings are all reconstructed. While you're there, take a side trip to nearby Santa Claus, Indiana, and enjoy the Holiday World Theme Park (I've never been there, but it sounds like another Indiana sight, along with the Children's Museum mentioned above, that provides the setting for lots of fun).

[Honorable Mention: College Football Hall of Fame (South Bend) – What better place than the home of the Fighting Irish to house this particular museum? I have been to the nearby Basilica of the Sacred Heart on the campus, with its large relic collection, as well. I love college football (WE ARE ... PENN STATE!), and found that this place proves somewhat different in approach from the Pro Football Hall of Fame in neighboring Ohio, with its A-to-Z collection (26 in all) of multifarious exhibits, many interactive. (Too bad it is currently moving to Atlanta, unaccountably.)]

[Second Honorable Mention: Auburn Cord Duesenberg Automotive Museum (Auburn) – I have passed the sign on the interstate for this museum many times, and, since I like classic cars, made the timing work for me in 2012, on the same day I visited the College Football Hall of Fame. It was certainly worth a stop, especially since these three makes were among the most luxurious cars ever produced. I saw a Deusenberg recently, a real rarity, at the Nethercutt Museum in LA; and here there are several of them. In fact, that's where we get the saying, "That's a real Dusie." They have done a fine job converting an old dealership into this venue, preserving the art deco building in the process. It's a straight shot south off I-80 on I-69; so if you find yourself in northeastern Indiana with a couple of hours on your hands, do what I did last year: take it in.]

Iowa

Bily Clock Museum and Antonin Dvorak Exhibit (Spillville) – You may not be aware that Czech composer Antonin Dvorak of "American Suite" and "From the New World Symphony" fame lived in Iowa for the summer during a period (1892) when he generally resided in New York City, and even filled-in at the small local Catholic church as the organist for daily mass (!), which church, right down the street, is still functional and open to the public. This is the house where he stayed, which contains not only an exhibit about him on the second floor, but an interesting collection of clocks on the first. (He was inspired by local Native American dance rhythms while there, which he tried to incorporate into that well-known symphony, his Ninth.)

Herbert Hoover National Historic Site (West Branch) – This is the first of the mandated presidential libraries. The location encompasses several buildings important to the former president, including his birth house. His ornate tomb is also located on the site. He is generally remembered for being the president when the Great Depression hit, but learn here how much he did for Europe after the two World Wars, and his start as a mining engineer in Australia.

Living History Farms (Urbandale [yes, that really is the name of the Des Moines suburb in which this farm site is located]) – This attraction presents farming in several different years, to show the development of agriculture in Iowa over the past three centuries. It is also the site where Pope John Paul II celebrated mass back in 1979, although I would not take it personally if Pope Francis does not show up to greet you the day you choose to visit.

[Honorable Mention: <u>Des Moines Art Center</u> (Des Moines) – The most impressive work of art here is the structure that houses this excellent collection of modern pieces. Granted, it is not a large museum. Still, it was an enjoyable and educational way to get out of the summer sun after the prolonged Living History Farms experience.]

[Second Honorable Mention: <u>Iowa State Capitol</u> (Des Moines) – I saw this impressive building on a Sunday, with its gold-leaf dome, so I was not able to check it out inside. Still, its four ancillary domes around the main structure make it unique among state houses. On a subsequent drive through I was able to experience the posh inside as well, which seemed to be competing with the mansions in Newport, Rhode Island, what with its 29 kinds of marble throughout. Practically next door is the Iowa State Historical Building, with some interesting artifacts from the state's past, including an authentic Conestoga wagon (which were first designed, I might add, in Pennsylvania).]

Kansas

<u>Kansas Cosmosphere and Space Center</u> (Hutchinson) – This place does a seriously good job with the history of space. Not only is its museum excellent, but it packs some high-end hardware, such as the actual Apollo XIII command module and a full-size replica of a space shuttle. If that's not enough, try an IMAX theater and planetarium. When I was there the hours just flew by (believe it or not, no pun intended). (There is also part of a German wall, although the young woman on the phone subsequently was not sure if it was the Berlin Wall or not [the Munich Wall, perhaps?].)

<u>Rolling Hills Wildlife Adventure</u> (Salina) – One half of this sight is a zoo. It may not be the largest zoo in the country, or even the state, but the species represented are well-chosen. The other half, unique among zoos in my experience, is a collection of animal dioramas, depicting various creatures in natural settings. Since I love both types of presentations, this sight was a natural (sorry) for me. And the animals in the latter section are never hiding out-of-sight in their dens.

University of Kansas (Lawrence) – This college actually sports two GEMs on campus: the Spencer Museum of Art, and the University of Kansas Natural History Museum. I recall that the latter featured one item that grabbed my attention: a beehive of glass (or some clear material), making the many busy insects on the inside visible, while they passed to and fro through a tube connected to the outside. (As it happens, I saw a second, similar one subsequently at the Turtle Bay Discovery Center in Redding, CA.)

[Honorable Mention: State Capitol (Topeka) – This is not only an impressive building on the outside, but features a famous mural inside, of abolitionist John Brown, which picture graces the cover of the first album by the seventies band Kansas, of "Dust in the Wind" fame. There is even a 22-foot statue atop the building of a Native American warrior of the Kansa tribe, with the Latin name *Ad Astra*, reminiscent of the Kansas state motto, "*Ad Astra per Aspera*," meaning that we can reach the stars only by being willing to overcome difficulties, sound wisdom no matter what state or tribe you're from.]

[Second Honorable Mention: Eisenhower Presidential Library and Museum (Abilene)–This sight not only features a museum about Ike, as other presidential libraries do, but his boyhood home and his final resting place as well. Indeed, the location of his and Mamie's internment is named a Place of Meditation, which I think is a nice touch. While you're in town, check out the Greyhound Hall of Fame, from which I sent a post card to friends of mine and their rescued greyhound Belle Vernon, back in the state where this former presidential couple retired (you guessed it: Pennsylvania).]

Kentucky

Abraham Lincoln Birthplace National Historical Park – Illinois likes to claim him, but Honest Abe was in fact born south of the Ohio River. While the actual birth cabin no longer exists, another one has been reconstructed, which itself resides inside a larger memorial building. A video on his early life is offered as well. The site itself stands on the original farm of the Lincoln family at that time.

Kentucky Derby Museum at Churchill Downs (Louisville) – What is more symbolic of the Bluegrass State than the Kentucky

Derby, run on the first Saturday of May? Here you will not only learn everything you ever wanted to know about "the most exciting three minutes in sports," but will be immersed in it through a 360-degree multi-media presentation. If that's not authentic enough for you, you actually can get a walking tour of the world-famous racetrack as well.

Mammoth Cave National Park – As the name implies, this place is huge. It is not that it contains the largest known rooms in caves, but rather that it contains miles and miles of caves. The guide introduced us to the site by having us imagine a cubic foot of space filled with cooked spaghetti, which model gives some idea of just how extensive these caverns are. If you prefer life in the sun, a number of surface hiking trails are also available.

[Honorable Mention: National Corvette Museum (Bowling Green) – You don't need to be a car buff to appreciate the beauty and performance of this American automotive icon. An introductory film explains such questions as why they are called Stingrays. Then there are several dozen of these deceptively attractive beasts on the floor for your perusal. (My only complaint: they wouldn't let me drive one, the way they did in the now-defunct car performance track in Las Vegas {which, admittedly, doesn't do *you* much good}.) Then, when you're done, get back into your own machine and take the Bowling Green Civil War Driving Tour.]

[Second Honorable Mention: Newport Aquarium (Newport) – There is quite a bit to see in this attraction, filled with various marine types, from piranhas to alligators, sharks to poison dart frogs (gee, is everything underwater that dangerous?). When you're done, you can perambulate on the city's Levee complex. (It was there, in a music store, after touring the aquarium, that I bought the classic Offspring album {I know I'm dating myself with that word}, *Smash*, which a couple of teenage guys nearby assured me was "awesome." They were right: about the album, and about the aquarium.)]

Louisiana

Norton Art Gallery (Shreveport) – I don't think I've ever seen such a concentration of phenomenal art per square foot anywhere as in this small (*CW) treasure trove (which may explain why it's the only museum of any sort I have also ever encountered with an armed uniformed local policeman walking the halls). Indeed, the four hours I allotted to experience it was not enough time to enjoy everything. The two Houdin marbles, of Washington and Franklin, are themselves worth the trip to Shreveport. Add the incredible selection of Rodin and Remington bronzes (for some reason the main Russell Gallery was closed, although his watercolor room was impressive), a number of Steuben glass animals, an original double-elephantine set of Audubon's bird books, a small Bierstadt Gallery, a delightful children's area, and a Peter Ellsworth room of monumental nature paintings that (*CW) need to be seen to be believed, and you are about halfway there.

Oak Alley Plantation (Vacherie) – On the day I planned to tour New Orleans on a cross-country drive, a Monday, all the GEMs were closed (any seasoned traveler would have anticipated this eventuality). Thus, after striking-out *in* the Big Easy, I struck-out *to* the northwest and visited old plantations instead. Oak Alley was particular striking because at one point in the house tour, on the second floor, the period-costumed guide opened a door to reveal what is literally an alley of stately live oaks festooned with Spanish moss, a marvelous sight. The informative tour itself helped me to understand the days of the plantations of this state better.

Preservation Hall (New Orleans) – This hole in the wall is the home base of the world-renowned Preservation Hall Jazz Band. I had seen this Dixieland-style ensemble twice in other cities on tour (they feature more than one band) before finally hearing them on their home turf. The building is not air-conditioned, they only accept cash, there are no reservations (so that you need to stand in line), and less than half the people who get in get seats (which are wooden benches anyway). So why go through all that hassle? Because the music is that good, and you are never more than 25 feet away from the band (and if you stay for more than one of the three different nightly sets, you can usually grab a bench vacated by some tourist who didn't really appreciate what he or she just heard). You can find it, of course, in the French Quarter, off Bourbon Street.

[Honorable Mention: Jungle Gardens (Avery Island) – Some of you may recognize the name Avery Island from bottles of McIlhenny

Tabasco Sauce. This is where it comes from, and you are able to take a rare post-9/11 food factory tour of the place and visit their museum. However, even more impressive, at the right time of year, is espying thousands of [Department of Redundancy Department] white snowy egrets (I got lucky).]

[Second Honorable Mention: <u>Longfellow-Evangeline State Historic Site</u> (St. Martinville) – You are now in the heart of French Acadian Louisiana, a word since transformed into the familiar epithet "Cajun." Henry Wadsworth Longfellow penned a poem about the removal of the Acadians from Nova Scotia (formerly called Acadia), by the English, and to this day they maintain many of their former customs down here. This sight will provide you a good introduction to the history and charm of the area. Afterward, make sure you take-in the nearby, historically-significant, eponymous St. Martin de Tours Catholic Church (Tours in this case being an ancient French city, not a travel concept).]

Maine

<u>Acadia National Park</u> – This Park contains the only authentic fjords on the east coast of our country. Several overlooks afford spectacular views of both the land and the water, and how they interact. I was fortunate enough to arrive at the top of Cadillac Mountain just at sunset, where that heavenly body turned the place into a wonderland. Then, after dark, there are plenty of restaurants in the general area that serve lobster. (If you get to Thunder Hole, so I am told, when the tide is right, you will discover why it has earned that name.) There are few full National Parks east of the Mississippi, and this is the only one in New England.

<u>Maine Maritime Museum</u> (Bath) – Maine's heritage is inextricably tied to sailing, and this museum presents that relationship over the generations. You may even find someone working on a sloop while you're there (the John B. or otherwise). One fun aspect of the place is its lobster section, sponsored by the legendary L. L. Bean, whose flagship store you can visit in Freeport, where you may actually catch and release fish indoors (I remember visiting it with my priest-friend in 1985, when it was this mail-order company's *only*

retail store). A building tour and cruise are also available in season (I was apparently there out of season, or in a hurry, or got there late, or was in one of my cheap stages, unfortunately). The name has great alliteration too.

Mount Katahdin (Baxter State Park) – At 5268 feet, this is the highest point in Maine, a solitary mountain towering over the surrounding countryside. It took my friend and me 10½ hours to climb to the top and down (in August rather than June, which meant that we arrived back in the dark), along a trail originally blazed by none other than Theodore Roosevelt. That night we tented at a local primitive campsite, and needed to chase two bears away from our food. A local ranger advised throwing rocks at them, but we were satisfied with yelling and banging metal pots until they got bored and left.

[Honorable Mention: Cole Land Transportation Museum (Bangor) – I've seen buildings full of antique cars, but nothing quite like this large edifice packed with everything from horse-drawn wagons (*sans* horses) to rigs, over 200 in all, plus an authentic covered bridge for atmosphere. If that's not enough for you, there is a collection of military memorabilia as well.]

[Second Honorable Mention: Victoria Mansion (Portland) – It must be in the name, because both this brownstone mansion in Portland, Maine, and the Oregon Historical Society building in the other Portland, sport *trompe l'oeil* effects (i.e., a two-dimensional piece made cleverly to look three-dimensional), the former on the inside, the latter on the outside. This urban villa also contains impressive stained glass, and such hotel-esque appointments as you would expect in a house designed for an ostler. The day I was there, the affable guide, noting our interest, extended the tour an extra half hour. Too bad that made me late for an appointment (I didn't wear a watch or a Fitbit in those days, or carry a phone), but it was enjoyable to see someone so excited and knowledgeable about what he was discussing.]

Maryland

Antietam National Battlefield – This important battle was called Antietam (after Antietam Creek) by the North (who tended to name battles after the local body of water), and Sharpsburg by the South (who tended to name battles after the closest town). It has the dubious distinction of being the bloodiest military encounter of the Civil War. Come take a driving tour of this important plot of ground, and learn why the victory here was crucial for the North.

Baltimore and Ohio Railroad Museum (Baltimore) – This sight is one of the best railroad museums in the country. Besides having a building that presents not only history but railroad miniatures, they display a large collection of old steam engines as well. However, as far as I am concerned, the centerpiece of this site is its wooden roundhouse, an architectural work of art, which impressed me both inside and out.

Chesapeake Bay Maritime Museum (St. Michael's) – The Chesapeake Bay is central to the Old Line State, not only geographically but economically as well; and this museum explains the history of this body of water, and how humans have navigated and harvested it over the centuries. It is certainly out of the way, but the goal is worth the search. While you're there, make sure you stop at a local restaurant for genuine Maryland crab cakes.

[Honorable Mention: National Aquarium in Baltimore (Baltimore) – (This is as opposed to the National Aquarium in DC, a small affair {by way of reminder} in the basement of the Department of Commerce Building.) I visited on a reduced-admission Friday evening, which meant that about half of Baltimore was gathered inside with me. However, after a tight initial run-thought, I took a second, more leisurely stroll after the crowd thinned, along the five floors of aquatic animals. I even enjoyed their half-hour dolphin show, which exhibited the relaxed sort of atmosphere for the animals that I associate with the Dolphin Research Center in the Florida Keys. Other highlights include a Kelp Forest; a requisite megaladon jaw; a life-size model of a breaching humpback whale; and several interesting videos on marine mammals, including the rare walrus.]

[Second Honorable Mention: Ward Museum of Wildfowl Art (Salisbury) – This specialized museum offers more than just duck decoys, although it showcases plenty of those as well. Some of the people who carve such items decided that there was nothing wrong with moving from functionality to art, and the results of this evolution are presented for your consideration and enjoyment. When you are finished with the copies, take a walk around the pond to see if you can spot (*CW) the real McCoys.]

Massachusetts

Lexington – When my frat brother and I did Boston in 1978, we visited Concord but by-passed this town because of timing. I took a personal evening tour many years later in the rain, trying to imbibe the spirit that sparked patriotism in the Thirteeen Colonies. Most everything is centered on an isosceles triangle of grass known as the Battle Green, with its iconic bronze citizen-soldier prepared to defend his own. It was kind of a magical evening for me, but I recommend that you do yourself a favor and go during the day, when the buildings are actually open. At least it is well-lit at night (unlike nearby Concord, which is also worth a daytime stop).

Norman Rockwell Museum (Stockbridge) – Here's an American icon of a different sort, the artist and illustrator Normal Rockwell. I suppose I can tolerate his museum being in the Bay State, even though he is best-known for his work on the Philadelphian publication, *The Saturday Evening Post*. Of particular interest to me was the room in which the "Four Freedoms" were housed in the four corners. The museum even contains his original studio. I remember getting there the same time as a bus-load of Japanese tourists did, making the place rather cramped for being so geographically isolated (still, I'm always happy to see other people traveling, especially folks from overseas who want to experience America). Nearby in the same town is the National Shrine of the Divine Mercy.

Plymouth Rock (Plymouth) – This is the iconic (another one) stone on which the Pilgrims disembarked from the Mayflower in 1620. It is estimated that about one-third of the original rock is left (it is now safely out of reach of souvenir-seekers). Like the Liberty Bell and the Alamo, there may not be a ton to do here, but it is a place to make your own personal pilgrimage. Then, while you're there, you can tour the rest of the delightful village of Plymouth. (Curiously, although I saw it in 1978, I went again years later and checked-out the town [you guessed it] at night. I also took their Colonial Lantern Tours-sponsored Ghosts & Legends Tour. Perhaps I'm part vampire.)

[Honorable Mention: <u>Battleship Cove</u> (Fall River) – This is one of the few places in the country where you can wander through a decommissioned battleship, specifically (and appropriately) the *USS Massachusetts*. If that's not enough fun for one day, there are other vessels waiting nearby for your touring pleasure, including a destroyer (a tin can in Navy parlance), two PT boats (Kennedy sailed on PT-109 until it was sunk), and even a submarine. I'm not sure I experienced all of them, given my rush to see the whaling museum in nearby New Bedford in my younger days, but make sure you stay and get your money's worth.]

[Second Honorable Mention: <u>Faneuil Hall</u> (Boston) –How could I pass over this important eighteenth-century building? Here there are not only portraits and other ancient appurtenances of the era: the day I visited, the main room was filled with tourists, while on stage a costumed man was conducting the equivalent of a town hall meeting, with certain of the out-of-staters doubling as actors and reading statements that supported either the king or the colony, with the rest of us providing appropriate cheers or boos. Where else are you going to enter into history in this way, and for free? And this is only a tiny taste of what this historical town has to offer.]

Michigan

<u>Fort Mackinac</u> (Mackinac Island) – It is pronounced "mackinaw" by the locals. The whole area of Mackinaw City (yes, it's spelled differently, just to confuse the rest of us) is worth seeing, but start here. The restored original buildings offer insight into life in northern Michigan two centuries ago. Costumed actors add to the sense of realism. (Try to avoid Labor Day, the occasion of the annual walk across the bridge connecting it to the UP [i.e., Upper Peninsula], when they close the bridge all morning, making vehicular travel in town difficult, and across the strait impossible [I know of which I speak].) When you're finished, you can explore another fort at nearby Colonial Michilimackinac, and then explore

a working water-powered sawmill and go zip-line riding at neighboring Historic Mill Creek Discovery Park (you're never too old to try something new).

Frederik Meijer Gardens and Sculpture Park (Grand Rapids) – The gardens alone would be worth the visit, and the sculpture alone would be worth the visit. Add the newly-installed Dale Chihuly monumental glass and you have a must-see.

The Henry Ford (Dearborn) – Do you think a high-tech factory tour, a huge, diverse museum, and a village of over 100 historic buildings will keep you busy for a while? It took me all morning and afternoon, and I only saw some of what there is to experience (they recommend two days to do it all).

[Honorable Mention: Soo Locks Boat Tours (Sault Ste. Marie) – Here you not only get to see working boat locks: you get to sail through them, as well as view other aspects of the waterway as well. If you save this sight until the end of your touring day, you can enjoy the relaxing dinner cruise. It's one of the many things that the UP has to offer you; and in this case you don't even need a passport to see Canada.]

[Second Honorable Mention: Motown Historical Museum (Detroit) – After I got home from Michigan in 2010, a friend asked me if I had seen the Motown museum, and I, with a red face that could be sensed even through the phone lines, had to admit that I had not. I had not avoided it: I just forgot about it in the rush of touring, since it is not a GEM. I have since remedied that omission, discovering a most informative tour of Studio A, where many of the tunes we know and love were forged.]

Minnesota

Grand Portage National Monument – I don't know why this site is not a GEM. I spent an entire day there waiting for Lake Superior to settle down so I could take the ferry to Isle Royale National Park, and I did not run out of things to do. A museum inside and costumed docents outside helped the voyageur lifestyle come alive for me. (More on this in Voyageurs National Park in the same state to the west, in the boundary waters with Canada, as mentioned above.) All this for $3 (or it would have been, had I not had my National Parks annual pass). (My only complaint was the summer black flies, which enjoyed munching on me most of the day.)

Minnesota State Capitol (Saint Paul) – Designed by the same man who gave West Virginia its own impressive capitol, Cass Gilbert, this building boasts one of the tallest marble domes in the world. I was fortunate enough, the day I visited it, to run into a free Fourth of July outdoor concert featuring eighties new wave band Blondie (the rain did not [*CW] dampen my spirits, especially when Chubby Checker made a stage appearance; but unfortunately it spelled the cancellation of the fireworks. [While I recommend a visit to this site, I cannot guarantee that Debbie Harry will be waiting to entertain you.])

Pipestone National Monument – Pipestone, also called calumet, was and is very precious to Native Americans, so much so that there was a general truce whenever any person or tribe came to this site to mine for this red material, from which peace pipes were made. After an orientation, you can walk to the actual areas that continue to yield it. They even sell crafts made from it in the gift shop (I bought a turtle, which I consider a sacred object).

[Honorable Mention: Great Lakes Aquarium (Duluth) – For a building full of water, this venue has a large number of interactive exhibits (but no, you can't go swimming with the fish). It also affords an excellent view of Lake Superior. What struck me most, on a day I was running behind and arrived there later than I planned (so what else is new?), was that, after closing time, they allowed visitors to stay pretty much as long as they liked, to make sure they saw everything. When I finally left I noted still other tourists inside.]

[Second Honorable Mention: Soudan Underground Mine State Park (Soudan) – It's not every day that you get to ride down into the earth half a mile, but that is exactly what awaits you at this former iron ore mine. If you want to know what you car looked like before the smelting process, come and take the tour. For all you fellow sciencoids out there: it houses a nuclear lab tour as well. (An incentive for a visit in winter is that the mine maintains a constant temperature of 50 degrees, positively balmy for the North Star State at that time of year; or for the summer, since it gets surprisingly hot up there, a meteorological fact that local sage Garrison Keillor opines just doesn't seem fair.)]

Mississippi

Elvis Presley Birthplace and Museum (Tupelo) – See the birth house of the King of Rock and Roll, along with a museum of personal artifacts. There is even a chapel on the grounds, which plays his religious music continually (his three Grammies are all for Gospel songs). When I was there they had just dedicated a statue of Elvis as a teenager, guitar slung over his back, as he was about to move to Memphis and into musical immortality.

Mississippi Sports Hall of Fame (Jackson) – This museum is done very well, making local athletes come alive for people visiting from other states. Believe it or not, it was here that I first heard of Bret Favre. (I had heard of baseball's Dizzy Dean before, but did not know that he hailed from the Magnolia State.)

Vicksburg National Military Park – Here is the most impressive battlefield I have seen in the South. Of course I just had to visit it during a heat wave in June of 1986, with the air conditioning off during the slow driving tour so as not to overheat the car (be smart: splurge, and take the park bus). Much from the time of the battle has been recreated to make the appearance realistic. This Union victory occurred at the same time as Gettysburg, and marked a significant shift in the war, although the carnage continued for two more years. If you get a chance to see only one battlefield south of the Mason-Dixon Line, this is the one to experience.

[Honorable Mention: Rowan Oak (Oxford) – This house, near the campus of the University of Mississippi, was the home of American novelist and Nobel Laureate William Faulkner. The day I made the pilgrimage, it was closed for refurbishment, so I only got to view the outside (like my experience of novelist Sinclair Lewis's house in Sauk Centre, Minnesota, since I arrived after hours {what a surprise}). After you tour the building, walk down the street and take a ramble across the campus of Ole Miss.]

[Second Honorable Mention: Natchez Trace Parkway – This road, which runs diagonally across the state from southwest to northeast, brings together both history and nature. It may not be so fast as an interstate to get you where you're going, but here the highway becomes the destination, with attractive scenery joined with items explaining the past.]

Missouri

Branson – This destination was indirectly featured in the 2010 Pennsylvania film, *I'm Not in Her League*. I arrived at the location once when I was on the way elsewhere and drove around, but it was off-season (January), and so I discovered a ghost town. In addition to 40 theaters with world-class entertainment, five GEMs are situated nearby. Admittedly, a week there could cost a few bucks, but you would certainly not be bored. It is one of my make-sure-you-go-back-and-do-it-right places. (True, I did get to several GEMs since then, but still need to do the theater thing.)

Forest Park (Saint Louis) – It's hard to argue with a single plot of land that contains four GEMs. No matter what you like, there is something for you here: art, science, history and animals, plus a non-GEM that features flowers. I don't usually like to present two sights from the same city, but there it is.

Gateway Arch (Saint Louis) – This is quite simply a necessary stop of American touring. Recall that Saint Louis was once called the Gateway to the West, as with the pioneers on the Oregon Trail on their way to jump-off point Independence in the 1840s (not to mention the Corps of Discovery in 1804). In fact, it's not enough to see it (which you can do from the interstate): you need to ride up to the top. They day I did so I was one of three Americans surrounded by a busload of Japanese tourists, God bless them (come anytime and bring those yen). I mean, if people from Japan take the trouble to see America, shouldn't we Americans?

[Honorable Mention: Mark Twain Boyhood Home and Museum (Hannibal) – There's a good bit to see here in addition to the actual boyhood residence (there are actually two technically, as you will find out when you tour here), such as other buildings that inspired aspects of Twain's fiction. Of particular interest to art lovers such as myself are 16 oil paintings by Norman Rockwell, used to illustrate two of Twain's books, in the non-original museum. When you're done, jump in the car and drive to where he retired, in Hartford, Connecticut.]

[Second Honorable Mention: The National Museum of Toys and Miniatures (Kansas City) – Kids will love this place, and so will you. After all, who can't have fun in a venue with over 100 doll houses, over a million marbles (some of which you are allowed to play with), and 38 rooms, each devoted to a particular type of toy (nice alliteration)? Maybe if you take the kids here, they won't complain so loudly when you suggest stopping at the nearby World War I museum.]

Montana

Cathedral of Saint Helena (Helena) – It was hard to pick a sight for Helena, since three are particularly impressive, including the capitol (one of the nicest in the country) and the Gates of the Mountains Recreational Area. However, this is the most impressive traditional Catholic cathedral that I have seen in the country. The stained glass is exceptional, and the inner pillars lend the worship space a majestic touch. I toured it in 1993, and so do not remember the outdoor statue garden of famous people (which gives me a reason to go back). (I did go back in 2016, took lots of photos of the church, and drove several dozen miles before I remembered the statue garden. Oh well ...)

C. M. Russell Museum (Great Falls) – Charles Marion Russell ranks with Frederick Remington as one of the possibly two most notable Western artists in our history (certainly sculptors). This museum does his creative contribution justice, by offering, in several galleries, his life's work, as well as other representatives of the genre. The last time I was there, I enjoyed an interesting temporary exhibit on the American bison (or, if you prefer, buffalo). As an added bonus, you can view his studio and house, both preserved on the museum grounds.

Glacier National Park – I consider this National Park the most beautiful in the NPS. The centerpiece of this area is Going-to-the-Sun Road, which is closed most of the year because of unimaginable snowfall. The scenery is absolutely gorgeous. You may even run into some wildlife, as I did the last time I was there: a mountain goat mother and baby feeding right next to the road. To the north is Waterton Lakes National Park, Alberta, together forming an International Peace Park with our close neighbor.

[Honorable Mention: Fort Peck Dam and Power Plant Museum (Fort Peck) – This large Depression-era earth-filled dam on the Missouri River still offers guided tours post-9/11. After spending time in the museum, you are taken on a walk-through of the power-house, the high point of which for me involved the unique experience of touching an actual turbine while it was spinning. Then the large lake is available for all sorts of outdoor activities. Just be prepared for a long drive, wherever you start.]

[Second Honorable Mention: Beartooth Scenic Highway (Red Lodge) – I was in Montana in June one year, and thought I'd take this road into Yellowstone (I had driven it in the past *from* Yellowstone, but some people say it's nicer the other way, although in the end it was [*CW] six of one and half a dozen of the other to me). There was a notice along the road in the town of Red Lodge that indicated that the highway was still closed because of snow, but I assumed that someone had forgotten to change the sign. Incorrecto. I got all the way up to the Wyoming state line, only to find a closed gate across the road and a ton of snow on the other side, with people playing in it. Rats! A month later I came back, and it was finally open. My point? Be smart and call ahead, or at least believe the sign (the snow was admittedly late that year). But if you want to pass through lots of beautiful snow-producing mountains after the snows have melted, and cross a pass over 10,000 feet, this is the drive for you. Then, when you're done, you can pick up the Chief Joseph Highway in Wyoming and take it to Cody, and its excellent museum complex.]

Nebraska

Chimney Rock National Historic Site – This landmark was an important stop on the Oregon Trail, since arrival there before July Fourth meant that the party would probably get across the Rockies before the snows set in. There is a spanking-new visitor center to it, one of those American spots you like to have seen at some point in your travels. Tourists who want more information can also stop by the nearby Scott's Bluff National Monument visitor center. (And for you latter-day late arrivals: the rock is lit most of the evening.) (Independence Rock, Wyoming, SSW of Casper, claims to be the Fourth of July marker as well, so they can duke it out, while you visit both and make your own decision. At least you get to climb on the latter.)

Strategic Air and Space Museum (Ashland) – This is one of the best museums of its kind in the country. I recall having a thoroughly enjoyable, in-depth tour by one of the docents, a former World War II air force pilot. Inside, they feature plenty of hardware to satisfy even the biggest airplane buff, including an actual SR-71 Blackbird, my first, itself worth the price of admission.

Stuhr Museum of the Prairie Pioneer: A Living History Experience (Grand Island) – This complex contains several different types of farming approaches from the past two centuries, which helps the viewer (well, walker) to understand better the development of horticulture in this very agricultural state. Native American and Western items are also displayed.

[Honorable Mention: Nebraska State Capitol (Lincoln) – If you asked me on the way into town, "Which is the only state to have a unicameral legislature?" I would have answered, Nebraska. So why, on the inside of this classic skyscraper-like building, did I ask a guide where the two chambers were? (he gently corrected me). What struck me the most, apart from my ignorance, was the statue of Abraham Lincoln outside, by Daniel Chester French, who also crafted the one in the Lincoln Memorial in DC. As a bonus, the Supreme Court meets in there as well.]

[Second Honorable Mention: Golden Spike Tower and Visitor Center (North Platte) – No, this is not the true albeit secret home of the famous Golden Spike that joined the two halves of the first intercontinental railroad, although that is its inspiration, since it overlooks one of the largest rail yards in the world, which does join east and west America by processing 15,000 train cars each day. The tower, which was originally going to look like a golden spike, gives a spectacular view of this facility, as well as the nearby Platte River. It's a quick on/off from I-80 if you happen to be passing by. A short talk orients you before your ride up the elevator.]

Nevada

Great Basin National Park – The Great Basin is one of the four deserts in the contiguous 48 states, and this National Park is a good introduction. I remember hiking to the edge of a small glacier (yes, in a desert). As a bonus, this Park, truly (*CW) in the middle of nowhere, offers a tour of Lehman Caves, so you really get two for the price of, well, two (but it gets you out of the sun for a while in a constant temp of 50 degrees). Still, the bristlecone pine forest is free, and contains some of the oldest trees in the world (but no, you can't cut one down and count the rings).

Liberace Foundation and Museum (Las Vegas) – My mother and I visited this museum while it was expanding, so we saw most of it, except for the classic cars. If you want a really good example of Las Vegas glitz at its height, come and see the costumes, furniture and pianos that made Liberace a household name. (Then, if you want some local natural glitz, Valley of Fire State Park beckons an hour away, with surreal red rock formations.) [The Web mentions now that this venue is currently closed, although the state park remains open.]

National Automobile Museum (Reno) – This place is just about the best car museum in the country, both for what it contains and how it is displayed. Of course, I got lucky: one of the owners was pinch-hitting for a sick guide, and gave a free tour that lasted almost three hours (no, his name was not Gilligan), exhibiting his vast knowledge of the autos along with his passion for them. A highlight is the only car ever to finish an around-the-world auto race (!).

[Honorable Mention: Nevada State Museum (Carson City) – Numismaticists will enjoy knowing that they are touring the old US Mint building, from the days when they were pulling silver out of the ground (*CW) hand over fist. Everyone else will stay because of the excellent exhibits in this newly refurbished site, featuring everything from woolly mammoths to Lahontan cutthroat trout (they are, I believe, native to the poker tables). While you're in town, catch the unique silver dome atop the state capitol.

[Second Honorable Mention: Hoover Dam – This is my favorite dam in the country, not only because of its reddish adobe color, but because what it lacks in breadth, in makes up in depth (reminding me of some of my more spiritual friends). National politics had the title of this structure rechristened Boulder Dam, so as not to be named after a Republican, but the US Congress later restored its original appellation. (Nearby Boulder City, by the way, is the only municipality I am aware of in Nevada that forbids gambling, a ban going back to the Depression days, so that the men working on the dam would not spend their paychecks each week at the poker and crap tables.) The highway between Nevada and Arizona now bypasses the dam itself, a response to 9/11; still, more than one tour of the largest mass of concrete in the world is still offered, including a hardhat version.

New Hampshire

Canterbury Shaker Village (Canterbury) – This is not the Canterbury that Chaucer wrote about. That lame joke is a way of covering the fact that I do not remember if I have actually toured here or not. I have been to a rebuilt Shaker village *somewhere*, and on the strength of that experience will recommend this one, since it contains 25 original buildings. These are the folks who brought you Fels Naphtha and the flat broom, a religious community of celibates who lived like a Catholic religious order. They are no longer a movement, but their handiwork, such as chairs and tables, resides today in museums across the country, pieces that have outlived the movement that spawned them.

Kancamagus Highway (White Mountains) – This scenic drive took a friend and me across the southern half of White Mountain National Forest in 1985, including the 2890-foot, aptly-named Kancamagus Pass. Rand-McNally also indicates several state parks along the route, allowing you to establish a base of operations for your own preferred outdoor activities. Among these, AAA recommends, besides overlooks, Rocky Gorge Scenic Area and Sabbaday Falls. Whatever you choose, you are up for some beautiful country, especially in the autumn.

Saint-Gaudens National Historic Site (Cornish) – Auguste Saint-Gaudens was a noted sculptor, whose best-known work (besides perhaps a US coin, the double eagle [a $20 gold piece]) is the Shaw

Memorial, of that premier Civil War Northern black unit, the 54th regiment. Ancient buildings house various works of the artist, although what struck me most was the bronze of Clover Adams (who had committed suicide), outside in the attractive formal gardens, which the archivist years later insisted over the phone was never in New Hampshire, but in Rock Creek Park, in Washington, DC, providing yet another reason to visit the District (well, at least I've narrowed the piece down to two possible locations). It was misty the day I was there (in more ways than one), which lent the grounds a pleasant atmospheric touch. (I have since encountered yet another casting of that poignant piece in the National Museum of American Art of the Smithsonian, so there.)

[Honorable Mention: Old Man in the Mountain (Franconia Notch) – I was greatly saddened when this well-known New Hampshire icon fell to pieces in 2003. If you viewed this rock formation from a certain angle, it appeared to be a bearded man. If you want to know today what it looked like, just glance at a New Hampshire license plate, or a state route sign. You can still go to the former visitor site and view a display of what it used to look like, what happened, and what it looks like now. Some people might wonder what the point is of mentioning a sight that no longer exists, but it was without doubt the best-known attraction in the state. (Franconia Notch is for that reason the best-known of the four main notches, or passes, that you can find in New Hampshire through the White Mountains, all of which still provide attractive scenery, and plenty of opportunity for various outdoor activities.)]

[Second Honorable Mention: Mount Washington Cog Railway (Bretton Woods) – My friend and I looked up at Mount Washington, the tallest point in New England, but passed on the cog railway, given the price. If you go for it, there is also a museum at the base included in the price. (Not recommended in winter: the strongest sustained winds in the world have been clocked at the summit.) Now you history types may recognize the name of the town as the place of the International Monetary Conference during World War II. We descried the luxurious Bretton Woods Hotel, but did not stop in to see their museum either. (Gee whiz! Then what's the point of traveling?)]

New Jersey

Grounds for Sculpture (Hamilton, Mercer County) – If you want a relaxing stroll through some well-manicured acres, replete with nature-made and human-made beauty, this is the place for you. It is one of the two best sculpture gardens I have ever seen, so it is probably no coincidence that it lies in the Garden State. (If it rains, there are things to enjoy under roof as well.)

Six Flags Great Adventure (Jackson) – I remember it when it was just Great Adventure. It was great then, but it seems to have gotten even better, with not only a national-class amusement park, but also a water park and a wild animal drive-through section. (When I was there in the 1970s they used to warn drivers with then-trendy vinyl roofs to watch out for the monkeys, since they liked to munch on them.)

Statue of Liberty (Jersey City) – Thanks to the United States Supreme Court, we now know that this American icon, a gift from France, resides in this former colony. You can view it for free, but if you want to get up-close-and-personal with it, take the ferry across to Liberty Island and climb to the top for a great view. Just recalling how many postage stamps this figure has graced indicates just how deeply we Americans value freedom. So come to New Jersey (or New York), gaze on the statue, and get a lump in your throat.

[Honorable Mention: The Wildwoods-by-the-Sea – What would this list be without mentioning the world-famous white sand of the Jersey shore? Before our family discovered the quiet residential seaside community of Brigantine, just north of Atlantic City, we used to vacation in the summer in Wildwood, sandwiched between North Wildwood and Wildwood Crest. It was said that whole neighborhoods from Philadelphia would transplant themselves to one of these three vacation enclaves. (So what was the point of leaving? It beat swimming in the Delaware River.) If you can do it in the water, you can do it in Wildwood. Then, when the fun in the sun is done (sorry), explore the extensive boardwalk, with several perpendicular piers devoted to rides and games. Make sure you eat at Mack's Pizza, the best I ever tasted. And don't be surprised if you end-up hearing the sentence, "Watch the tram car, please," in your sleep.]

[Second Honorable Mention: New Jersey State Museum (Trenton) – The year I saw this venue it was undergoing refurbishment, so that not everything was accessible. What struck me most forcibly were the actual (not casts) dinosaur eggs, the only time I have ever seen the like. There is also an example of what used to come out of dinosaur eggs, along with lots of Native American artifacts and a model of a mine. But why limit yourself to earth? Take in the planetarium show and reach for the stars. Or is that light a reflection from the gold dome of the New Jersey State House next door? History buffs will then want to enjoy the nearby Old Barracks Museum, complete with costumed docents, and muskets being fired.]

New Mexico

Anderson-Abruzzo Albuquerque International Balloon Museum (Albuquerque) – Learn anything you ever wanted to know about ballooning, from its history, to its varied uses, to how the latest mechanisms work. A treat for lovers of color is a large room displaying a number of actual non-inflated balloons. Come in early October and you get to watch them in action during the GEMmed Albuquerque International Balloon Fiesta.

Carlsbad Caverns National Park – I've been to many cave sights around the country, but this one impressed me the most. If you're lucky (or smart) and stay until evening, you can watch the bats emerge from the cavern *en masse*. It is close to Guadalupe Mountains National Park in Texas (if it is near anything).

Cumbres & Toltec Scenic Railroad (Chama) – This narrow-gauge railway travels terrain impassable to cars between New Mexico and Colorado. The full-day excursion involves a meal included in the price of the ticket. I visited when the aspen leaves were just starting to change to gold, but missed them at their height. An interpreter supplies regular information about what the locomotive is passing. The scenery, even outside of autumn, is beautiful, and you may occasionally observe wildlife. A bus brings you back to your car, whichever side you started on (by a different route, of course).

[Honorable Mention: El Sanctuario de Chimayo (Chimayo) – What else would you expect from a priest, since this site is a copy of the second-most-visited religious shrine in Mexico? Actually, this small building is known for physical cures, and the walls are lined with crutches and other items abandoned by people healed on the spot over the years. The nearby parish church displays huge strings of local peppers in the sanctuary, reflecting the area as the Chili Capital of the World. It is close to the town of Espanola, founded in 1598. The mountain ride to this sight is dramatically beautiful. It is a good way to immerse yourself in the culture of northern New Mexico. (I still have a hand-woven blanket from the eighth-generation Trujillo family displayed in my room.)]

[Second Honorable Mention: New Mexico State Capitol (Santa Fe) – I like this building for its simplicity, which blends into the overall atmosphere of this old, appealing town. No big dome, and no imposing columns, but just architecture that fits the state well, as is the case in Delaware also. As a bonus, there is a permanent display of local art on the walls inside, making the edifice come alive even more.]

New York

Metropolitan Museum of Art (New York City) – There is no collection of art in our country to compare to this one. I have visited several times and I have still not seen it all (not to mention the quality of their temporary exhibitions). (While you're there, drive to the Hudson River and see the religious branch called The Cloisters.) You name the style of art, from Etruscan pottery to Impressionism, and it is represented here, in spades.

Niagara Falls (Niagara Falls) – You cannot exaggerate how awesome these falls are, on both the American and Canadian sides. The boat, the Maid of the Mist, actually distributes plastic coveralls, and then sails you out into the midst of the mist of the Canadian side, as they have been doing since the nineteenth century (well, not in the same boat), an experience you will not soon forget. Right across the bridge in Canada are several GEMs waiting to be discovered, plus a non-GEM IMAX that I did not have time to squeeze in. If it is half as good as the IMAX of the Grand Canyon, it is worth twice the price to see it.

Corning Museum of Glass (Corning) – This is one of the foremost glass venues in the country, if not the very best. It encompasses a large museum of silicate, not surprisingly, and features a show of actual glassblowing. Included is a separate section for the high-end Steuben (STOY-ben) glass that is likewise produced there. You need to spend several hours to take it all in. Try to make this drive through mid-state New York in the fall, to see the leaves. (Nearby is the Rockwell Museum of Western Art [in the east, notice], which does include one painting by the unrelated Norman Rockwell.)

[Honorable Mention: Adirondack Museum (Blue Mountain Lake) – This area, in the huge Adirondack Park in upstate New York, is as attractive as the town's name. I had been to Whiteface Mountain earlier that day, and then Lake Placid of Olympic fame, where I ran into gridlock, the result of mixing a film festival and a biker rally. By the time I arrived at this excellent museum the first time, I needed practically literally to run through it to see everything by closing. What I encountered convinced me that I wanted to go back, so I could learn, through various sorts of exhibits and artifacts, about this distinctive section of the country. The staff were as nice as the displays, letting me in that first visit after the cut-off time, and for free. My subsequent return visit did not disappoint.]

[Second Honorable Mention: The National Shrine of the North American Martyrs (Auriesville) – It was here that Jesuit priest Saint Isaac Jogues and two companions were martyred in 1646 (although their remains have never been recovered). It is no coincidence that Saint Kateri Tekakwitha was born there only 10 years later, the first Native American to attain formal canonization in the Catholic Church. As the African writer Tertullian wrote centuries before, "The blood of the martyrs is the seed of the Church." There is plenty to see, whether your interests concern museums or chapels. My only minor disappointment the day I visited was to discover that Saint Kateri is actually buried, not there, but in Canada (in Saint Francis Xavier Mission in Kahnawake, Quebec), where I toured and said mass years later.]

North Carolina

Biltmore (Asheville) – After the excesses of Newport, Rhode Island, this building represented (*CW) a breath of fresh air. Compared to his grandfather Cornelius Vanderbilt's mansion, the Breakers, this house of George Washington Vanderbilt was designed with great taste and restraint (to the extent that you can describe a 250-room mansion as restrained). The grounds are as lovely as the house, designed by no less a landscape architect than Frederick Law Olmsted; if I lived in the area, I would definitely purchase an annual pass. It is pricey, but the place is maintained in pristine condition by a staff of 1500. A final note: the workers were both friendly and knowledgeable.

Cherokee – This town is aptly named, as explained in the musical about the events of the Cherokee Nation in the past entitled, "Unto These Hills." Those wanting to hear the Native Americans' side of the story would do well to drive out to the reservation and take-in this show. The Oconaluftee Village is located in the same area, where craft demonstrations take place during the day. And while you're out here, Great Smokey Mountain National Park is right next door

Wright Brothers National Memorial (Outer Banks) – History was made here in 1903. True, Orville and Wilbur were native Ohioans, but they came all the way to Kill Devil Hills, aka Kitty Hawk, to do what others said could never be done. A reproduction of the Flyer is featured on-site (the original is in the Smithsonian), as well as an earlier glider (at first I thought it was two models of the same plane, in case one broke). You can go outside onto the sand to walk precisely where these historic flights transpired. As a bonus, you're now in the Outer Banks. (When you see OBX in an oval on the front or back of a car or SUV from now on, you'll know what it means.)

[Honorable Mention: Old Salem Museums and Gardens (Winston-Salem) – This delightfully recreated town, right in the middle of Salem, transports visitors back two centuries to what it was like living in a Moravian village. Here you will learn, in this extensive hamlet featuring living actors in period dress, not only about this interesting Protestant sect, but about life in America when the likes of Thomas Jefferson and John Quincy Adams occupied the

White House. I do have one issue with them, however: as much as I like religion, and as much as I like history: was it really necessary to raze the original (and therefore historical) Krispy Kreme doughnut shop in the reconstruction process?!]

[Second Honorable Mention: Battleship *North Carolina* (Wilmington) – These sorts of ships were actually floating towns, with the captain the mayor of about 5000 "constituents" (I'm sure he was glad they never held an actual vote on the matter). Here you will learn, through touring nine decks, not only about the running of the ship itself, but about life during World War II, from which the *North Carolina* earned 15 battle stars. (I hope traffic is better for you than it was for me, since there was a local footrace taking place the Saturday morning I was there. Arriving on time somehow with no foreknowledge of that athletic event, I actually showed up earlier than some of the workers {and therefore showed the workers up}.)]

North Dakota

Fort Abraham Lincoln State Park (Mandan) – It was here that the Corps of Discovery, led by Lewis and Clark, wintered during their historic trip (in 1804-05), a season they could not have survived without the help of the local Mandan tribe (have *you* ever tried to spend a winter in North Dakota?). This area proved at one time the location of one of the largest Indian settlements on the continent. The actual fort, built in later years, was used by the US cavalry, ironically, to subdue the Native people. In fact, the 19-storey state capitol in nearby Bismarck is visible from here.

International Peace Garden – On our northern border the US shares this park with our neighbor Canada. You are actually allowed to walk into Canadian territory without a passport, as long as you have some form of ID, and stay within the garden boundaries. The evening I was there the weather was misting, and I was essentially alone, offering me a strangely peaceful feeling, especially while I spent time in the chapel. It's not all bells and whistles (well, there is a carillon), but a low-keyed way to celebrate and thank God for the peace between these two countries, with the longest unguarded border in the world. (Since my own visit they have added a 9/11 memorial, constructed of steel from the World Trade Center.)

Theodore Roosevelt National Park – I have visited both sections of this badlands-type Park, and have seen bison both times. On one occasion, you will recall, they got onto the trail I was using, necessitating my roundabout return to my car via hitchhiking. While tent camping there that same night I was awakened from a dead sleep by the howl of a wolf. In other words, there is a good chance you will run into some wildlife in this ruggedly beautiful enclave.

[Honorable Mention: North Dakota Heritage Center (Bismarck) – This state museum traces the history of the area from earliest geological times to the present. It was closed the first time I was there, when I viewed the skyscraper-like capitol, which sits on the same plot of land. Fortunately, they have recently refurbished the whole place, making it state-of-the-art, as I discovered in 2016, with its extensive collection of Native American artifacts, a particular interest of mine. If you've taken the trouble to come all the way to North Dakota, you owe it to yourself to find out as much as possible about the state in this museum.]

[Second Honorable Mention: National Buffalo Museum (Jamestown) – Now who wouldn't like to visit a facility dedicated to this American icon? In fact, nearby you will discover the largest buffalo in the world, an outdoor statue which serves as a great photo-op. Inside you will find everything from art to artifacts about the bison and the West. They even field a live buffalo herd with one rare white specimen, but they let the animals run free, so you will need to be luckier than I was to see the albino.]

Ohio

Armstrong Air & Space Museum (Wapakoneta) – Ohio declares on its license plates that it is the birthplace of aviation, since it was the home of the Wright Brothers. Is it simply a coincidence that the first American to orbit the earth, John Glenn, and the first person to walk on the moon, Neil Armstrong, were Ohioans too? This museum is a good introduction for the general tourist, what with extraterrestrial hardware and several video presentations, taking you through air and space travel from the beginning, through Kitty Hawk, to NASA and beyond. (Just try to say the name of the town fast three times.)

Rock and Roll Hall of Fame and Museum (Cleveland) – I liked this venue even before the TV show. The name pretty much says it all, with various displays highlighting important performers and songs in rock history. There is also space reserved for temporary exhibitions, as was the case when I toured there and got to see a presentation of John Lennon's papers and artwork. The Great Lakes Science Center, which featured a special major exhibit of Titanic artifacts when I was there, is right next door.

The Wilds (Cumberland) – This place goes beyond a mere zoo in allowing the animals to run free while the tourists travel through the several sections of the sight on a bus. Drivers narrate the experience, and are good at spotting animals that might otherwise go unnoticed. In fact, these guides make the furry beastums, as it were, come alive, in talking about their individual or group personalities as if they were close friends. It's a treat for animal lovers of all ages.

[Honorable Mention: National Underground Railroad Freedom Center (Cincinnati) – This name too says it all; and the five films scattered among the other exhibits in this handsome building make it a must-see for folks visiting the tri-state area (well, except for me, apparently, who didn't get here until 2013). A sight like this not only reminds us of how precious our own freedom is, but raises our awareness that there are people around the world, even in the 21st century, who do not enjoy the liberty we can so easily take for granted (end of sermon).]

[Second Honorable Mention: Museum of Ceramics (East Liverpool) – The building itself is a work of art, a converted turn-of-the-twentieth-century post office, from the days when public buildings were meant to lift the spirit of the citizens they served. However, the ceramics inside might at first seem prosaic, but they represented a large portion of East Ohio's economy in the nineteenth century, and everyday American life. You will note simple attempts and items meant for mass distribution, but also fine works that demonstrate that ceramics is itself an art form. There is quite a bit of an historical nature in east Ohio; and this museum, sitting as it does practically on the Pennsylvania and West Virginia state lines, is a good place to begin your investigation and discovery.]

Oklahoma

Fort Sill National Historic Landmark and Museum (Fort Sill) – This facility has been a continually-operating fort since 1869, when it was founded to quell Native unrest (the only surviving such entity built by buffalo [i.e., African-American] soldiers). It contains a number of exhibits that interpret different aspects of Oklahoma history. Of greatest interest to me was Geronimo's grave. In that particular cemetery each Chiricahua Apache interred had a tombstone explaining who he was; but one cairn of stones had only a single word inscribed: Geronimo. Comanche chief Quanah Parker is buried there as well.

Oklahoma City National Memorial and Museum (Oklahoma City) – The tragic bombing of this federal building in 1995 is commemorated here, at the actual site of the domestic attack. Outside there is an area displaying chairs for each person killed in the blast. The museum itself presents the terrorist assault from a number of angles, to make the event as real as possible for the viewer. It hardly seems possible that 20 years (and counting) have passed since 168 persons died there. As with the Alamo and Pearl Harbor, it can be approached as a place of pilgrimage.

Woolaroc Museum and Wildlife Preserve (Bartlesville) – If the American West had an attic, it would be located here. What began as a hunting cabin became an extensive collection of Western and local Native American artifacts (Oklahoma was once called "Indian Territory"), housed in a rustic building. If that's not enough, animals roam free on the property (you are instructed not to get out of your car on the drive from the front gate to the museum). I don't remember the multimedia show, so this feature must be new. (I do remember that it was a bear [no pun intended] to find, but worth the effort).

[Honorable Mention: Gilcrease Museum (Tulsa) – I keep going back and forth as to whether this museum or the Amon Carter in Fort Worth is the best Western art museum in the country. Not only are all the big Western names represented, but there are Western studies by the likes of Winslow Homer, James A. McNeil Whistler and Pennsylvanian N. C. Wyeth as well. It doesn't end there, since they also display a number of Native American artifacts. In fact, my coffee mug, which I am looking at now, is covered with a painting of glowing wigwams at dusk, an eerily beautiful effect. (Sorry: a ceramic mug is not included in your entrance fee.)]

[Second Honorable Mention: Jasmine Moran Children's Museum (Seminole) – It's nice to have a place designed primarily for the kids, and a straight shot down from I-40. This creative sight includes an entire town with children-size places where the young'uns can pretend to be grown-ups. It is very hands-on, but still contains items of interest for the old folks, such as an aquarium, model airplanes, and model trains, so that the rest of us can pretend for a few minutes to be kids again.]

Oregon

Crater Lake National Park – If tall mountains and blue water appeal to you, come and refresh your soul amid this natural beauty. You can drive completely around the lake, with a number of lookout points along the way. Two visitor centers explain the formation of this high and deep body of water, and the surrounding mountains' volcanic past.

National Historic Oregon Trail Interpretive Center (Baker City) – It is worth a drive into eastern Oregon to experience this excellent museum. I have a great deal of admiration for the average Americans who nonetheless braved the Oregon Trail in the nineteenth century, and this creative and technologically-advanced venue does these settlers justice. As a bonus, there are even actual ruts from the pioneers' wagons, preserved a medium walk away from the building.

Washington Park (Portland) – This acreage contains a number of attractions, as diverse as an arboretum, a zoo, a children's museum, a forestry museum, and a holocaust memorial. Come enjoy the scenery, and take in the various sights at your own pace.

[Honorable Mention: Astoria Column (Astoria) – The column itself, with its painted bas-reliefs, offers the viewer a taste of local history. However, if you want to see one reason people came out to this part of the country to make that history, climb the 164 steps to the top (sorry, there is no elevator) and view the surrounding country (which can be done, you will be happy to know, from the bottom as well, since it rests on a hill), as the Columbia River, under the shadow of the local mountains, surges toward the Pacific Ocean. Right across the street is a fine maritime museum, also a GEM. Then drive the lengthy bridge to Washington State and descry the river from high atop the middle, a sight not to be missed.]

[Second Honorable Mention: Oregon Caves National Monument – Be prepared for a winding drive into the mountains (a bonus for outdoor types). As caves go, this one is brisk at a constant 44 degrees, so dress accordingly (although negotiating the 500+ stairs inside should warm you up). You encounter all the usual formations, and maybe some unusual ones, and for about half the price of a commercial operation (or free with your annual National Parks Pass). The time I was there, forest fires were raging, so close that the morning of this visit there was a layer of ash on my car. For your sake and for the people of southwest Oregon and nearby California, I hope your own trip is less problematic.]

Pennsylvania

Carnegie Museums of Pittsburgh (Pittsburgh) – One museum not enough for you? Then try this sundry collection, which includes a natural history museum, a science museum, an art museum, the Andy Warhol Museum (well, I guess that's art too), and even a submarine. My visits have once again confirmed that anything with the Carnegie name attached to it tends to be done well. (If you don't want people to know you're from out of town, be sure to place the accent on the second syllable.)

Gettysburg National Military Park (Gettysburg) – As a preserved military battlefield, this park, with its four GEMs (not counting Gettysburg Civil War Heritage Days in July, and the nearby Eisenhower National Historic Site), is without peer. As President Lincoln asserted, it has been hallowed by the blood of the men who fought and died there, and should be approached accordingly, since this was the price for maintaining our Union. It represented also the

High Watermark of the Confederacy, the farthest north the South penetrated militarily. Of particular interest is its cyclorama, one of only two remaining in the country (the other is in Atlanta). The Eternal Light Peace Memorial can be said to shine for all the battlefields of this voracious and contentious war.

Liberty Bell (Philadelphia) – It was hard to pick from among Philadelphia's historic sites, but this one sums up all the others, and has been an icon on such things as US postage stamps for years. The other major contenders, such as Independence Hall, Congress Hall and the National Constitution Center, are all within walking distance (good luck parking), in Independence National Historic Site, which itself encompasses six GEMs.

[Honorable Mention: Fallingwater (Mill Run) – This recently-refurbished house, designed by Frank Lloyd Wright, is so well-known that it too graced a US postage stamp. He considered it for so long, that when the client came on a surprise visit to his office in Wisconsin, he drew the plans from memory on the spot. Come to the beautiful Laurel Highlands of Pennsylvania and see why his cantilever idea caused such an architectural stir.]

[Second Honorable Mention: Johnstown Flood Museum (Johnstown) – In the name of full disclosure, I must admit that I once lived here (well, not in the museum). Still, the film used at the site actually won the Oscar for Best Short Subject. Ironically, the building used to be a Carnegie Library, paid for by one of the men who owned the South Fork Dam. It has been said that, for 30 minutes, it was as if the volume of Niagara Falls emptied into the valley, heading toward the unsuspecting city. Remarkably, after 2209 people died and downtown was destroyed, the steel mills were running again after a mere six weeks, a tribute to the iron will of the local inhabitants. Drive north to where the dam used to be, to the Johnstown Flood National Memorial in St. Michaels, where their own film complements this one very well.]

Rhode Island

The Elms (Newport) – You could name the whole town of Newport as a sight, but I like this mansion the best. It actually demonstrates some restraint, and is designed with what I consider to be good taste (although a couple of idiosyncratic statues in the gardens might call that estimation into doubt). But don't take *my* word for it: get a package ticket of mansions to visit, a day well-spent, and then decide which one is *your* favorite (I mean, you are allowed to like The Breakers).

International Tennis Hall of Fame (Newport) – This museum fooled me: I stayed in the Hall of Fame near the entrance, thinking that was all there was to see, until about ten minutes before closing, when I discovered lots more. If you like professional tennis (which I do), you will recognize many names. Even if you haven't followed it yet, this place is a well-designed introduction to the sport.

Museum of Art, Rhode Island School of Design (Providence) – This nice little collection was founded to give the students in the school examples of what they were studying. It is not so comprehensive as, say, the Met, but the pieces are well-chosen, giving students and non-students alike a good introduction to the visual arts over the centuries. Don't be surprised to find groups of young persons, from grade school to college, in any given room.

[Honorable Mention: Touro Synagogue National Historic Site (Newport) – I first learned about this historic building from yet another US postage stamp, in the same four-item block as Fallingwater. The year I visited it, it was closed for renovations, so I only viewed the outside. It is not surprising that such an old (pre-Revolutionary War) synagogue would exist in this city, since Rhode Island was the only original colony to grant full religious freedom. The only problem: it is located in a maze of streets (although visiting it during the day will no doubt make the feat of finding it easier than it was for me).]

[Second Honorable Mention: Hunter House (Newport) – This relatively humble building is a definite change-of-pace, and in some ways (*CW) a breath of fresh air, for Newport, built as it was in the 18th century and housing early American furniture and other period artifacts. Afterward there is a small garden to enjoy. I seem to recall that you can walk there from the visitor information center, where you can buy your package of tickets for this interesting town.]

South Carolina

Boone Hall Plantation and Gardens (Mount Pleasant) – Hear and see what an antebellum plantation was like. The stately house has been preserved, and offers tours. More rarely, the slave quarters, by exception constructed of brick (the owners ran a factory that made these items), have also been preserved and offer insights into slavery conditions through several exhibits and audiovisuals. The grounds are quite impressive, including an extended avenue of ancient live oaks with hanging Spanish moss. An added treat is an outdoor theater presentation on Gullah [slave] life.

Fort Sumter National Monument (Charleston Harbor) – This is where it all started (you can call it the War Between the States or the Civil War [in the seminary a southern friend of mine referred to it as the War of Northern Aggression]). A ferry takes you to the island on which the structure is located. The site was captured by the Confederacy, which maintained it pretty much throughout the war as a thorn in the Union's side. Come and find out the details through exhibits and ranger talks.

South Carolina State House (Columbia) – This Cass Gilbert building sports a copper dome, as well as six stars covering the cannon holes it earned during the War Between the States (I missed them when I saw it [no, that was not because of my age]). Make sure you walk the landscaped campus, which contains a number of monuments and statues, including South Carolina's copy of the Liberty Bell (every state and possession, and DC, has one, many around their capitols). Nearby is the state museum, also a GEM.

[Honorable Mention: Huguenot Church (Charleston) – Since it was a Saturday, I only got to see the outside of this historic worship center. (The Huguenots, by the way, were a small French Protestant sect, about whom I first heard on a yet another US postage stamp as a boy {I am not making this up}.) The current structure is antebellum, but built in the Gothic style. (In other words, don't expect it to look like the preserved houses and mansions in the area, for which Charleston is rightly well-known. Indeed, you could spend all day just going from tour to tour downtown, as I did that fortuitous day.)]

[Second Honorable Mention: <u>Mepkin Abbey</u> (Moncks Corner) – I know I seem to be on a religious binge here, but this sight offers a rare opportunity to visit the inside of a Trappist monastery (a Catholic religious order, also originally from France; for some reason, my biased spell-check accepts "Huguenot" but not "Trappist"). You won't get into the cloister; still, if you take the guided tour you will see quite a bit of the modern church and attractive grounds (and, if memory serves me correctly, some of the monastic buildings). The abbot when I visited was a concert pianist, who would regularly offer recitals in nearby Charleston. Then, when you're finished, there are two GEMs in town waiting just for *you*.]

South Dakota

<u>Badlands National Park</u> – These formations originally received their name, not because desperados fled there to hide (which they did), but because the ground breaks up easily when walked on in places, making it treacherous. However, you can be sure that any hiking paths are safe for perambulation today. Not in a walking mood? The loop drive itself offers spectacular views of this beautiful country.

<u>Mount Rushmore National Memorial</u> – This iconic mountain needs little introduction from me. Still, they actually improved it between visits of mine with a spanking new visitor center. Make sure you ask them where to drive to be able to view the profile of George Washington from side/behind. (While you're there, tour the rest of the Black Hills, which should take about a week, if you hurry. Of note is the huge but incomplete Crazy Horse Memorial, by way of comparison.)

<u>Redlin Art Center</u> (Waterton) – I grew up in suburban Philadelphia, but after visiting this museum, I found myself homesick for a farm I had never lived on. Such is the magic of painter Terry Redlin, who plants a nostalgia in his viewers for an older, simpler lifestyle, some of whom couldn't tell a turkey from a duck. It's not just that he's an accomplished artist, or that he likes agricultural themes, but that there are four large floors of these windows-into-another-world, leading to a cumulative effect. You can view the video before or after you see

the paintings, to learn about the man behind the creations. (Speaking of creation, there was a planetarium when I was there, but now that space is utilized for some more Redlin productions, specifically, artist's proofs.) The cost to enter this world? Just the gas it takes to drive there. The lesson? That the people in the paintings are living in their present, not somebody else's past; I can learn from them by living in my blessed present, and finding happiness in the Now.

[Honorable Mention: <u>Corn Palace</u> (Mitchell) – This is not the most impressive sight in America, but it is a real piece of Americana. I mean, what other building have you ever seen featuring murals on its facade and one side constructed entirely from ears of corn, which images change every year, giving you a reason to go back? One time I saw the building filled with temporary booths on the floor, while another time it was empty except for some info on the place, contrasting Rodeo Week from the rest of the year. Still, it is right off I-90 (more or less), is free to look at, and is near another GEM in town, the Mitchell Prehistoric Indian Village and Archeodome. (There used to be a doll museum GEM there as well, the Enchanted World Doll Museum, but AAA now makes no mention of it, and its phone number has been disconnected {sorry, girls}.) (In 2016 the theme was music, a favorite of mine, with several American icons featured, most notably Willie Nelson.)]

[Second Honorable Mention: <u>National Music Museum</u> (Vermillion) – This distinctive museum is located on the campus of the University of South Dakota. I discovered standard instruments, interesting versions of familiar instruments, and instruments I had never heard of before. It is reminiscent of the days before TV and radio, when family entertainment was essentially supplied by the residents, often in the form of home-made tunes. Who knows, it may inspire your kids to start making music with something other than an MP3 player. Another freebie for you from your friends in South Dakota (well, they do accept donations).]

Tennessee

<u>Hermitage</u> (Nashville) – This iconic residence, which I learned about as a boy collecting (you guessed it) US postage stamps, was

the home of President Andrew Jackson and his wife Rachel, the first Washington outsider to be elected to that office. The site preserves not only the actual 200-year-old building, but many family furnishings. A video explains who President Jackson was, and an audio tour points out various structures and sites on the property.

Museum of Appalachia (Clinton) – As with Woolaroc for the West in Oklahoma, and the Shelburne Museum in Vermont for New England, this place could easily be Appalachia's attic. (By the way, I pronounce it with a long A in the third syllable, but that's just me.) There are lots of buildings filled with all sorts of things that offer a taste of what it was and is like living in this region of the country. Not surprisingly, they feature a section dedicated to instruments, since bluegrass is just one of the several musical styles that can be traced to the Volunteer State.

Women's Basketball Hall of Fame (Knoxville) – It's about time that female athletes received the attention that is due them. This museum does just that, presenting a number of fun exhibits on the subject. Indeed, it's hard to miss the building, as it has a huge orange basketball surmounting it. (In the name of full disclosure, I need to mention that, of the handful of coaches of whom they have audio clips, one, Rene Portland, was at the time the head coach of the Penn State team, whom I met once at a Pro-Life fundraiser dinner in State College, and who played for the Mighty Macs in the seventies; and a high school classmate of mine, Harry Perretta, was at the time the coach of Villanova. {*CM} Small world.)

[Honorable Mention: Grand Ole Opry (Nashville) – I regret that I, a self-confessed music lover, took so long finally to visit this piece of Americana. Even if you can't be in town for a show (which I did, and was blown away by it, a country music smorgasbord), there are tours of this musical icon daily. In fact, it is part of a larger concern called Gaylord Opryland, which includes such items as a museum, a series of gardens, and a riverboat. By way of trivia: it produces the longest-running radio show in the world. (Curiously, my spell-check accepts Opryland, but not Opry.)]

[Second Honorable Mention: Jack Daniel's Distillery (Lynchburg) – I finally made the pilgrimage to this piece of Americana (another one) a few years ago, sending my frat Bro a postcard and gloating.

If you want to learn about how Tennessee sour mash whiskey is produced, and also about the colorful man for whom the product is named, take the tour and be enlightened by the spirits (sorry). The good news is that the tour is free; the bad news is that there are no free samples (well, the lemonade is complimentary, which was more welcome anyway by me, a teetotaler, on a hot day). Further, they have no need of new taste testers as of this writing.]

Texas

Alamo (San Antonio) – This is less a national attraction than it is a national shrine, which needs to be approached with reverence. Remember, not one American survived that siege, kind of like the 300 in Greek history. Then take a drive down I-10 to the Houston area to see the result of the Alamo resistance, at the San Jacinto Monument and Museum of History (in la Porte). We lost the battle, but won the war.

Amon Carter Museum (Fort Worth) – What better place than Texas to have what may very well be the best Western art museum in the country? They don't just display a couple of Remington bronzes, but two or three of the same figure for comparison, explaining how different castings affected how the finished product appeared. Even the campus on which it sits is attractive.

Fossil Rim Wildlife Center (Glen Rose) – It is simply the best animal facility I have ever seen. Even the café, at the driving halfway point, is creatively designed. They provide you a color-printed photo-guide to the animals, and I was able to espy at least half of them. If you want endangered species mobbing your car, this is the place to go. (Then drive down the road to see full-size models of extinct species in Dinosaur World, as well as the Creation Evidence Museum.)

[Honorable Mention: McDonald Observatory (Fort Davis) – I stopped in here one day to check it out for an hour, and remained there the entire day and evening. You wouldn't think an observatory would have so much for families to do, both before and after the stars come out, but it was spring break, and the place, as out of the way as it is, was packed. If you ever wondered where those Stardate bits on National Public Radio originate, this is the source. They even have a Stardate Café to keep you well-fed and -hydrated the whole time you're there. (The only other observatory I have seen with so much to do is The Griffith Park Observatory in LA, at the opposite end of the population spectrum.)]

[Second Honorable Mention: Petroleum Museum (Midland) – What could be more Texan that an oil museum? This excellent attraction focuses on the technical side of this universal product, following it from the ground to your car. The Petroleum Hall of Fame lists, among others, both Bush former presidents (yes, they were each involved in the oil industry before turning to politics). Not satisfied with doing this well (no pun intended), they also have oil paintings of the history of oil, a large room full of ancient maps (I'm sure there's a connection somewhere), and an exhibit on locally-built race cars. Then step outside to see what is probably the largest collection of old oil rigs on public display anywhere. Finally, when you're finished, drive down the way and tour the George W. Bush childhood home.]

Utah

Bryce Canyon National Park – I could have chosen any of the five National Parks in southern Utah, except perhaps Capitol Reef, since it involves hiking to see its treasures. However, I think this Park is the most visually stunning, with the red rock canyoned (is that a word? my spell-check doesn't think so) to make it magnificent, and spired (spell-check veto here too) to form its many signature eerily humanesque (let's make it a hat trick) *hoodoos*. Anyway, you're not far from the other ones if you have an entire day or two to spare.

Museum of Ancient Life at Thanksgiving Point (Lehi) – This is the most impressive dinosaur museum I have ever seen, with dozens of full skeleton casts of various species. There is also a Mammoth Screen Theater with several offerings (I happened to enjoy a film about the Ernest Shackleton voyage to Antarctica). They feature a good deal for kids to do, but (*CW) kids of all ages will enjoy it, because who doesn't like dinosaurs?

Temple Square (Salt Lake City) – Here you get to see, not only one of the Mormon Temples (from the outside), but the unique, musically-famous Tabernacle as well. They provide not one but two visitor centers, where you can check if your family is on record. Tours of the Square are available. It is essentially the Vatican of the LDS church. The attractive Catholic Cathedral of the Madeleine, and the Episcopalian Cathedral of Saint Mark, are only a few blocks away, as is the impressive state capitol. Access to everything just mentioned, of course, is free.

[Honorable Mention: Rainbow Bridge National Monument – Why did I relegate one of the seven natural wonders of the world to the status of honorable mention? Because it's a major challenge to access. Still, since the creation of Lake Powell, you can avoid the 14-mile one-way hike over rough terrain (the way Theodore Roosevelt experienced it) and take a boat that makes the round trip (with a moderate walk from the water to the monument) in less than six hours. I had wanted to do it for years, and finally went for it in 2010. It is as impressive as you have heard, the largest and perhaps most perfect natural bridge in the world, in a stunning red, sacred ground to local Native Americans. A ranger at the site explains its formation and answers questions. The ride There and Back Again on the Colorado River is pretty as well.]

[Second Honorable Mention: Kennecott Bingham Canyon Mine (Bingham Canyon) – I thought twice about recommending what is essentially a huge strip mine, but the desert terrain around it is a far cry from the tortured mountains of Appalachia. After all, if a hole in the ground is large enough to be viewed from space, it's probably worth a visit while on earth. The main mineral involved is copper, and they explain the operation to you in several media. I mean, haven't you ever wanted to see those dump trucks that can crush a pick-up, they're so big? (If you want to sit behind the wheel of one of these monsters, however, you'll have to travel to the Hull-Rust Mahoning Mine in Hibbing, Minnesota. If you want to drive one, you'll need to apply for employment.)] [As of April, 2013, a huge landslide has indefinitely closed the mine for tours.]

Vermont

Bennington Battle Monument (Bennington) – This tower is reminiscent of the San Jacinto Monument in Texas, both because it is tall, with an outstanding view of the surrounding area, and because it commemorates an important victory in our history. This particular skirmish, which included the Green Mountain Boys of Vermont (a name that literally means "Green Mountains") was decisive in the Revolutionary War. Nearby is the Bennington Museum, which contains, besides a good deal of Grandma Moses' artwork, a very rare British redcoat. While you're there, take a moment to visit the local cemetery where poet and American icon Robert Frost is buried.

President Calvin Coolidge State Historic Site (Plymouth) – Here you can find out all you want to know about our 28th president, and visit some of the buildings that were important to his life, including his birth house. He is the only US president to have been sworn into office by his father, while on vacation as vice president, right after getting news of President Harding's death (his father was a Justice of the Peace). Known for his paucity of words, he continues in death as he did in life, with a simple headstone among those of other family members. (Perhaps it was Vermont winters that were behind the "Keep Cool with Coolidge" slogan during his subsequent presidential campaign.)

Shelburne Museum (Shelburne) – Strolling around this museum, with its 25 buildings, is like rummaging through a very rich person's attic. I don't mean that you will find expensive treasures so much as that you'll find just about everything here, a real collection of Americana. It offers a broad taste of New England life since Europeans arrived. True, it's something of a drive to get there (crossing almost the whole height of the state), but it involves a pretty US-7, and puts you near Lake Champlain. You'll find things you haven't seen in years, things you've never seen, and things you'll not want to admit you've seen before because of their age.

[Honorable Mention: Billings Farm & Museum (Woodstock) – This is one of three dairy operations I have toured in my travels (the other two were in {predictably} Wisconsin and {unpredictably} California {I can't believe I have never visited one of the many in Pennsylvania, as often as I have passed signs touting registered Holsteins here}). This place gives you (*CW) two for the price of one: a working dairy from 2011, and a dairy farm museum from the 1890s, demonstrating the actual processes, past and present, of producing all those calcium-rich products. This is not a farm factory, either, but one in which the animals are treated as well as the people. (Speaking of dairy: for ice cream lovers, the Ben & Jerry's factory {visited by friends of mine a few years ago} is located in Waterbury to the north, and offers tours complemented by free samples {slurp}.)]

[Second Honorable Mention: Porter Music Box Museum (Randolph) – I discovered this quaint museum years ago, and it may have been a GEM then, or else I simply noticed a sign while driving to somewhere else and stopped. In any case, I was happy I did. The music boxes in question are the large ones that play metal discs more reminiscent of juke boxes of later generations than what you grandmother may have displayed on her living room table. As a further treat, there are various unrelated artifacts, from antique toys to Sitting Bull's medicine pouch. An introductory video helps contextualize everything. The only drawback: to hear what the boxes sound like, you need to feed real, live quarters into them. But at only $7.50 to get in, you can splurge to hear these rare and distinctive devices.] [While the museum itself closed in 2012, the Porter Music Box Company remains open for business, and features a shop/showroom of their distinctive products in the same town.]

Virginia

Cumberland Gap National Historical Park – This site marks the place where people from the east coast (both before and after Columbus) first moved through the mountains to settle the lands beyond. The morning I stopped there the area behind the gap was filled with mist, which was slowly emptying through the gap and downward, creating the illusion of a giant pot boiling over. It was eerily impressive. Even if you don't get to share that experience, there is still good information available at the visitor's center, with tours and hiking available.

George Washington's Mount Vernon Estate and Gardens (Mount Vernon) – This was George Washington's home during his adult life. I remember this edifice and Jefferson's Monticello from collecting postage stamps as a boy (but you knew that), and was somewhat surprised that, after visiting them both, I preferred Mount Vernon (although Monticello is worth a visit too). Just getting to look at Houdin's bust of Washington is worth the price of admission. (A friend of mine was actually hired to work there back a few years ago: how cool would *that* be?)

Museum of the Confederacy (Richmond) – Here is a (*CW) treasure trove of information and artifacts about the South's participation in the War Between the States (including items owned by Jeff Davis, Robert E. Lee, JEB Stuart and Stonewall Jackson). If that's not enough for you, they throw in the refurbished White House of the Confederacy as a bonus.

[Honorable Mention: Busch Gardens Williamsburg – This is one of those places I can't believe I've never visited (except for their Christmas extravaganza, which is also worth the trip). AAA makes it sound like a cross between a museum and a Six Flags rollercoaster park. Everything is themed European; and those not interested in traveling 70 mph backward all day can choose from the nine stage shows. There is quite a lot of history to investigate in the surrounding area as well (I *have* been to Old Colonial Williamsburg, Jamestown and Yorktown).]

[Second Honorable Mention: The Mariners' Museum (Newport News) – This is one of my *déjà vu* experiences. It was the remarkable, larger-than-life-size metal statue of Leif Ericson that convinced me that I had been there before. I was not really disappointed to have made that mistake, since it is now my favorite maritime museum in the country. The docents really make the various artifacts, including a first-order (that's the largest) Fresnell (pronounced fre-NELL) lighthouse lens, and the mastheads, come alive (as it were). A bonus for me the second time around was the building that I missed (or which did not yet exist the first time around): the collection of large miniature ships (is that an oxymoron?). They had also made some more headway on restoring the USS *Monitor*, of *Merrimac* and *Monitor* fame.]

Washington

Chief Joseph Dam (Bridgeport) – I was heading to the Grand Coulee Dam a number of years ago when I discovered this hidden treasure. In fact, it was my introduction to Chief Joseph, the peace-loving Nez Perce leader of whom I later bought a poster. The dam is as impressive as the man, and is still, in this post-9/11 era, willing to offer guided tours. And it's free. (I did get to see the breast of the Grand Coulee Dam later that day, but that was all, given how far behind I was on my floating itinerary. A visit years later confirmed my intuition that the latter is one of the premier touring dams in the country [it even offers a laser light show at night in the summer].)

Olympic National Park – I have viewed the mountains in this Park both from the east and from the north, and either way they are extremely impressive. Imagine the view from the tops when, weather permitting, you can drive up into the mountains, to Hurricane Ridge, which affords magnificent panoramas of the entire area. If you get as far as Seattle, why not make an incursion onto the Olympic Peninsula and enjoy some impressive natural beauty, far from the traffic on I-5?

Space Needle (Seattle) – This carry-over from the 1962 World's Fair has become the icon of the city. It presents great views both day and night, and you can buy a reduced-price combination ticket. I have come to look upon this benign structure as the city's guardian angel. From there, the rest of this great town beckons.

[Honorable Mention: Mount Saint Helen's National Volcanic Monument – I can still recall the day in 1980 when the top literally blew off this (*CW) sleeping giant. I made the trek some years later, receiving an interesting ranger presentation that took us to the lake (well, one of them). This individual emphasized that the pumice, which now lay all around the body of water, while good for your bathtub, was federally protected, and so could not be used for your calluses, unless you chose to bathe in the lake (which no doubt was frigid). I was not so adventurous as to climb to the top, but such activity is possible, with permission and an added fee. It's not every day that you get to watch geological history in the making (the volcano is still technically active).]

[Second Honorable Mention: Underground Tour (Seattle) – I have never seen, or heard, the like. There is actually a city under the city, the reason for which the tour, accessed from Pioneer Square, will explain. It is not only interesting but hilarious, and I found myself guffawing at jokes the entire time. Indeed, I laughed so much that afterward the guide made it a point to come over and ask me what I did for a living (I told her I too worked in front of crowds). If a Las Vegas stand-up act were half this funny for double the price, you would have gotten more than your money's worth.]

West Virginia

Harper's Ferry National Historic Park – It was here that abolitionist John Brown made a raid, and penultimately a last stand (just ignore the contradiction). A number of buildings have been restored, some of which contain historical exhibits. (Side note: the officer sent to lead the attack on Brown was the then-Colonel Robert E. Lee, back when the Mountain State was still part of the Old Dominion.) The nearby view of the Potomac River has long been considered one of the most beautiful natural sights in the country.

Smoke Hole Caverns (Petersburg) – An interesting aspect of these caves is that it is documented that Native Americans used them in times past. The guided tour introduces you to the world of stalactites (the ones on the top) and stalagmites (the ones on the bottom), as well as other natural formations. (The vintage still, a throwback to the perpetual flight from revenuers, is not a natural formation, nor is it currently operational.)

West Virginia State Capitol (Charleston) – This is one of the state houses that I saw at night, since that's the time I pulled into town, so I have no first-hand idea what the inside looks like. However, I can attest that the outside is most impressive, in the typical dome style, and is made even more so by its sitting on the bank of the Kanahwa (pronounced Ka-NAW) River. How do I know what it looks like, if it was night? The place was (*CW) lit up like a Christmas tree. In fact, it was designed by Cass Gilbert, also known for the US Supreme Court Building, as well as the imposing Minnesota capitol, the Arkansas capitol, and the South Carolina capitol (none of which I have seen the inside of either, although it does sound like we both got into respective ruts). The governor's mansion is next door (I knocked, but nobody answered).

[Honorable Mention: <u>Theatre West Virginia</u> (Beckley) – This summer venue features a couple of standard rotating shows each year (one on the Hatfield-McCoy feud, and another on the split from Virginia), plus a Broadway show, in an outdoor facility right on the New River Gorge National River. Too bad the evening I made the trek all the way from Pennsylvania, lightning forced the show's cancellation (fortunately I had bought insurance against such an eventuality). Still, under roof, the cast put on a delightful impromptu concert of four-part harmonies. Now come on, where else can you see all that for a mere $17?]

[Second Honorable Mention: <u>Blennerhassett Island Historical State Park</u> (Parkersburg) – Here you will find a museum and video presentation on the mainland, followed (or preceded: it's up to you) by a stern-wheeler ride to the island and the rebuilt mansion. The history involved is most interesting even to the nonprofessional. You can do all that, plus take a horse-and-wagon ride, for just over $20.]

Wisconsin

<u>Circus World Museum</u> (Baraboo) – After seeing two other GEMs in this town (Devil's Lake State Park, and The International Crane Foundation, the latter featuring each of the 15 species of cranes), I spent the rest of the day here. There are regular circus performances more or less continuously, with time in-between to tour the museum. It is the only circus in the world to feature a giraffe. And the clowns are funny. The famous Wisconsin Dells, with their scenic boat tours, are nearby.

<u>House on the Rock</u> (Spring Green) – You have never experienced a place like this, the oddest and most interesting museum I have ever visited. Where else can you see and hear a room full of large (five-foot) music boxes that still work, a huge model of a whale and a squid joined in (*CW) mortal combat, and the coolest, most hypnotic carousel ever? Nearby is Frank Lloyd Wright's Taliesin.

Mitchell Park Horticultural Conservatory: "The Domes" (Milwaukee) – It's not just that the three large glass pyramids are impressive from the outside. Inside they contain mini-environments, and associated flowers and plants (that's not really redundant). The desert dome was my favorite, of course, but the tropical dome is also well-done. The third dome features changing themed exhibits.

[Honorable Mention: Wisconsin State Capitol (Madison) – The building itself is impressive, at the confluence of about eight different streets. What sticks in my mind, however, is that every Saturday there is a farmers' market on the sidewalk that circumscribes the structure. I can still taste the loaf of herb bread that I bought, which served me for meals over the next 24 hours. (It took me an embarrassingly long time to realize that everyone else was walking the opposite direction from me around the edifice.)]

[Second Honorable Mention: Apostle Islands National Lakeshore – I have passed this sight several times in driving through the region, but only noticed now that there is a scenic, narrated boat tour, itself a GEM-within-a-GEM that includes passage by the islands, light-houses and caves. There is also a visitor center that includes a video and exhibits. Naturally, there is plenty of space for any marine activity you can imagine. Just a word to you swimmers: it is not without reason that Harry Chapin makes reference to Lake Superior's "ice-water mansions" (Brrr!).]

Wyoming

Buffalo Bill Historic Center (Cody) – This site is actually comprised of five excellent museums in one, a mere hour east of Yellowstone: a Native American museum, a natural history museum, a gun museum, a Western art museum (all the big names are represented), and (of course) a Buffalo Bill Cody museum. All this, over two days, if you wish, for a mere $15.

Devil's Tower National Monument – Anyone who has seen *Close Encounters of the Third Kind* is already familiar with this landmark. Still, there's nothing like seeing it in person (as it were), which my brother and I did, climbing as high as we could without technical support. Properly-equipped people (about a thousand per annum) do manage to scramble to the top, but that's (Cliché and Pun Warning) above and beyond the call of duty, although I imagine the view from up there is dynamite. We missed the visitor center, as well as the prairie dog colony. (Sorry, there are no helicopter rides to the summit.)

Yellowstone National Park – This is the (*CW) granddaddy of them all, the first National Park in the world, founded in 1872. It is a national must-see, with the iconic Old Faithful geyser a double command performance. The last time I was there I saw both bison and elk, so there is a good chance you'll stumble across some wildlife. Staying overnight will be a challenge during the summer (it really gets crowded, and approaches gridlock, which hardly seems fair, out in the middle of nowhere), but my Pittsburgher friend and I tented in Shoshone National Forest to the east in the summer of 1986 with no lead time at all (first come, first served), where a couple of moose walked by. To the south is Grand Teton National Park, included in the same seven-day admission price.

[Honorable Mention: State Capitol (Cheyenne) – I found this statehouse to be quite tourist-friendly, both in terms of personnel, and written information. They are proud to be the first state to offer the franchise to women, with two pertinent monuments; and of course they display a statue of the iconic cowboy on the bucking bronco outside, as on their license plates (recently voted the most attractive in the country). The golden dome is impressive, and I particularly liked the taxidermied wildlife inside.]

[Second Honorable Mention: National Museum of Wildlife Art (Jackson) – If you're already in Yellowstone, drive south into world-famous Jackson Hole and experience this underrated museum. True, the day I was there, one of the curators admitted that it was the best configuration of art they had ever displayed, with an incredible traveling exhibition by world-renowned Swedish animal sculptor Kent Ullberg. Even so, I don't understand why the permanent collection of this sight does not deserve GEM status. If you go in winter, which I did, you can jump into a sleigh or wagon (depending on the depth of the snow that day) right there and head across the highway to the National Elk Refuge, something I had been wanting to do for almost 20 years (in those days I was driving an AWD standard with studded snow tires). After all, in Wyoming, isn't it all about the wildlife?]

CONCLUSION

A CONTINENT AWAITS

So, have you had your Rand-McNally Road Atlas out, pouring over the national map, starting to decide where you're going to go on that first trip, or that next trip, cross-country? I hope you've at least been storing up ideas, perhaps one from the chapter on Seattle or Philadelphia, or several from the 50x5 chapter. After all, I was not (*CW) waxing eloquent about all the places I've been, simply to show off (although that is no doubt one of the reasons), but to get you to want to see these places, too. After all, if I have *not* motivated you to start planning such an experience, I will consider that, in your case at least, this book has failed in its primary objective.

Still, in spite of my obvious control issues, I want you to see this vacation as a suggestion, not a demand. After all, who wants to be forced into doing something that's supposed to be fun? One of the reasons that stuff is fun is that you're *not* required to do it, but simply *want* to do it. So, rather than (*CW) trying to lay a guilt trip on you (welcome to the sixties), I've been hopefully motivating you to want to pursue this project on your own. However, I did not want it simply to be a (*CW) warm fuzzy idea that goes nowhere, literally, but one that gets you onto the road. After all, if you don't get out and see some of our wonderful country, this book will ultimately prove to be frustrating for you: another collection of someone else's travel stories, while you go to the Wisconsin Dells, or to the Jersey Shore, or to Huntington Beach, for another conventional summer vacation, even while your heart lies elsewhere.

Indeed, you need to listen to your heart. Don't let your head veto your desire to see new places again, insisting that it's too expensive, or too complicated, or simply too new, to do. Don't let your acquaintances put the kybosh on the trip by wondering why you need to be different this year, the way that the average hobbit looked at Bilbo when he would take his occasional adventures outside the Shire. If the other hobbits don't want to meet elves, that's there business; but should they keep *you* from doing so? And don't let your vacation default setting deflate the idea, lulling you once again into a sleepiness that makes you just want to veg-out for a couple of weeks on a beach, or a couch, somewhere. Tell this chorus of nay-sayers that (*CW) there's a new sheriff in town, and he's deciding on the itinerary for this year's holiday. If you try it and end-up hating it, Fine. At least you tried, and now you never need to do it again. However, I think that, if you try, you'll realize just how much there is out there to see, and will want to keep finding these treasures, year after year. And if you never try it, you'll never shake that feeling that you're missing out on something that some people have discovered, and are happier for.

Remember, you don't need to travel the way I have traveled in the past: sleeping in my car, munching peanut butter crackers as I drive, and seeing as many sights in one day as possible, even if that meant rushing through them, checking off items on a list. I can see that maybe I unwittingly needed to travel that way, in order to be able to amass enough material for this book, even though that literary idea developed later. You can see as much or as little as you want, as quickly or as slowly as you desire. Unless you intend to write a book of your own, you don't need to log a quarter of a million miles in North America. One practice I do suggest you imitate, however, is to pray for safety whenever you start-up the car: it's the only reason I'm still alive.

The choice is yours. I give you credit at least for reading the book, and so for allowing some new ideas to challenge your old notions of what a vacation needs to look like. I don't make any more money at this point if you chose the cross-country trip. It would simply make me happy to know that my own experiences were not totally for me, but were meant to be shared with others, so that they too would start producing their own cool travel tales. True, you can read the book and just decide to enjoy the stories vicariously, and that is one legitimate approach, I admit. However, what I would rather discover – through your letter, or perhaps postcards, or your own tome – is that you took your big trip, and now want to share it with others, beginning with me. Indeed, I've had my say: it's time for you to have yours, in writing to me, since I genuinely enjoy hearing about anyone's road adventures. And who knows? Perhaps one day, in Yellowstone, or Key West, or SoCal, we'll run into each-other, and start a travel version of Can You Top This? And if that happens, I won't mind if you've gotten to a place or two that I have not seen yet. After all, I need to get new travel ideas from *somewhere*.

Godspeed!

EPILOGUE

THEODORE ROOSEVELT

As you may have noticed at the beginning of this volume, I have dedicated the book to our 26th president, Theodore Roosevelt. Why? A fair question. There are two reasons for the choice.

For one, he was a conservationist. He, although a politician, had the same mind-set as people such as iconic proto-environmentalist John Muir. He had been born into wealth, but saw his privileged position as a call to serve his fellows. He had been a sickly boy, so his parents made him spend a good deal of time outdoors, which toughened him up well. Indeed, he was the man who led the charge of the Rough Riders up San Juan Hill in Cuba in the Spanish American War. (When he ran as a third-party candidate in his own Bull Moose Party in 1912, the logo for the organization was a bandana, from this period in his life.) He was a reformer while governor of New York when Boss Tweed ran New York City, and it was said by one historian that he was afraid of no one.

In other words, he loved the outdoors, not just in theory, but in practice, visiting a number of unenclosed places, spots that had already been or would one day be designated as National Parks. This was when those sections of the outdoors were not yet developed, so that it took a good deal of physical hardness and courage to make these visitations.

His breeding taught him that there are things that we receive that need to be preserved for the future. He saw our natural beauty as one such thing, and took active steps while president to do just that. Congress voted in the National Park Service under a successor, Woodrow Wilson, but he was the president who enabled it to move forward when vested interests wanted all that wilderness to be developed economically, at whatever cost to the surroundings. He saw himself as a strong man who had a duty to other Americans to make things right, and so often took the side of the underdog, as with workplace safety reform. He wanted to make a difference, and he did make a difference. It is no coincidence that he is on Mount Rushmore with the likes of George Washington, Thomas Jefferson and Abraham Lincoln. To put it another way, he loved nature and travel, and wanted to make sure that there would be attractive places to visit for generations to come.

The other reason is that he was a writer of travel books. In fact, in the Presidential Museum and Leadership Library in Odessa, Texas, there is a shelf with his political works on it. He also wrote memoirs of his travels, adventures in places such as Africa, where he went on safaris, and in South America, where he braved the Amazon River. In fact, he is the most published president in history. Yes, he loved to hunt, but he always wanted to give the animal a fair chance. In one book I read, he contended that a responsible hunter would never shoot a deer in a river, but would let it get out first where it could run before opening fire on it, giving it a fair opportunity to escape. As with the underdog humans, he wanted to give animals a fighting chance as well; and he wanted to write, not only to share his travel experiences with others, but to invite others to share these experiences in a responsible way.

I have never been much of a political guy, but I do love history, and learning about politicians. I am always happy to find that a particular statesman or -woman is more than simply someone trying to garner votes, and I believe TR was one such person. I am, however, a writer, and in penning this book I have had two goals in mind (well, besides earning a meager supplemental income): to share with others what I have experienced, and to encourage others (*CW) to follow in my footsteps, or at least tire tracks. With these goals in mind, when I think of TR, I believe that I am in good company. I hope that you, like me, will allow him to be the president who encourages you to travel around this great country of ours, and to leave it safe and beautiful for folks in future centuries to enjoy as well.